D0997925

PATHFINDER

Air Vice-Marshal D. C. T. Bennett
C.B., C.B.E., D.S.O.

During the grim years of World War II the
Pathfinder Force of the R.A.F. won an
admirable reputation as an élite strike force
with its precision bombing of targets in Nazi
occupied Europe. The Pathfinder squadrons
were the brainchild of one determined man:
Air Vice-Marshal Bennett, whose foresight
and genius brought into being one of the most
effective bombing forces in the history of
military aviation. This is D. C. T. Bennett's
own story, a personal account of a remarkable
man.

PATHFINDER

To Squadron-Leader A. P. Cranswick, D.S.O., D.F.C.
– one of those who died.

"Better be not at all than be not noble"

Pathfinder
A War Autobiography

AIR VICE-MARSHAL
D. C. T. BENNETT, C.B., C.B.E., D.S.O.

First published in Great Britain in 1958
by Frederick Muller Ltd.
© Air Vice-Marshal D. C. T. Bennett, 1958 & 1983

*Conditions of Sale – This book shall not without
the written consent of the Publisher first given
be lent, re-sold, hired out or otherwise disposed of
by way of trade in any form of binding or cover
other than that in which it is published.*

*The book is published at a net price and is supplied
subject to the Publishers Association Standard
Conditions of Sale registered under the Restrictive
Trade Practices Act, 1956.*

Printed in Great Britain by
Hazell Watson & Viney Ltd,
Aylesbury, Bucks

Contents

Illustrations

Preamble

TEN-YEAR TEST

THIS day of August, 1955, is V.J. Day plus ten years, and a decade has passed since peace was supposed to have come to the world. This is the period which I always intended should pass before I would set pen to paper concerning my war experiences. I had recollections of the flood of war memoirs which were published after the First World War, and I was determined that I would write nothing which was not mellowed by time and adjusted to its right perspective. Particularly I felt that this delay was important as I had many critics who would have been very happy to call me a hot-headed youngster should I have been tempted to write something which might be described as "critical" concerning certain aspects of the conduct of the war.

The intention and the result turn out to be worlds apart! I had hoped to write in a calm, unbiased atmosphere of peace 10 years deep; instead I find myself torn by the disappointments of a lost peace. Admittedly the second German war was officially fought as a "war without aim" (I wanted to call this book *War Without Aim*, but my wife would not let me; she said it would be misunderstood). Our own Prime Minister in the many statements which he made during the war to the effect that we had no war aims, always stuck to his statement "except to destroy the enemy". In fact, he made frequent statements to the effect that Germany would never rise again to be a scourge against mankind. Thus we asked our young men to fight and die without any clear ideals such as liberty, fair play or justice; we simply asked them to fight to destroy a nation which twice in a lifetime had proved itself to be a murderer. Ten years afterwards, we find that the self-same politicians in their same high offices are telling us that the Germans are our well-beloved friends, that they must be rearmed in full and with our help, and without the slightest safeguards against the probability of their plunging the world into a war again. To suggest that we must have their strength on our side against our recent supposed allies be-hind the Iron Curtain is right, but to say that there is no other way of having this help except by the unconditional rearma-ment of twice-murderous Germany, is sheer hypocritical non-sense, and both our own and the American leaders should know it. We could and should have German strength on our side, but it should be as junior ranks only in a fully integrated European force which contains no national units. Such a force or better still a world force, is the only hope of preventing another world war on an even greater scale than the last. In short, unless we take some such steps within the next few years, a world war is inevitable within the next 12 years.

So after 10 years it is clear that having won the war, we have failed completely to achieve our only declared war aim.

Against the other things which we appeared to be fighting —namely, the tyranny of the Nazi bureaucrats, the suprem-acy of the state over the individual and the injustices and dis-tortions of Germany—we seem also to have fought in vain. Our allies, the Americans, have used every possible pressure against us, the French and the Dutch to destroy our empires which we have governed so beneficially and justly for so long; and we and the Americans have done precisely noth-ing to stop our other late allies, the Russians, in their open aggression against France in Indo-China. On the Home Front we find much in comparison with which Hitler appears almost saintly! We find that freedom and justice are dead in many walks of life. For example, a man cannot work at his trade unless he agrees to accept the private tyranny of some trade union. Similarly, trade associations fine both their members and people who are not their members, and the so-called courts of justice of England uphold such fines as legal. One such association, to which I am forced to be affiliated, begins its rules with: "The rules of this Association apply to members and non-members alike". And the courts of justice themselves outrage the most primitive instincts of justice. For example, in a case of contempt of court the court acts as judge in the case to which it is itself a party. Moreover, they will not allow the free giving of evidence, nor will they allow a defendant to be represented by the person of his choice. In an English court I have seen the unbelievable sight of official witnesses committing deliberate and obvious perjury, and although this fact was clear to the court I have seen such witnesses walk away free and unpunished.

And in these ten years I have seen many actions in England reminiscent of Nazi Germany. To come home one night to find a compulsory purchase order nailed to a tree outside my front door, throws doubt on my navigational reliability, while to be forced by a surfeit of regulations out of the profession which I have followed for a lifetime also makes me doubt the success of our fight for freedom. Moreover, when the British Foreign Secretary solemnly tells the House of Commons that he had no power whereby he could stop the issue of United Kingdom passports to two traitorous diplomats, and yet is able to refuse absolutely and finally the issue of a United Kingdom passport to me, an ex-R.A.F. officer, and an ex-United Kingdom Member of Parliament, who has held very many U.K. passports in the past, simply because I will not sign a form saying that I am a "citizen" of Great Britain, I wonder whether a war is still raging, and whether black despair in the hearts of freedom-loving Britons has driven them "underground".

But I hope, also—I hope that freedom and fair play will be reborn and that permanent peace will be achieved.

It could be—easily.

PREAMBLE TO 1983 EDITION

World War I was fought in order to create a world "fit for heroes to live in". The bitter disappointment which followed World War I made us somewhat cynical when again we had to fight for our freedom and independence in World War II. We did not pretend to any pious hopes nor to any specific conditions of surrender from Germany. We did however make it clear that we were fighting for the free world in order to establish freedom and fair play for humanity. By freedom we quite clearly meant freedom as individuals and as nations. Certainly neither of these two objectives have been realised and indeed we see ourselves as individuals more heavily burdened by bureaucratic dictatorship than at any stage in human history. Moreover as a great nation, we in Great Britain, have given away our right of self government in about 75 per cent. of our human activity. This is not a question of opinion but of fact. We have given away this right of self government almost entirely to those against whom we had to fight.

We lost many thousands of human lives, mostly of our very best young men. Pathfinders lost more than 3600 dead. They must be lying in their graves in agony to see how totally wasteful their sacrifice has been. The very people against whom they were compelled to fight now have control over our destiny in almost every walk of life. As an English Court has ruled on Appeal "the laws of the EEC are superior to and take precedence over English law passed at Westminster".

As for fair play and justice we see our Courts of Law making a mockery of every normal human right. We no longer have the right of choice in sex, colour or anything else. Moreover the Universal Declaration of Human Rights which gives a man the right to work is completely ignored and ridiculed by our labour laws.

We must recover our right of self government and with it loyalty to our own kith and kin throughout the world and we must re-introduce honour and freedom.

1

EXTRA-ORDINARILY ORDINARY

As I begin to write this book I am forty-five years of age, British, married and alive—and if you are a discerning reader, you will now quickly skip to Chapter II! To those more determined sufferers who think that, if I am to tell them the story of the war as I know it, they would like to know something of the storyteller, I say, read on.

I was born on 14th September 1910, in Fairthorpe, our home in Toowoomba, Australia, deep in the rich mud of the Darling Downs—often literally so during the rainy season. I was "the last hope of the Bennetts", as my mother used to say, being the youngest of four boys. This had the undoubted advantage that if there were any danger of my parents spoiling "the baby of the family", my big brothers ensured that there was plenty of corrective treatment. My father was a cattle man, of which as a youngster I was intensely proud. Amongst my earliest recollections I recall the smell of burning flesh as the red-hot irons branded the writhing young steers and heifers with my father's registered brand U∾4. But of all the influences which have left their mark on my make-up, undoubtedly my mother came first. She was English-born and had an intense love of the home country, as indeed most Australians have. Her father, Dr. T. P. Lucas, took her to Australia when her mother died, and brought her up as a strict Methodist and teetotaller. In his fight for medicine as opposed to surgery in those days of carbolic acid and the high mortality rate under anæsthetics, Grandpa

Lucas had offended the B.M.A., and he it was who first taught me the fact, which my R.A.F. squadron commander repeated on my arriving in England twenty years later, that "the only crime an Englishman cannot forgive is to be right" It is easiest to summarise my mother's teaching by quoting the two hymns which were perhaps the earliest she taught me: "If I were a beautiful twinkling star" and "Dare to be a Daniel".

In addition to his cattle station, in which his heart was really set, my father also ran an agency business, first of all in Toowoomba and subsequently in Brisbane, the capital of Queensland. He taught me to ride a horse and to drive a car, though my brothers took a fairly active hand in these proceedings as well. There were ten years between me and my eldest brother Clyde; then came Aubrey, eighteen months younger than Clyde, followed by a gap of six and a half years before Arnold, who was born two years before me. All my elder brothers were brainy types, and I was officially the disgrace of the family from my earliest days. Both Clyde and Aubrey were in turn "dux" of their school, and I am not sure whether it was an inferiority complex or something much simpler which made me the complete opposite. In fact, at school I was somewhat of a loafer, and except for subjects in which I was interested, such as chemistry and physics, I generally did fairly badly. Subsequently both Clyde and Arnold qualified as barristers and Aubrey as a doctor—and all did wonderfully well in their professions, as they still do.

Boyhood in Australia is freer than in the United Kingdom, and children have the advantage of being allowed to display their initiative earlier and in more numerous ways. As teenage youngsters, we drove ourselves to school in a sulky, drawn by a dear, sweet-natured chestnut mare called "Frollic", and we were allowed to ride or to go swimming or shooting quite freely, provided we observed reasonable rules of safety and punctuality. We lived in Toowoomba and later in Brisbane, but frequently visited my father's cattle station at Condamine, 30 miles south of the railway at Miles. At home we had every sort of hobby, and played a variety of wild and unusual games. As the youngest of the family, and generally the youngest in the games which we played with our numerous friends in the district, I was accustomed to being one of the weaker brethren, and I recall the carefully suppressed pleasure I derived by impressing my elders with the first "Lantana jump". It occurred in a game which we had devised, which we called "Sneaking." I cannot remember the rules exactly, but I do know that one side were virtually the police and the other side were the bushrangers. On one occasion I was one of the hunted, and I was stalked into a position where I had no alternative but to climb a fairly substantial tree in order to escape. My pursuers had me cornered. They swarmed up the tree after me—all of them. I was about 25 feet from the ground, and as they all left mother earth and got closer I jumped into a dense bush of a lantana, a prickly unpretentious shrub which grows prolifically around Brisbane. It broke my fall, and the effect was like magic. My pursuers were dumbfounded, and I was free. But the lantana jump lived on—for we found that quite high jumps could be made safely on to a well-developed lantana.

But of all the influences which affected my young life, the cattle station "Kanimbla" was perhaps one of the most important. My father used to take me sometimes by car, sometimes by rail, on visits lasting from a few weeks to a few months, and he taught me not only how to ride but also about the bush and about cattle. Old Steve Patch, the station manager, and even more so young Steve, his son, carried on the good work. My environment at Kanimbla was of horseflesh, of 180 square miles of sandy soil often parched and spoilt by prickly pear. It was sleeping on the ground with a saddle for a pillow, hearing the howl of the dingo, and the raucous screams of the cockatoo. In short, it taught me the toughness of an outdoor life.

The environment at home was the opposite. Cars soon

took the place of horses. In fact, I was almost born in the car my father first owned, an old De Dion. My first driving lessons were taken sitting on my father's knee, steering a model T Ford with beautiful brass headlights with candles, and polished black leather straps to retain the high altitude hood. One of my earliest recollections was jacking up a front wheel of the Ford, at the age of four, spinning the wheel and by some adroit magic pushing my hand through the revolving spokes so that a finger caught in the open cog wheels which contrived to drive the speedometer. Thus my life was a mixture of horse-flesh and austerity on the one hand, with steel and comfort on the other.

At the age of eleven, by which time we had moved to Brisbane, I was allowed complete control of a car on the road. It was a very early Overland, with an enormous 4-cylinder engine, and my dimensions at that time were quite inadequate in comparison with the seating arrangements. From then on I had an ever increasing opportunity of driving cars, and even although licensing had begun by that time in Queensland, I was able to drive surreptitiously in Brisbane and openly out west, to gain experience of driving in all sorts of conditions. I learnt to wind cars out of flooded streams with the starting handle, and to haul them out of the mud by a dozen different methods. As I grew older, my father was always generous, letting us boys have cars, and we often had private races with our friends. To give us our due, we did in return do much to care for the cars with which we were entrusted.

The east coast of Australia is well blessed with surfing beaches. All young Australians soon learn to swim, and I was early able to surf—without a board—as well as my big brothers. It is a wonderful sport; to master the gigantic strength of the breakers and shoot shorewards with such an apparent speed is more exhilarating than one's first slow roll. The danger of under-tows, or of sharks, adds spice. Almost equally thrilling is surf-canoeing. We, Arn and I, had seen the big surf boats going out through the breakers—and shooting wonderfully on their way back. We had also built our own canoe for ordinary calm water use, and, indeed, had undertaken long journeys in it. We soon put the two ideas together—and had wonderful fun, to the horror of the onlookers. Outward bound was hectic enough. Two held the canoe prow on to the breakers crashing on to it while the lucky one leapt aboard, and then they shoved him hard at the next breaker. With strenuous paddling there would be just sufficient forward speed to cut through the apparently mighty crest and to leap out the other side, ready to paddle madly to get through the next one. And then, beyond the surf, there was perfect peace. The tiny craft rose and fell on the great Pacific swell, utterly removed from the world.

The return journey was, however, the whole object of the exercise. Heading gingerly for the shore, one endeavoured to choose a good big breaker which would shoot well but not be beyond one's ability! The big point was to keep straight as the tiny canoe rushed down the steep slope of the wave and the crest curled over mountainously just behind the nape of one's neck, and the canoe shot forward. For if the prow, digging into the lower stationary water, was not straight as the canoe shot forward, it would swing uncontrollably one way or the other, and the canoe would roll. And roll it did on many occasions. It was, unconsciously, good training for a future seaplane pilot.

My schooling began at a private prep. school run on strictly English lines by a Mr. Gill. It was situated on the brow of the range of the Great Divide, with the hills falling away steeply to the east, whilst to the west there was only a gentle slope merging on to the flat plains of the Darling Downs. I was a day-boy, and therefore the strict English outlook made little difference compared with that of the ordinary Australian school. In Brisbane, however, we reverted to normal, and like 99·9 per cent. of all Australian children we went to the State school provided completely free of cost by the generous government. Both socially and educationally the State schools of Queensland were excellent. Like all other boys I passed my Scholarship examination, and subsequently my Junior, with subjects intended to be useful for the medical profession into which I hoped to graduate. By this time my eldest brother was a barrister, my second brother was a doctor, and my third brother was also studying for the Bar. I was supposed to be the second doctor in the family, but unfortunately a year before my Senior matric my father received a school report which, with every justification, he regarded as disgraceful. I had indeed been taking things easy at school with the intention of putting in a spurt as the exams drew nearer. To my father, however, the report was one which hardly justified the expense of a university course for a further five years. This report had arrived whilst I was out at "Kanimbla", and when I arrived home I was greeted with the news that I was to start work in my father's agency business the following morning. This I did. But after a few days' thought, I decided that work on the cattle station was more the life for me, and at least to give myself time to think, I would prefer to work there. To my surprise my father not only agreed to this request but positively welcomed it, for—much to my embarrassment—he envisaged my being some day able to take over the management of the station.

For the next three months I was an ordinary jackaroo, and did the everyday work of a station hand. Armed with an axe, a coil or two of barbed wire and a good pair of pliers I did boundary riding. I joined the others in mustering the cattle, branding and earmarking, and did short droving jobs, moving stock from one part of the station to another. Once a fortnight I would help with the killing of a steer for home consumption, and for about a day we would have the luxury of fresh meat. The rest we would salt down and store in a strong brine bath to be used until the next killing I learnt to make a green hide rope and a stock-whip. . . . But mostly, I thought. I realised that my ambition to be a doctor had largely been taken for granted both by myself and by my parents, following the footsteps of Grandfather Lucas and of my brother Aubrey. I was not unduly sad at having to forsake this ambition. On the other hand, I realised that the life of a station hand or even of a station manager in South Central Queensland was utterly devoid of prospects, and although it would be sublimely happy, it was a dead end—absolutely. To become a business man, on the other hand, appealed even less, and so I was forced to cast around and begin to put in some basic thought. Thus it was that I deliberately chose aviation as a career.

After three months as a jackaroo I made for Miles, and there jumped on a train to Brisbane. My father was obviously disappointed that I should leave the station, but he was even more disappointed that I should take up flying, and he and my mother opposed it not merely on grounds of danger but also because they considered it would simply make me an "aerial bus driver". Knowing that my brother Aubrey had a big influence over me, they invoked his assistance in trying to dissuade me. His letter told me of the many dangers which beset flying in those days—of which he had learnt through his close association with many of the Qantas pilots in Western Queensland (he flew with them before the flying doctors' days). He told me of the effects of thunderstorms and many other things, but there was only one thing in the letter which mattered, and it confirmed my ambition completely. He used the phrase which appears on the title page of this book, "Better be not at all than be not noble", and he admitted that to forsake one's ambition at the dictate of fear would indeed be ignoble.

Incidentally, I often wonder whether I was influenced by the great pilots I had seen. Before I was 4 years of age—and I can remember it—I saw an American give a flying display at Toowoomba. Later I saw Hinkler arrive on his flight from England, and also Amy Johnson, the first woman to do that flight (she overshot on landing at Eagle Farm and ran through into some corn, where she turned over). I also saw the arrival of Kingsford-Smith at the end of what I consider one of the greatest flights in the history of aviation—across the Pacific.

Age was the next stumbling block, for I was too young to apply to join the Royal Australian Air Force, and I therefore worked in various capacities in my father's office, gaining invaluable experience in every way. I did a little as an office boy, I became a salesman, I learnt the elements of book-keeping, and, most valuable of all, I was eventually promoted to be a half-baked conveyancer, and thus early lost any awe of the mysteries of legal language. Eventually the great day came when I was old enough to apply for flying training with the R.A.A.F. Of the several thousands of entries, fifteen were to be picked, and the selection committee travelled by Southampton flying boat to each of the State capitals in order to interview applicants. My "Merit Pass" in physics and my subsequent attendances as a night student at Queensland University, taking science subjects, together with my knowledge of cars and the fact that I had already become an N.C.O. in the Australian Citizens Forces, all carried weight, and to my intense delight I was selected.

I was immediately given a medical examination, and the doctor concerned declared me to be a 100 per cent. O.K. with the exception of my tonsils. I was horror-stricken, but determined to give the R.A.A.F. little chance of refusing me. I, without delay, had them removed that same day, and reported the fact to the Air Board in Melbourne. Unfortunately this minor operation cost me a six-months' delay. So I went "soldiering on" in my father's office, but taking at the same time every opportunity to learn all I could about aircraft. I had, several years earlier, helped a neighbour rebuild an old Farman biplane, and to overhaul its engine. I had read all the flying books I could find, but I was madly anxious to get into the air.

In·due course the six months dragged by, and one day the post delivered the letter instructing me to report to Melbourne and enclosing a railway warrant. I was almost delirious with joy, and prepared for the departure. To my dismay and embarrassment, just before I was due to leave I received a letter cancelling everything that had been said, and informing me that as I was medically unfit I could not be accepted for the R.A.A.F., but could apply again in a year's time. It was "a bolt from the blue", and I think my parents realised that, however pleased they might be, I was in fact very deeply affected by this bombshell.

My mother suggested that she should take me on a visit to Sydney. We stayed with relatives in Sydney, but the next day I left my mother there, bought a second-class railway ticket without sleeper, and continued on to Melbourne. I rushed straight from the train to the Air Board, and I think the surprise that a youngster should react so violently impressed them so much that they felt out of sheer kindness they had to do something about my case. They blankly refused to accept me for the course just starting, but instead of making me wait a year they agreed to a six-month's delay only, and to my having a medical examination there and then at the Air Board. I breathed again; there was hope, and indeed apparent certainty, that I could begin the course in a further six months. Thus it looked certain that I would get started, although I had lost six months through tonsils and a further six months through what I subsequently learnt to be political interference, a little Nepotism on the part of a politician. Apparently this politician had a nephew who was very keen to get into the R.A.A.F.; as he had influence, he used it appropriately and the nephew concerned was accepted. Somebody had to make room for him, and as I was one of the furthest away from Melbourne it seemed most convenient to cancel me. To the best of my knowledge there never was any question of "medical unfitness" in my case— then or now!

It was cold and wet in Melbourne that morning in
July, 1930, when I reported with 14 others to the headquarters of the R.A.A.F., Victoria Barracks, Melbourne. I had
been born and lived all my life in a hot climate, and it was
indeed a bleak welcome to my new career. But there was
bleaker news in store for us. After a few administrative formalities we were ushered into an office and were given a talk
which showed the characteristics in its initial stages of a
simple pep-talk. Soon, however, the main point was reached.
Australia was experiencing an economic depression—a depression which subsequently affected the whole world—and
economy was the order of the day. Of the 15 of us selected, it had originally been intended that most would remain
in the R.A.A.F. with a possible transfer of two or three to the
R.A.F. Now, however, Government economy compelled a
change of policy, and unless the majority of us would volunteer to transfer to England at the end of our training then it
would be impossible to continue with the full fifteen then
present. I, strangely enough, had never had any urge to
travel, and had no desire to leave Australia. A few moments
brief thought, however, convinced me that the only safe
course of action was to volunteer for the R.A.F. In fact, only
two decided otherwise, both for domestic reasons. Thus
a division was struck from the outset compatible with the
economy drive and agreeable to all concerned. We were
bundled with our baggage into a heavy covered lorry, and in
cold drizzle which would have been a real credit to London
we drove to Point Cook on the western shore of Port Phillip.

Point Cook was a mixed land and marine station. It had a
pier and a slipway for its two Southampton flying boats and
its five single-engined Seagull amphibian boats, with moorings completely exposed except from westerly wind. Its aerodrome was clear and flat, but its surface in those days lacked
any form of drainage, and in wet weather it cut up badly
into mud holes of the most delightful nature. Its hangars and
workshops were on the side of the aerodrome nearest the

sea, whilst the living accommodation and the parade-ground were on the far side—a healthy arrangement for unwanted exercise, but enormously wasteful in man-hours, to the delight no doubt of all regular officers. For I was to learn there, and at all future stations, that the Air Force has no thought whatsoever for economy in manpower in matters such as station geography. On our first Sunday about 6 or 8 of the 15 Cadet-Officers left the Officers' Mess for a walk. Being ignorant of station standing orders, we walked straight across the aerodrome to the hangars. When within about 200 yards we saw the Duty Officer walk out of his office in our direction. One of us guessed—and guessed rightly —that "we should not have walked across the aerodrome". Two or three "beat it" back towards the Mess as hard as they could go, and heard no more of the matter, whilst the rest of us felt the more honourable thing to do was to face the music and walk on. The Duty Officer gave us a brief telling-off and a temporary present of some picks and shovels, and for our sins we did one hour of aerodrome levelling. Thus it was that I learnt the first law of the Air Force, "Thou shalt not be caught."

Our first weeks' activities were very remote from aviation. As in all other weeks of that one-year Course, a whistle blew at 6.30 a.m. in "Canary Cottage", our quarters, and we each leapt to the door of our room and stood outside in our pyjamas, smartly to attention in the bitter cold. Then, after showering and dressing, we polished our floors to a mirror finish, ensured that our leather equipment was jet black and polished, that our beds were made with "straight edges" and that there was no dirt or fluff within miles of the place. Each of us, moreover, had particular responsibilities in the bathrooms and lavatories. Then, breakfast in the Officers' Mess, and out on to the parade ground with the rest of the station (less officers) by 08.00 hours! The rest of the day for that first week was extremely simple. We had drill with rifles, we had drill without rifles, and then we had an hour's P.T. After lunch we repeated the morning's programme precisely, except that the P.T. finished with a short run "over to the trees and back, and the last one home does it again". The trees were over two miles away, but the supreme penalty of having to do it again if one was last home was only applied on two or three occasions. This week of "toughening-up" was no doubt well meant, but it was completely absurd to embark so fiercely upon such extreme physical exertion, particularly for one or two of the older pupils, who had allowed themselves to become a little soft.

We survived this week, and as a reward flying training began. During each morning, having marched from the parade ground the distance of approximately three-quarters of a mile to the hangars, we spent the morning partly on flying training and partly on practical ground instruction. This latter included, of course, a high proportion of washing down aeroplanes with soap and water, but practical rigging and fitting and other trades were covered fairly thoroughly. The *ab initio* flight was commanded by Flight-Lt. Jerry Waters, with two Flying Officers and two Sergeants as instructors. I was allotted to Sergeant Preston, a solid average type, by no means a genius, but with a simple direct approach to the job of teaching flying which suited me admirably. He made no pretence at heavy theory, but taught the practical job extremely well. A year earlier Point Cook had been cleared of all its obsolete First World War aircraft, owing to a spate of fatal accidents. We therefore were lucky, and were trained on De Havilland "Moths", a type of aircraft which proved to be one of the greatest trainers the world has ever known. We marched back to the Mess for lunch, and over again for the afternoon session of lectures. Comparing the Point Cook course with other flying training courses which I have known, I realise now that we were fortunate in having practical training quite as good as the average, and theoretical training far superior. At the time, however, quite a number of cadet officers were more than tired of the surfeit of theory which was being forced down our throats.

The period of dual instruction was as at any flying training school, one of competition to be the first to go solo. One of our number, Norman Littlejohn, had already done some 600 hours flying, and he was forced to do dual instruction like the rest of us. Naturally, he was off first. I was not particularly quick, taking nearly eight hours before I was allowed the thrill of my first flight alone; and there is no doubt about it, it is a real thrill. For a youngster of reasonable enthusiasm and susceptibility the sheer delight of solo flight—alone for the first time—is hard to equal. But even our flying was not all fun and games. After going solo we still did a large proportion of dual instruction as well as solo flying, and although in due course we went on to learn loops and stall turns and slow rolls, we were at the same time always made to practice forced-landings, and were in fact subjected to forced-landing tests on every dual flight. We were strictly forbidden to do flick rolls, owing to the strain which this manoeuvre placed on the wing structure, but we were taught the half-flick roll very accurately and with a full theoretical explanation—a piece of knowledge which I subsequently found very useful when I became a fighter pilot a little later in my career. (In an ordinary slow roll the aircraft rotates around its fore and aft axis by the force of the ailerons. In a flick roll, the rotation is caused by the stalling of one wing due to low air speed and is induced by pulling hard back on the stick and kicking on rudder just as the stall is approached. This causes the inner wing to stall before the outer, causing the aircraft to rotate violently round its fore and aft axis. In the half-flick roll the manoeuvre is quickly countered, so that the aircraft stops its rolling motion when upside down, and the stick is held back to complete the second half of the loop.)

My only pre-Air Force friend from Queensland, Howard Berg, was unfortunately failed for alleged flying inability and sent off home. I have never agreed that it is possible to tell whether a person is likely to be a good pilot or bad one in the early stages of his training. and I think that this, like many other cases, was a deplorable waste of talent. Howard Berg was by far the best brain on our course.

During this initial training period of six months we carried no guns or bombs, but concentrated purely on flying itself. My judgment then reached a standard higher, probably, than it ever reached subsequently in my flying career. We used to do much unauthorised low flying, which is, of course, great fun. We also, in our forced landing practice, landed quite often in odd uncertain places, and I wonder to this day at the tolerance and good nature of the local farmers. I also wonder to this day whether the girls hanging out the washing at the local farmsteads every Monday morning were as attractive as they looked during a power-dive to fifty feet.

Ernie Klose, the only commissioned officer on our course, a lieutenant from the Army, fell by the wayside mainly through poor eyesight. He had been automatically and universally disliked by the rest of the course at the outset, owing to the fact that he was a "Duntrooner" (a graduate of the Australian military college, Duntroon). However, his early exhibition of the snobbishness which in those days seemed to emanate from that distinguished academy, had soon mellowed, and we were all genuinely sorry when he was forced to leave us.

Play time was included in the course. Our weekly P.T. continued, and before the long cross-country run we were allowed to play "all-in rugger". Gouging was not permitted! The ball, a very large medicine ball, could be carried, kicked or otherwise transported, and the object was, as in rugger, to reach the enemy base-line. The pitch was a small piece of well-kept lawn in front of the Officers' Mess, approximately fifty yards long and twenty yards wide. To see two opposing teams of half a dozen each, locked and interlocked in all-in wrestling, with a ball lying unmolested on the grass, did not give a very true picture of the rugger which it was. On very rare occasions somebody might attempt to break away and score, but the consequences of such an attempt were so violent and so quick that it was never tried unless the chances of success were extremely good. I often think that if an aggressor such as Hitler had played that game, and if the rest of the world were organised appropriately, then he would never have attempted so dangerous a goal. Our casualties in this game were high, and eventually the time came when the majority of the course reported to sick quarters as the result of a quiet game—and a complete prohibition ensued. But there were other pastimes equally, if not more, absurd.

Guest nights, even when we had distinguished visitors from the Air Board, were conducted in what was then the tradition for the R.A.A.F. After a strictly formal and well-mannered dinner, and with great restraint until after the coffee, the party would begin to liven up. One sport was to grab a Cadet Officer and force him to climb up into the rafters of the ante-room. There was a steel ring in the centre of the rafters, supported from above by a piece of $1\frac{1}{2}$ in. round steel and similarly with bracing to each side of $1\frac{1}{2}$ in. steel. Each steel support was attached by a large nut on the inside of the ring. As the total diameter was only about 15 in., and even this was impaired by three large nuts, and as there was no means of supporting oneself in the process, I can assure all those interested that it was an extremely difficult task to get through it. However, a really determined effort over a period of ten to fifteen minutes would satisfy the cheery onlookers below, and in any case they were tired of throwing things by that time. Another form of rugger was also played in the ante-room with a beer bottle as a ball. As a teetotaller I found Australian "drunks" fairly unpleasant company, and therefore I was usually out of the Mess before this beer-bottle rugger began. The casualties in it were often quite serious. I recall particularly watching Ron Rae run the full length of a long table, to dive on to a scrum centred upon the beer bottle. Unfortunately, just as he took off from the end of the table, the scene of activity suddenly shifted to one side, and he came down on the hard polished floor, banging his head violently. He was knocked out cold, and was off flying for a few days with mild concussion.

None of these antics compared even mildly with our initiation night, which took place early in our first term. Each initiation was organised by a few of the flying instructors, with the senior course to carry out their orders. We heard of the impending danger, and immediately after dinner deserted the Mess and our quarters, to the great annoyance of the senior course. They shouted into the blackness that we should come back and take our medicine, but we thought that it was only fair that they should come and get us—and we said so. With what we thought was great unfairness we were eventually ordered back to our quarters and the fun began. We were taken one by one, and in the first room into which we entered we were stripped naked. We then went through a succession of tortures. We ran the gauntlet with two R.A.A.F. red, white and blue roundalls painted on the appropriate portion of our anatomy, whilst the fronts of our bodies received suitable decorations. Sitting on a block of ice about $3 \times 2 \times 2$ ft., we were forced to recite a very unofficial oath of allegiance, all very improper, but in the best poetic form. One of the best of the ordeals then took place. The victim was held close to the very hot fire whilst a large poker was brought to a good cherry red heat; this poker was passed under the nose of the victim for test purposes on three or four occasions and plunged back into the fire. In order to show appropriate reverence for this "test of fire" the victim was then made to kneel down. The poker, properly heated, was extracted from the fire and passes were made at the victim's chest. With much chatter and discussion it was eventually decided that this particular victim was too much of a "softy" and must therefore be blindfolded for the ordeal. The poker was put back into the fire, and the blindfold was applied. Then suddenly there was deathly silence. The poker was once more passed under the nose of the victim, so that the heat would be felt, and then suddenly it was plunged! A sharp pain in the centre of the chest indicated—but before one knew what it indicated there was a strong smell of burning flesh. It took a moment or two to realise what had happened. A piece of ice had been jabbed into the centre of the victim's chest, whilst the poker was stuck into a piece of beefsteak a few inches below his nose. The wreck was then tarred and feathered, except that the tar was not quite so unkind as real tar, and thrown out of the window. Even this, to be thrown out of the window into the pitch blackness, had its reaction, but fortunately our kind tormentors had arranged a canvas swimming pool below the window, into which we fell. The cleaning process with dope solvent, petrol and every other method known in those primitive days was not sufficient to get us clean for some days to come. The only serious casualties were when the sheepshears, used to remove all the hair from one particular place, slipped and cut something very important on one cadet officer. Incidentally, those pupils with moustaches did not lose them, but only half of them.

The second six months were more mundane and down to business. To our disgust the "initiation ceremony" of Flying Training Courses in the R.A.A.F. was formally banned. Thus we never had the opportunity of demonstrating our imaginative ideas of welcome to the new course. We would dearly have loved to do so, as it consisted entirely of Duntroon Cadets of all levels thrown out of Duntroon because of the economy drive.

In this term we moved on to another type of aircraft, the Wapiti, a large single-engined biplane. It was the post-war successor of the DH 9, and did roughly the same job. In it we not only carried on ordinary flying training, but did front gunnery on to ground targets; we did rear seat gunnery, with a single Lewis gun on a Scarf ring mounting, on to targets in the bay. We carried out camera gun work on each other, and we actually flew photographic runs sufficient to make up reasonable mosaics of the area which we had covered, and subsequently we developed the film, made our own prints and pieced them together. We did stereoscopic analyses of these photos, and made out interpretation reports. Our bombing practice with Wapitis consisted not only of dropping practice bombs on the land target, but also on one occasion we were permitted to drop live 112 lb. bombs on a target in the bay.

One of the greatest days of the second half was a long cross-country. In this we went off solo and flew to Deniliquin, actually across the border into New South Wales. It was quite an adventure, and what with one or two pupils going astray and one or two overdoing the low flying business, it was amazing how such a simple flight could produce so many episodes—and on one aircraft, so much telephone wire!

Eventually the end of the year approached, and a very hard year it had been. The early rising, the spit and polish not only of our own uniforms and equipment but also of our quarters, to live immaculately as officers and at the same time to be on all station parades often with rifles and side arms, to have the long fast march four times a day, to carry out our flying, to cover all our lectures and to study every evening, was fairly hard going. To make it more surely hard, no cadet was ever permitted to walk on the tarmac; all movements of a cadet on the technical side of the station had to be "at the double". The final flying tests and the examinations loomed up, and just before the end of the course we received the final results. I had been beaten by Clary Smith in the examinations, but fortunately, to my delight, I came out top in the actual flying. With this news we dispersed for our pre-embarkation leave prior to leaving for England and the R.A.F. Home I went, proud as a peacock, to be, as I thought, a qualified pilot. The only comfort in having little knowledge is to have little knowledge of how little knowledge one has!

2

A KOOKABURRA MIGRATES

WE were shipped first class P. & O. to England by the old *Narkunda*, a ship which years later became famous for its gallant but hopeless fight against great odds in the Atlantic. We called at Ceylon, Bombay and Aden, saw the Suez Canal, Malta and Gibraltar.

The voyage was not only educational from the point of view of geography, but also gave us our first-hand knowledge of Englishmen in reasonable bulk. In Australia, our only experience of that rare bird the "Pommy" was the very occasional. visitor from England, but on the *Narkunda* we met droves of them all together, consisting mostly of that august circle known as the "Indian army". We had been warned by the ship's officers that we should not take the "Indian Army" as typical of the average Englishman; we had been led to believe that they were like Duntroon graduates only considerably worse. This unhappy description did indeed fit some of them, but in general the men were not too bad. Of their wives, however, I can say little good. Mostly they were loud-mouthed, overbearing, pompous and stupid, and I must say I felt that if English ladies were like these examples then every Englishman must indeed be an unhappy creature. Later on I was to learn better.

There were also on board many more normal English people, both male and female, and from them we cadets tried to learn all we could of the land to which we were going, and of its inhabitants. It is a strange fact that we were more self-conscious of our relationship with the people of the country than we were doubtful of our own ability to do our jobs in the R.A.F. We discussed the question of how we should behave, and of the details of etiquette and formalities, in a way which you would not expect from apparently rough-skinned young Aussies.

On arrival in England we reported to the Air Ministry, and eventually to Uxbridge, where we had our first taste of R.A.F. life. In those days the R.A.F. was extremely small, and there was only one Officers' Mess at Uxbridge. We were, therefore, over-awed by the heavy weight of "brass" at dinner each evening. It was the H.Q. of Fighting Area, and we changed for dinner every night. We learnt the whereabouts of London tailors, and within a week we had all supplied ourselves with R.A.F. uniforms, although we still had the right to wear R.A.A.F. dark blue. This latter subsequently proved to be a source of unpopularity for us, because most of us liked it better, and therefore went on wearing it.

We reported to the Flying Training School at Seeland, near Liverpool, for flying tests, which apparently were satisfactory, and we were packed off to our squadrons, after a short instructional period on the type which we were intended to fly. In my case it was the Siskin, undoubtedly one of the worst aeroplanes ever produced. I believe its history was that it had been intended as a parasol monoplane (i.e., with the wing above the top of the fuselage), but that this proved unsatisfactory and therefore a tiny lower wing was added to convert it into a biplane. This lower wing was about half the chord of the upper wing, and about two-thirds of its span. Its angle of incidence in normal flight was about eleven degrees, and it carried no aileron. Most specimens of the Siskin were not stable in any plane, and they generally carried a directional bias as well as a one-wing-down tendency. I am glad I flew the Siskin.

I was posted to 29 Squadron at North Weald in Essex, and

I was more than pleased to be "a fighter boy", which for some unknown reason seemed and still seems to carry with it an aura of glamour—goodness knows why! My Squadron Commander was short, tubby and maintaining a fairly strong Irish brogue, and seemed to me to be a million miles from the picture I had always imagined of an R.A.F. fighter squadron-leader. The degree of restraint he exercised over all our aerial activities, and his tendency to avoid flying soon confirmed the innuendoes of the other pilots in the Squadron, that he did not much like the idea of flying a Siskin. But he was also a most conscientious C.O., and apart from fits of temper he was kind-hearted and helpful.

There was no other member of my Course posted to 29 Squadron, but I was delighted to find an earlier ex-Point Cook type, called Ron Lees, already established. I hoped to be allotted to C Flight, which was graced by his presence, but instead was put into B Flight. Nevertheless, his help and advice in those early days in strange surroundings helped me tremendously, and stopped me from dropping innumerable "clangers". Flight-Lieutenant Duke was my Flight Commander. He was rather old to be holding the rank of Flight-Lieutenant, and his promotion had obviously been slow, but so far as I was concerned he was an excellent Flight Commander, an experienced and very useful pilot, and whilst able to give orders and have them obeyed without question, he was extremely human.

A new Annual Squadron Training Programme had just been introduced from Fighting Area, and I stayed in 29 Squadron long enough to complete it. Its early stages consisted of individual training, concentrating subsequently on Flight training, and eventually Squadron work. We did considerable camera gun work, particularly air to air. We spent many long hours in the air, trying to induce a new-fangled device known as Radio Telephony to work. The R.T. of those days was reminiscent of the early crystal sets with which I had played as a boy ten years earlier. Whilst flying in an open cockpit, with a fairly noisy engine and a headset not so well fitting or efficient as present-day equipment, it was extremely difficult to decide whether one could hear a voice from the ground station or whether it was wishful imagination. Ranges of five to ten miles were, of course, quite satisfactory, but it was somewhat of an historical occasion when I managed to work both ways at a range of forty-three miles. In our formation flying, which we all enjoyed thoroughly, we naturally wanted to emulate the displays which were becoming famous at Hendon every year. Unhappily, however, we Siskin boys were heavily discouraged. We were not permitted to do aerobatics of any significance in formation, and if a Flight passed over the aerodrome in even moderately tight formation, all the pilots would be "on the mat" for it when they landed.

At about this time I saw for the first time a demonstration of the ineffectiveness of medical examinations. I am sorry to say that a graduate from Point Cook gave the demonstration. He was one Course ahead of me at Point Cook, and he was now in 56 Squadron, also stationed at North Weald. His was a clear case of Australian alcoholism in its classic form. He drank whisky. After crashing a couple of Siskins, which was not abnormal in those days, he was sent for medical examination at station sick quarters. Being a good friend of the medical officer, he often would drop in to pass the time of day, and had taken the precaution of learning the letters on the eyesight test card which was always exhibited there. His medical examination, therefore, showed that he was entirely fit. Admittedly Siskins would drop a wing on landing if you let them. This wing-dropping tendency was instantaneous when it occurred. There was, therefore, only mild surprise when "X" from Point Cook piled up another Siskin. When, however, he continued the programme until he had written off four aircraft, Fighting Area Headquarters took a hand and ordered that he should be sent immediately to Central Medical Establishment for a thorough check-up, and that his history be sent with him. Not to be outdone, X went to sick quarters and obtained every eyesight test card used in the R.A.F. He then learnt them off by heart, and with the greatest of glee went off for his examination. He passed—and came back to crash a 5th Siskin. Fortunately for him, the Squadron was re-equipping with Bulldogs, an aircraft without vice, which required less accurate judgment in landing and no high-speed corrective reaction. After a few weeks' rest he was back in the fold—only, alas, to come to an untimely and dishonourable end so far as the R.A.F. was concerned, by paying his mess bill with a "rubber cheque". He was the only case of which I have ever heard of a Point Cook Graduate proving to be a disgrace.

Squadron training continued, and one of the most interesting episodes was night flying. To its interest we had the added attraction of the spectacle of our Squadron Commander himself doing his night flying. Whilst we all agreed that he was right that the Siskin was far from ideal for night landings on the very primitive flarepaths of those days, we also realised that his own lack of flying practice made it a thousand times worse for him—he was obviously shaken, but he gallantly did his stuff. A flarepath was laid out on the aerodrome in the prescribed manner of three flares in a line, with the fourth flare to the right of the last flare and spaced from it a distance of about fifty yards. These flares consisted simply of a body of felt wired together, soaked in paraffin and then set on a steel tray and ignited. They gave no illumination on the ground, but simply indicated a level. I am glad I learnt my night flying on such flares, for they taught a principle of landing by level and not by focusing—a principle which I found of value in later life, not only when landing without proper facilities at night but also useful on glassy calm water with a flying boat. On night flying, our Squadron-Commander proceeded on lines somewhat as follows: he would have the flarepath laid in broad daylight, which we youngsters jokingly referred to as "just

after lunch", for his dusk landings. The principle of training
was that, as we had no dual aircraft, all pilots would land on
the flarepath at dusk for two or three evenings until they
finally carried on into true darkness. His dusk landings were in
broad daylight, and on his declaring that he was intending to
carry on into full darkness we saw him, to our surprise, continue into moderate dusk conditions. We were quite impressed, but unhappily he taxied in just before dark and
declared that since he had now himself tried out night flying
in a Siskin in full darkness, he was in a position to convince
Fighting Area that the Siskin was unsafe for the purpose!
Fortunately for us, his powerful argument was not accepted
by Fighting Area, and we continued with our night training.
Not only was this a most valuable flying experience, but it
also gave me an opportunity of frequent flights by night over
the lights of the mightiest city in the world, a privilege
shared by very few in those days. It also taught me a new
technique, map-reading by night.

In those days of intensive peace conferences and high-
pressure disarmament, we in the fighter squadrons of the
R.A.F. were not normally permitted to fly with live ammunition in our guns. Once every year, however, at our annual
air-firing practice camp, live ammunition practice was permitted. For this the squadron moved as a whole to Sutton
Bridge, where we landed on a small grass aerodrome and
enjoyed two weeks of most delightful summer weather with
the good sport of firing at ground targets on the shores of the
Wash at frequent intervals. In those days, the most cherished
part of a fighter aircraft was its guns, and as they were as
temperamental as most highly valued possessions, they were
placed in a position where they could be dealt with by the
pilot. To dive at the ground target in this open cockpit
machine, so carefully lined up with the open sights exactly
on the target, and then, as the trigger was pressed, to have
the violent chatter of two Vickers guns just in front of one's
face, was one of the most war-like experiences I have ever

met. Stoppages were, of course, quite common, and had to be dealt with in the air by the pilot without undue delay. In fact, this question of technical knowledge of one's guns and ability to clear stoppages was a major part of ordinary training in those days.

On one occasion one of our pilots had a failure in the Constantinesco gear, which meant that the bullets from his guns made a nasty mess of his propeller. He returned, however, to Sutton Bridge without further accident. I should perhaps explain for those who have not had the pleasure of firing guns through the propellers of an aircraft that the Constantinesco gear was a hydraulic mechanism which worked off cams at the back of the propeller, and this interrupted the application of the trigger mechanism in the guns so that they would only fire at the moment when the propeller blade was exactly in front of the gun. By the time that the bullet came out of the gun, the propeller had moved. There fore, the Constantinesco gear ensured with reasonable certainty that the blade would not be hit by the bullet. As the machine guns of those days were so unreliable, it was so absolutely essential to have them in the cockpit with the pilot, and it was therefore essential that they fired through the plane of rotation of the propeller. The Constantinesco gear was the most successful method of achieving this with safety. On the occasion which I have described, one of the rare technical failures occurred which meant that the guns "ran away" and fired without any nice discernment as to the whereabouts of the propeller blades at the time!

Incidentally, by this time we had had the misfortune to lose our Flight Commander, Duke, and his place was taken by John Merer. I am afraid the change was, from the point of view of all pilots in the flight, a most unhappy one. John Merer was a very nice man and all that. Never before or since, however, have I ever met such a bureaucrat. Translating the orders of every other bureaucrat at higher levels as generously as he could, he produced every order in writing, he insisted upon signature *ad neuseam* and reduced our flying, both in frequency and in duration. He allowed no discretion and no action other than that which he had ordered in detail and in writing. Cleland, Widows and myself, the three officers in the flight, were all soon talking of applying for postings, and even the two sergeant-pilots, without any undue show of indiscipline, made their view fairly clear. John Merer's orders for a flight would read something like this: "1500 hours. Siskin . . . Flying Officer Bennett, aerobatics, minimum height 6,000 ft., no more than 10 miles from North Weald, practice loops and slow rolls, land before 1530." This order would be signed by him and I would then be required to sign it, to show that I had understood it. I then had thirteen other places where I had to sign or initial, most of this being due to the new maintenance system which had been introduced by Fighting Area. All this was intended to produce safety, the only ambition then existent in the R.A.F. and the only basis on which promotions were judged.

It is somewhat ironical, therefore, and even perhaps educational, that as an indirect result of these restrictions, I was guilty of the only aircraft accident in my flying career. It happened, believe it or not, that John Merer one day sent up Widows and myself for formation practice and forgot to put his usual restrictions on the order. Having signed his instructions, we rushed out of his office, and grinning from ear to ear we mutually agreed that we would go somewhere—and go we did. I was the leader, and I wanted to have a look at a place about sixty miles south of London. There was a good deal of heavy shower-cloud around, and we dodged amongst the heavier part of it until we had reached my pinpoint. Then we headed for home, but in front of us there towered a mighty cold front, with cloud coming down to very low levels and there were hills ahead of us; the range of a fighter was strictly limited, and I soon realised that I had to go through the weather if I were to reach base on our petrol. Widows tucked in close, and into it we went. It was very turbulent, and Widows did a wonderful job holding tight formation with me in thick turbulent cloud. I tried to climb over it, which was the obvious remedy. Unfortunately the snow in the cloud grew heavier and heavier, and both air-craft were soon carrying a coating of 4 to 5 inches of ice on the leading edges of their wings. This was bad, but not impossible, as I knew from previous icing experience with the Siskin. What was serious was that my engine was losing power, and in those days, I, like most if not all other pilots, did not fully understand carburettor icing. Eventually, quite suddenly, my engine stopped altogether. Widows overshot me and was gone, and I had the nasty thought that I was on the southern outskirts of London and I could not therefore bale out. Moreover, the modern invention of a turn indicator which was serviceable at the beginning of the flight (a rare event on a Siskin) now went unserviceable, and with a partly iced-up air speed indicator, heavy ice on the wings, no engine, an uncertain cloud base and probably a suburban terrain, life was far from happy. During the long and silent descent I carefully undid my safety harness and tightened it one notch on each shoulder strap. I switched off the ignition, turned off the petrol and long before I broke cloud I had arranged my left arm to brace myself and got my toes well into toe-straps on the rudder pedals. I broke cloud over a small wood with about 200 feet of height. There was a field straight ahead, but the distance was too much for the small height remaining, bearing in mind the ice load that I carried. I remember registering that by a remarkable coincidence, Widows' Guardian Angels had brought him out at almost exactly the same spot, and I caught a glimpse of him as he broke cloud, pulled the stick back smartly to avoid hitting the ground, and then happily having engine power, flew round the field. I, in my dilemma, could do nothing. I held the aircraft just clear of the trees as the speed dropped, and as I cleared the edge of them, with the aircraft sinking violently, I whipped the stick hard back to try to save the undercarriage. The strain was too much for it, and over I went on to my back. The Sutton harness held perfectly, and without the faintest scratch or damage to myself I came to a standstill, inverted, with my head dangling six inches from the ground. How many thousands of lives have been saved by Sutton harnesses, and how many have been wasted by waist-belts!

I had heard the story of the fighter pilot who, in similar circumstances, had pulled the safety pin on his harness and had broken his neck, so I lowered myself out carefully, divested myself of my parachute, judged that the field was long enough for Widows to land and then got into a position in which to signal him the direction of landing. He came down satisfactorily, and without damage. What had happened was simple enough. Whilst the carburettor itself had some heating arrangement around the venturi, there was a "smart Alec" arrangement half-way up the intake, consisting of a medium wire gauze intended to prevent stones passing through the induction to the super-charger. In the steady throttle conditions under which I was flying, the impact-type of ice had soon packed on this screen until it had completely stopped the entry of all air to the carburettor. Widows' aircraft, presumably because he was so constantly changing his throttle opening, as was necessary in a tight formation in turbulent conditions, did not ice over. I had certainly much to thank providence for that night, and it was an expensive, though valuable lesson to me for the rest of my flying career. Needless to say, a formal enquiry took place which, although quite rightly blaming me for having gone so far south, did admit that the strong north-westerly wind, carrying with it this very bad weather, had not been forecast, and that in any case there was a severe icing danger with a Siskin in such circumstances. Bureaucrats, of course, will say that had their champion not failed to give me detailed instructions, as a bureaucrat should, I should not have crashed. To this I would reply that when I was a real captain of an aircraft, I always considered what I was doing, and in particular knew what the weather was doing. I felt responsible, and I used my head. When, however, I was regimented into a mere auto-pilot, I lost my initiative and air sense. Then at the first moment of a relaxation of the bureaucracy, I did something thoughtless and irresponsible without bothering to exercise my mind or my legs to find out what weather was coming or even what winds were blowing. My airmanship and my captaincy were barren as a result of the period of my subservience.

About six months after this event, when I had been with 29 Squadron for one year and had already completed one short course on parachutes (including my first jump), I applied for the Flying Boat Pilots Course. Incidentally, my first parachute jump was quite an experience—though, in fact, it was not a jump at all. At the end of the Course on Parachutes I went up with one of the instructors, each of us on the wing tip of a Vickers Vimy, he on one side and I on the other to keep the aircraft balanced. A small wooden platform was arranged round one of the outer wing struts of this old biplane. We each wore two parachutes, one to be used and one for emergency. Taxiing out required a considerable amount of tenacity, as the uneven surface of the aerodrome threw us about rather violently out on the wing tips. We stood facing backwards with the strut firmly clutched, so that when we took-off the force of the wind would blow us on to the strut. We climbed laboriously to about 1,500 feet, and on a signal from the pilot we gently and carefully turned round so that we were standing behind the strut and were holding on to it with our two hands. On a second signal, we held on with one hand and took the rip-cord handle in the other hand. On a third signal from the pilot, when he thought he was in the right position for us to drift to the confines of the aerodrome, we did not jump, nor did we fall off, but we simply pulled the rip cord. The result was most astounding. It was as if an almighty policeman had taken one's shoulders and pulled violently backwards. So violent was the tug that one's body simply rotated around its middle and then swung down under the parachute. The experience thereafter was peaceful and pleasant, and while floating to earth I was able to call to the instructor, who told me that the pilot had mis-judged the position and that we were going to land outside the aerodrome. He tried to demonstrate how to slip in the direction required, and this we both attempted to do as hard as we could go. The net result was that instead of drifting well outside the aerodrome, which would have been quite safe, we very nearly landed on a barbed wire fence on its boundary. The impact with the earth, partly because of attempts to slip, was fairly severe and far more abrupt than I had expected. All was well, and my log book was duly endorsed "parachute jump carried out".

My application for the Flying Boat Course proved to be an event of considerable importance to my subsequent activities. I confess I had made the application largely with the deter-mination of getting as many Courses as possible. In fact, it turned out to be my last Course in the R.A.F.

I reported to the only "Base" then existent in the R.A.F.— at Calshot, a colourful station in those days with a few hangars at the end of the spit of land sticking into Southamp-ton Water, dominated by the old Castle. The course was for a mixture of pilots, the most senior being Squadron-Leaders, with a few Flight-Lieutenants, a number of Flying Officers and one or two Sergeant-pilots. The course lasted six months, and consisted of half theory and half flying. We started life on the practical side with dual instruction on the old wooden-hulled "Southamptons". These boats were the most beautiful examples of wooden construction I have ever seen in aircraft, and they were certainly a delight to fly. Yet it was a terrible change to come from a fighter to these, the heaviest of all aircraft then in the R.A.F.

My instructor was Laddie Clift, who was the Flight Commander of the initial training flight of the Flying Boat Squadron at Calshot. He was a real "old salt", with a great pride in the fact that the albatross on his cap-badge was deep green from the salt sea spray—in fact, everything about him was deep green from the salt sea spray! He was, however, so far as I was concerned, a very thorough instructor, and I am very glad that I had him, though at the time I was a little impatient that others went off solo quickly whilst I "soldiered" on and on and was one of the last in the Course to be allowed to take a flying boat into the air on my own.

The flying side was intensely interesting, as we used to do many things other than simple flying, particularly on the seamanship side. The down-to-earth nature of the seamanship in flying boats is far "saltier" than the seamanship which ordinary sailors learn. We had open cockpits, and anchoring or mooring in difficult conditions almost always produced exciting moments. The pupils not only did the flying, but also acted as bowmen when picking up moorings, and a large part of the Course consisted of navigation training. In fact, apart from the flying, the navigation was the biggest part of the course, coupled with a little naval co-operation and the like. In the navigational subjects it so happened that I did well, and this was to affect my subsequent postings.

In due course we finished at Calshot, after a very happy six months, and I was posted to 210 Squadron at Pembroke Dock. I loaded all my worldly possessions on to my aged Morris and set out for "little England beyond Wales." As I crossed the high Welsh mountains that night, in pitch black darkness, the lightening flashed and the thunder roared, an excellent baptism to my new station.

Pembroke Dock township consisted of stone walls and bleak, wet, empty streets. The station was completely surrounded by a high stone wall, and by careful navigation I eventually found the one and only gate—a heavy forbidding structure which opened carefully at the noise of my car.

After due examination I was permitted to enter; it seemed almost like a prison. The next morning my first impression was one of desolation and despondency, but how wrong first impressions can be! Pembroke Dock turned out to be one of the happiest stations I have ever struck. The squadron was equipped with Southampton metal-hulled flying boats when I arrived, but we soon got Singapores, which were a great thrill. Shortly after my arrival we had the privilege and pleasure of getting Bert Harris as our Commanding Officer, and he certainly made things move. Night flying became a normal routine, though previously it had been a most rare activity for flying boats. Milford Haven was narrow at the dockyards, but we taxied 5 miles down the estuary so that we could get sufficient runs in all directions, and there we carried out our flying. To this activity we soon added fishery protection patrols, dropping flares—and on a number of occasions, with the help of fishery protection vessels, very nearly managed to make arrests of French fishermen inside our territorial waters! At one stage we did a six weeks' exercise in night flying, taking off from Dover Harbour and landing back at Calshot—a most interesting occupation which had something to do with Air Defence.

On one occasion I was flying as second pilot to a more senior officer in the Squadron, and on the way back to Calshot his ability to fly on instruments, even in the fairly good weather which prevailed, was not all it should be! When I saw the compass spinning and the air speed climbing, I rushed for the cockpit to find him rolled half over—and with all flying wires screaming and wings flapping, he was heading for the sea. I grabbed the controls in the rear cockpit, and righted the aircraft without any resistance from the first pilot. It was an interesting moment, and a very surprising one for an old hand.

In due course, this happy life at Pembroke Dock came to a sudden end. I was posted to Calshot as a lecturer in the R.A.F. Navigation School, and back I went. The idea of being a lecturer was repulsive to me, though I should have been delighted at the honour. I not only lectured to the Flying-Boat Pilots who went through that Course, but in some subjects I also took the specialist Long Navigation Course. This went on for some time, but I had no particular desire to remain a navigation lecturer all my life, and in due time I was able to transfer to become an instructor in the Flying Boat Training Squadron. I still continued with lecturing in a number of subjects, but I had the great pleasure of flying a large part of my time.

Gill Saye was Flight Commander, one of the best I have ever had. He allowed a remarkable degree of freedom to both me and to Crackers Carey, who was the other instructor in the Flight for most of the time I was there. The three of us remained together for a very long period, in contrast to the usual chopping and changing. I was still there at the end of my service with the R.A.F., and during that time I had carried out a very large number of cruises around the British Isles.

On these cruises each instructor took two or three pupils, one fitter, one wireless operator and occasionally one rigger, together with a large number of spares. The squadron of usually 4 aircraft (sometimes 5, if the C.O. of F.B. Training Squadron came), went off for a period of 10 days. It was excellent for initiative, as we were often left very much to ourselves, and if in trouble we had to take the appropriate action entirely on our own initiative. We usually night-stopped at flying-boat stations of the R.A.F. where available. Otherwise we used moorings which were provided for us at various harbours around the British Isles. Each day we would move on one stage, and during the day's flying would carry out a navigation exercise and possibly anchoring trials at lunch-time at places of our own choice—and the variety of places chosen was amazing. We usually stopped at Felixstowe, Queensferry, under the shadow of the Forth Bridge, Inverness, Oban, Stranraer, Londonderry, Pembroke Dock and Plymouth. Most of the time was spent in Scottish waters, and we did these cruises every three months, including the depth of winter. Being in open-cockpit flying boats we often were drenched with spray or worse, and it certainly taught one how to ignore the weather. Moreover, engine failures were frequent, and I had a good many forced landings in many odd places. These were sometimes fairly serious. The performance of the Southampton on one engine was rather that of an over-weight brick, and, therefore, if an engine failure occurred over a heavy sea the result was generally fairly catastrophic. We never flew overland except for the shortest possible journeys.

On one occasion, I had a perfectly happy and amusing incident occur when homeward bound from a cruise. I was steaming eastward up the Channel, about fifteen miles south of Portland Bill, when suddenly, bang went one engine with a complete seizure. There was a destroyer about a quarter of a mile away, and we parked close by, having managed to stay airborne on one engine just long enough to get off a signal announcing our forced landing. The destroyer was delighted to have the opportunity of rescuing a flying boat, and came alongside hailing us with obvious glee. Of course we, on our side, were equally delighted to accept their help, and soon we had a large steel hawser attached to the com-paratively diminutive bollard on the front of the boat. I was doing my stuff as the big instructor, seeing that everything was done correctly and properly, but I managed to drop a real "clanger". The destroyer set off at a speed which I con-sidered was far more than was safe for the strength of the bollard. Soon a matelot on the stern of the destroyer sig-nalled in semaphore: "Can we go faster?" I was already considerably disturbed at the strain, and thoughtlessly and abruptly said: "Certainly not." My wireless operator, stand-ing on the centre section, signalled "certainly", and before he could send the word "not" to the destroyer the matelot had disappeared and in no time at all we were practically planing. The destroyer was really going as fast as she could, and never in my life have I seen a flying boat go so fast at the end of a piece of string as on that occasion. Fortunately it was beyond the hump speed. In fact, the strain on the bollard was reduced by higher speed, and, therefore, I let matters proceed as they were; we arrived in Portland Harbour in the finest spirits and in the shortest time. They put us on a mooring and we then changed the engine, as was our custom, with one fitter, three pupils, one instructor and one wireless operator—and no outside help.

On 1st January 1934 I sat at my study-desk in my bedroom up at the Mess at Calshot, and solemnly made some New Year resolutions. A certain Mr. McRobertson had offered a large prize for a race from England to Melbourne to mark the Melbourne Centenary Celebrations. I was keen to be in that race. Admittedly I knew something about navigation, and had flown different types of aircraft, but comparatively I had little to offer as a pilot in asking for some exceptional aircraft in which to compete. I decided, therefore, that I must get my First-Class Navigator's licence, a qualification then extremely rare anywhere in the world, even in Great Britain. The examination took place in the middle of March. I began studying that day, 1st January 1934, and worked as I had never worked before. The Station Commander had at that time introduced dressing for dinner five nights of the week, and this meant formal dinner with a lengthy procedure. The President of the Mess Committee, P. D. Robinson, however, was both human and intelligent, and he turned a blind eye to this requirement, whilst I cooked sausages on my open coal fire in my bedroom and kept at my study from the moment work ceased in the afternoon until 2 a.m. every morning. In two and a half months I took the examination, and to my great surprise I passed. I was, I believe, then the seventh holder of the licence in the world.

The attempt to get an aircraft for the McRobertson race

was, however, a battle far from won. Captain Baird, of early Schneider fame, joined forces with me, and he managed to get an offer of a Rolls Royce engine on loan if we were able to build an airframe round it. Unfortunately, this came to nothing, in spite of a number of interviews and journeys. The final outcome was that after the entries had closed, I was happy but disappointed in having to accept a post as navigator with Jimmy Woods, an Australian, flying a Lockheed Vega with a single engine and a high wing. Basically it was a good aeroplane, but unfortunately we did not fare too well. The preparations were extremely hurried, and Jimmy Woods was obviously harassed by lack of sufficient funds to do things properly. The aircraft was second-hand, and he arranged for a number of modifications and other work to be carried out. On the day we should have arrived at Mildenhall, the starting point, the aircraft was still not complete, but late that afternoon we managed to get it out on to the aerodrome at Hanworth ready to take off. In spite of the late hour, Jimmy was quite unperturbed. In fact, even whilst we still had time to reach Mildenhall, he went to the phone, telephoned through to the Air Race Committee, and got permission to arrive one day late at the assembly point. It was fortunate that he did, as an undercarriage leg jammed solid and nothing we could do would move it. Even this did not interfere with Jimmy's tranquillity; he went off to London for some social reason and left me and one mechanic to try to rectify the trouble. Hydraulics are a specialised subject, and neither the mechanic nor myself had ever seen a similar oleo leg. Nevertheless we took it apart, released the gland which had been binding and put it together again. We were well into the small hours of the morning by the time we got it back on the aircraft apparently serviceable. The next morning we reached Mildenhall, and then there followed a few hectic days preparing maps, compass swinging and passing the race inspection. Unhappily, our chances of the speed event were poor, owing to the very short range of the aircraft when flying within its normal category weight limitations.

Eventually the great day arrived, and it certainly was a magnificent sight to see the aircraft taking off in an English early morning on a race half-way round the world. We were off at 0639 hours on 20th October 1934. We had no radio, and 90 per cent. of the first leg was over the top of clouds, so that we had to rely entirely on dead reckoning. All went well and we landed at Marseilles 3 hours, 45 minutes after take-off, a very fast trip for those days. Incidentally, Jimmy Woods had implicit faith in my navigation, and was under the happy delusion that a navigator could work magic. Fortunately the fates were kind, and his reliance on my navigation did not go astray. We pressed on to Rome, and thence in the dark to Athens. As we were doubtful of our range being sufficient to reach Aleppo, and as the only intermediate stop, Nicosia, had no night-flying facilities whatsoever, we decided to sleep a little in Athens. The Greek Air Force kindly put us up in the local barracks, and after a few hours' sleep we pressed on to Aleppo. As we took off I was under the impression that the undercarriage had jammed again, as it had done at Hanworth. On arrival at Aleppo, in Syria, Jimmy brought the Vega into land, whilst I took up my position as far aft as possible. He hit the ground with a fair wallop and the undercarriage collapsed; down she went, and the nose went in as we whipped over on to our back. I was in the tail of the machine, and my velocity from one end of the cabin to the other was remarkable. Even more astounding was the degree of "concertina-ing" of my body which took place at the far end. I rolled out into the dust of the aerodrome and then helped Jimmy Woods out with his forehead bleeding rather badly. He looked an awful mess, but he was not really as badly bent as I was. I had done a fair bit of damage to one knee and could not move my head or shoulders, due to what I subsequently discovered to be three crushed vertebræ. We were taken to a convent, and some

Syrian nuns patched us up. The Air Attaché had come up from Beirut, which was very fortunate for me, as he looked after me magnificently and subsequently drove me, a very forlorn character, down to Beirut, where I caught an American ship via Alexandria to Naples. I had to leave poor Jimmy Woods with practically no money, and a badly broken aircraft, waiting for funds to be cabled to him from Australia. He did eventually manage to rebuild the aircraft, and he continued the flight many months later.

On the ship between Alexandria and Naples an ear infection, no doubt acquired whilst in Aleppo, gave me absolute agony. I repeatedly asked to see the ship's doctor, but could obtain no definite news of him, however much I pressed. At last things became so bad with my ear that one of the ship's officers took me to the doctor's cabin, where I discovered the reason for his mysterious non-appearance. He lay on his bunk under the influence of dope, and we could not get more than a word or two out of him. We therefore helped ourselves to what we thought might be good for my ears—and I survived.

A week later, back at Calshot, I passed my annual medical with one stiff leg, three crushed vertebræ, an·abscess in the ear and immobility of my head and shoulders! It took me months of treatment with a specialist before my backbone was fully recovered.

My premature return to Calshot coincided with a start of another cruise round the British Isles with pupils, and Gill Saye quickly readjusted the plans so that I could take my pupils on this cruise as usual. Within a fortnight of the crash at Aleppo, I was flying my favourite Southampton S1234 ex-Calshot.

It was at about this stage of my chequered career that a poor innocent girl from Switzerland, visiting England, found herself unable to avoid me. Inevitably and inexorably I ultimately fell for the job of teaching her English—and I have been doing it ever since.

During the three years that I was an instructor at Calshot, I not only obtained my First-Class Navigator's Licence, my B Pilot's Licence, Ground Engineer's Licences in A, C and X categories, my Wireless Air Operator's Licence and my Instructor Certificate in preparation for the day when I would enter civil aviation, but I also took the precaution of trying to gain civil flying experience and to keep slightly in touch with aeroplanes on wheels.

In 1933 I purchased my first private aircraft, a single seater DH 53. This low-wing monoplane, powered by a twin-cylinder Bristol Cherub engine, was highly delightful and highly dangerous. It was as light as a feather, but it had a stall like the crack of a whip. It cruised at sixty-five miles per hour, and could land in about fifty yards. Literally it was ideal transport with which to go out to tea on Sunday afternoon! It used two and a half gallons per hour, which was just within the financial limitation of an impecunious junior officer. I bought it for £115, and sold it two and a half years later for £130. My annual overhauls cost one guinea for the A.I.D. fee. £1 to my fitter at Calshot who helped me, and about 5s. for material.

They do say that civil aviation is now fortunate that annual overhauls are in the kindly and understanding hands of the Air Registration Board—and private owners, if any survive in this land, know all too well what the costs now are. Not only are the fees five to ten times more, but "licensed" certification costs a fortune, whilst material and components are approximately five times the price of similar materials and components when they are used commercially and are, therefore, uncertified. The result is that Britain today has less private flying for her population than any other civilised nation.

During the time I was at Calshot I also gained a little air line experience by flying for Jersey Airways, Ltd., every Saturday and Sunday. This gallant new airline operated from Heston, Southampton and Portsmouth to Jersey, where we landed on the beach between tides. Jersey Airways owned eight aircraft—twin-engined DH Dragons. We were operating into Jersey twice each day. Each pilot did his own paper work and everything else, including looking after his passengers and their baggage, and running the aircraft singlehanded. It was good experience. The tide at Jersey rises a mere twenty-six feet, and the beach becomes covered like a flash once the water starts its inward race. Never was any aircraft lost to the tide, in spite of many close shaves, but the derelict bus which was driven down on to the beach to act as our office was eventually lost.

My flying with Jersey Airways was very valuable experience for me, but it came to an untimely end when some M.P. asked the Secretary of State for Air whether it was true that a regular Air Force officer was flying for a civil airline and thereby depriving a civil pilot of his livelihood. I had never taken any reward for my services, and I was, therefore, entirely in the clear. I felt, however, that discretion was the better part of valour, and discontinued my week-end flying.

During the rest of my service in the R.A.F. I remained at Calshot lecturing and flying. Occasionally we would do anchoring practices—for lunch—at St. Helier and at St. Peter Port, and the cruises every three months were always an experience, if not a pleasure. I managed to fly a good many other types of flying boats during this period, so that by the time I left the service I had 1,350 hours flying to my credit on twenty-one different types, of which eight were marine aircraft and the remainder land planes.

When I left the Air Force there were many regulars who regarded me as a thoroughly bad type for not wanting to stay in the Service. What I did, however, was done not in any spirit of dissatisfaction with the Service—for I had been both happy and well rewarded by a wealth of experience during my years in the R.A.F.—but more because I fully realised that a peace-time air force has its limitations, and if I were to continue real progress in aviation I must look elsewhere. Moreover, I felt quite certain that if there were a war I should be not less but more valuable to the R.A.F. by widening my experience. This I believe proved to be true—almost dramatically so. When I left the Service, in August, 1935, I was a young man of very mixed feelings. Determined to move on and not to fear an outside world, tremendously grateful for all that the R.A.F. had done for me, I was filled with hope for my future career, very sad to leave the R.A.F.—but more than anything else I was scared and happy, for in ten days' time I was to be married.

I married a beautiful and wonderful girl, and she has helped me and stood by me ever since, and therefore she has a share in all that follows in this book; but as I am writing about my war activities, my private life is omitted.

3

WORLD WAYS

HAVING left the Service on 11th August 1935 I became one of the unemployed. I spent the next five months as a gentleman of leisure. In fact, for one so poor as myself a five months' honeymoon might sound a little extravagant, but circumstances demanded nothing less. First, we had to go to be inspected thoroughly by all my wife's relatives in Switzerland, and then to be fair we had to give an equal opportunity to my relatives in Australia. We took the s.s. *Hobson's Bay* from Southampton to Brisbane—a long and tiresome trip had it not been for the fact that we were on our honeymoon. Before leaving London I had taken the precaution of calling upon Sir Isaac Pitman's, the publishers, and had their assurance that if I were to write a book on air navigation in a fairly complete form they would be only too pleased to publish it. During the six-week voyage to Australia my wife and I managed to write one whole chapter of this book, but even that was a struggle with a ship full of passengers violently and aggressively engaged in the waste of time.

Our voyage to Australia was not simply a honeymoon jaunt. For six months before leaving the Service I had been in close touch with a London finance house, who had purchased a number of aircraft for New England Airways, a company operating between Sydney and Brisbane. This finance company, having had a little contact with me over small technical matters, kindly armed me with a letter to the managing director in Sydney, requesting him to find me a suitable appointment in an executive capacity in the airline. Thus I not only had the pleasure of having a prolonged honeymoon in my visit to Australia, but the prospect of finding work there as well. I had, however, also taken the precaution of contacting Imperial Airways, who at that time had never heard of somebody who held all civil licences as I did and were therefore quite anxious to have me join them, though old Sir Tom Webb Bowen, who was the Personnel Manager, almost fell over backwards trying to avoid any appearance of keenness.

On our arrival in Brisbane the whole of the Bennett clan turned out to meet us, and I was so nervous that I shaved with toothpaste—to my wife's delight. Friends and relatives filled the wharf as we docked, and for the next four weeks gave us a wonderful time. During that period I flew down in an Avro 10 with the chief pilot of New England Airways to meet their managing director. He was most anxious to co-operate with his financial colleagues in London, and was very fair to me. He offered me an appointment as navigation superintendent, at a salary which was very just and reasonable in relation to that of other members of the company, but was somewhat less than half the remuneration which I could obtain on entry as a First Officer in Imperial Airways. What was more important, however, was that the experience obtainable would be very limited, and therefore advancement would be similarly circumscribed. So we decided to return to England. My wife and I finished writing the navigation book on the return journey—and it is still going strong, twenty-one years later.

In January, 1936, I joined Imperial Airways, Ltd., and Major Brackley, who was Air Superintendent of the company, sent me first to Croydon for three weeks, where I did training flying on the DH 86 and the two experimental mail carriers which had been produced at that time by A. V. Roe, Ltd., and by Boulton and Paul, Ltd. What was more important, however, was that at Croydon I saw for the first time a

real airline in full-scale operation. I did two trips as a super-
numerary first officer, and then had the pleasure of going as
first officer to Captain Horsey with no other first officer to
show me how to do it. It was an interesting occasion, for it
was a late-night service to Paris in a HP 42 with a full load of
passengers. Captain Horsey, who was not only a colourful
character (like all the old Imperial Airways pilots) but also a
lovable one (unlike some of the others), had a friend amongst
the passengers, and immediately after take-off he handed
over to me and disappeared. As we joined the circuit at Le
Bourget old Horsey came into the cockpit, climbed into his
seat and did the landing. I must admit I was a little impressed
myself that I should be left alone in control of a large four-
engined aircraft of which I had practically no experience, to
fly blind on what was then a quite bad weather route. Old
Horsey was even more disturbed when he asked me, as we
drove into Paris, how many trips I had done, and I replied:
"It was my first as a first officer." He had been away and was
under the impression that I had been operating out of Croydon for some months! Later, while still based in England
with Imperial Airways, I was on a Croydon-Cologne trip on
the day when the Nazi military forces marched in, re-occupy-
ing the Rhineland while Britain refused to join France in
preventing it—the beginning of the end!

Major Brackley, the Air Superintendent, was a character
to whom the British Commonwealth owes much. "Brakles"
was the person most directly responsible for opening up the
Empire Route from England to Australia and from England to
South Africa. After a distinguished career in the First World
War, and subsequent work in flying in Japan, he became the
Air Superintendent of Imperial Airways when it was formed
out of five small civil operating companies, and his work
during the 1920s and on into the 30s was of the greatest
importance. Whilst not in any way a striking or sparkling
personality, he was always calm, always immaculate and extremely proper in all his conduct. Above all else, he upheld the

prestige of the pilot, and in doing so I believe added greatly to the safety of British aviation, for there is no doubt that the captains of Imperial Airways were in those days—even though I say it myself—the best in the world, with the greatest self-reliance and ultimately the highest competence. So far as "Brakles" was concerned, captains had the first and last word concerning all decisions with regard to cancellation; their word was law. Admittedly others in Imperial Airways, notably Area Managers at some stations along the route, were the opposite, and committed what I considered to be one of the worst of all crimes, interference with the decision of captains. Indeed, some years later I saw one such Area Manager directly cause an accident with the loss of life of all those on board. Brackley, on the other hand, protected and preserved the integrity and the authority of his captains of the line. He was largely responsible for the choice of aircraft, which were always of British construction, always thoroughly sound and reliable, and also, incidentally, reasonably economical. He did great work for aviation as a whole.

After a few such trips I was posted to Egypt, where Brackley assured me I should be put in command of a flying boat between Alexandria and Brindisi. I arrived at the beginning of an era of intense training and evolution. The few flying boats then in Imperial Airways were to be replaced by a fleet of twenty-nine four-engined Short S 23 "Empire" flying boats, large four-engined monoplanes of considerably improved performance. The competition to be first in command of these boats was already intense. Frank Bailey, alias "Bill", and Donald Drew (who died shortly afterwards) were functioning in command, but others of my own vintage had just been given acting command as I arrived. They were Gurney, Oscar Burgess and Kelly-Rogers. All were paid on the basis of the amount of flying they did, and the keenness to get flying was almost "cut-throat". I pushed into the roster with considerable difficulty and consequent unpopularity

Unfortunately at about this moment, possibly due to our sanctions against Italy (for it was at the height of the Abyssinian war), *Sylvanus*, one of our four-engined Kent-type flying boats, was "accidentally" burnt at moorings in Brindisi whilst refuelling. This left two Kent boats to operate 4 services a week in each direction, Brindisi—Athens—Mirabella—Alexandria, an impossible situation. The old Calcuttas (three-engined) were therefore pressed back into service, 2 of them to fly instead of one Kent. With open cockpits life was not very easy going in the Calcuttas, but what was more tiresome was the fact that with their 75-knot cruising speed and their limited range the prevailing north-westerly between Crete and Egypt was often too much for us. On many occasions one found it necessary to cancel the early morning departure from Alexandria and send all the passengers back to their hotel because of forecasts of strong headwinds. On other occasions, however, I have set off and done 2 or even 3 hours, only to find that it was impossible to reach Mirabella on the fuel, and so have to turn back to Alexandria.

Nearly all our flying was done "under the weather", and we became very familiar at close quarters with many Greek mountains, particularly up and down the Gulf of Corinth. The Italians in Brindisi were very anti-British, which sounds more serious than it was. Indeed, in general it was our sole source of amusement when night stopping in Brindisi. There were times when the anti-British demonstrations got a little hectic. On one occasion the local Italians threw our engineers into the harbour. On several occasions they besieged the hotel with the intention of lynching all English present. This happy pastime was staged with true operatic thoroughness, and we were well warned. The crowd assembled at the top of the town with a great deal of noise and shouting, and, with Fascist flags flying, marched down the main street and turned left along the waterfront to the Albergo Internationale, where we and our passengers were having dinner. The passengers were not allowed to be flown across Italy at that time, and at Brindisi, therefore, we put them aboard the train for Paris. The hotel staff would solemnly put up all the shutters and close the big front doors. The chief of the Fascists, who lived in the hotel, would be disturbed at his dinner to be told that a demonstration was taking place. By this time the crowd were outside chanting "Il Duce, Il Duce" and throwing stones at the hotel, generally egged on and aggravated by irresponsible Imperial Airways staff making faces from the windows. This would go on until the head Fascisti boy finished his dinner, when he would take himself very solemnly to the balcony on the first floor over which a large Italian flag had been draped. He would then make a fiery speech, after which he would tell the crowd that to prove their sense of responsibility they must allow the English passengers to proceed on their journey safely. The bus would draw up at the front door, and the passengers would get on board and drive away. All very good fun but for the occasion when one of the traffic trainees was caught red-handed throwing a jug of water on the crowd from his bedroom window! It was good experience for him to see the inside of an Italian gaol for a short period. He knows the Italians now even better than I do!

During the period when I was operating out of Alexandria, the routine was normally to fly up to Brindisi in one day, rest there one night or three nights, and then fly back to Alexandria in one day. Irregularities on other parts of the route (from Australia or South Africa), coupled with the weather, often resulted in our stopping for the night in Athens, and generally having a much more irregular life.

On one occasion I had five days in Brindisi, and in that time wrote a complete book—on the handling of flying boats (*The Air Mariner*).

I also occasionally flew HP 42s through to Karachi and down to Kisumu, as part of the company's policy of giving as wide experience as possible to all its captains, whenever practical.

The first of the Empire flying boats, *Canopus*, for which we were all waiting so enthusiastically, eventually arrived in Alexandria in the hands of Bill Bailey (Capt. Frank Bailey) about January, 1937, and this truly was a sign of change. Soon more of the type were ready for collection, and the Imperial Airways policy of stationing crews along the route was changed so that we were all based at Hythe, near Southampton, in England. The second boat was allotted to Egglesfield, and the third, to my annoyance as he was a newcomer to flying boats, to Jimmy Alger. I was given command of the next one, G-ADUX *Cassiopeia*, with D. F. Satchwell as my First Officer and a permanent crew. This system, introduced by Brackley as part of the new scheme with one captain and crew on one boat on a more or less permanent basis, was undoubtedly the happiest flying arrangement I have ever encountered. Unhappily, it soon proved impractical and had to be dropped. Whilst it lasted, however, it added to efficiency and safety in scores of ways.

At first we operated Southampton-Alexandria, but soon the "all-up mail scheme" whereby all first-class mail was carried throughout the Empire by air, was in full swing, and the Empire boats operated right through to Durban on the South African run and to Singapore on the Australian run. Sir Kingsley Wood, who was one of the originators of this system together with Woods Humphrey, the managing director of Imperial Airways, deserved the highest honour for this system, which proved to be so beneficial to aviation and to Commonwealth business and personal relationship. Needless to say, they received no recognition whatever for this, a milestone in British history.

The interest of these far longer routes was an improvement both for crews and for passengers. The handling of a flying boat at Wadi Halfa with a five-knot stream running with a twenty-knot wind, was often extremely tricky, with the mooring buoys swinging and thrashing, with drogue lines breaking, and the bowman terrified of missing the pick-up, but even more terrified of falling into the boiling muddy water where crocodiles lurked and were almost certain to get him in a matter of seconds if he fell in. Unhappily on one occasion a native boy fell off the refuelling barge at Wadi Halfa and was taken by a crocodile before we could save him.

There was interest all along the line, particularly beyond Khartoum. We often used to fly low to show the passengers the Bor herd of elephants, then about one hundred and fifty strong, or to give them a view of a charging rhino not knowing which way to charge, or of the stately loping canter of giraffes. One of the most popular sights was the river just below Murchison Falls, which teemed with hippo such as I have never seen anywhere else at any time. From Lake Victoria down to the coast we nearly always went close to Kilimanjaro, a true primary school-book shaped mountain with its beautiful snow peak.

We had our moments of achievement. I picked up a load at Alexandria on one occasion on a service which was running late. We had no night-flying facilities at Southampton in those days, but nevertheless I aimed at doing the trip in one day. I made an early start, and the passengers grumbled a little, but before we were half-way through their spirit of "charging and cheering" was even more enthusiastic than that of the crew. We had strong head-winds between Alexandria and Athens, and again from Athens to Brindisi. We rushed our refuellings and our formalities on the ground and kept going—Bracciano and on to Marignane. As I went ashore there I really felt that it was impossible to reach Southampton until well after dark, and I should therefore be forced to give up the attempt. In the Met. Office, however, they forecast following winds, and on we went. Half-way across France the passengers were in such a state that I had to report ground speed every quarter of an hour, and even then they sent the steward up to wait for more news long before we were ready to give them any. We landed at South-

ampton with twenty minutes of daylight to spare, the first
aircraft to fly from Egypt to England in one day.

Shortly afterwards I was the first to fly from Dar-Es-Salaam
to Durban in one day, making an early start which necessi-
tated a night landing in Lindi before daylight. As they had no
flare path, to do this I used the passenger launch as a single
datum, and "felt" the boat down with a little engine on to a
calm sea. It was certainly something one could not have done
in a land plane!

Early in 1938 I applied formally in writing to be put in
command of *Mercury*, the top half of the Mayo Composite
aircraft. It was Imperial Airways policy that during 1938
flights across the Atlantic would be carried out using the
Mayo composite, and also using S 30 flying boats with flight
refuelling to assist them. Unfortunately, the flight refuelling
system and the S 30 boats were not ready for the job, and
therefore the sole Atlantic effort of the company that summer relied on the Mayo composite. The testing by Short
Brothers test pilots went fairly well, and they did the first
separation of *Mercury* from its parent flying boat, the *Maia*.
Mercury was a small four-engined monoplane on floats, with
a tiny fuselage, sufficient for one pilot and one radio operator. In the floats there was space for mail and freight.

The Mayo Composite was designed and built by Short Bros.,
Limited, but Major Robert Mayo, who was then Technical
Manager of Imperial Airways, was the holder of the patents
covering the separating technique and of mechanism involved in the process. The basic principle was that at slow
speed the lower half of the composite would carry most of
the load, and would assist the upper half off the ground.
Moreover, the lower half being lightly loaded and having
very powerful engines would substantially assist the thrust
problem, because of its great surplus of power. The take-off
was, of course, simply that all eight engines, four on the
lower half and four on the upper half, would all be working
to full throttle, but the amount of power taken out of the

engines of the upper half would not be unduly arduous for them and greater reliability was thus ensured. Moreover, the propellers of the upper were designed for cruising conditions without any great consideration for take-off, and thus achieved a lightweight without the complications and weight of the two-pitch propellers which were then coming into vogue. After the take-off, when in level flight, the speed was allowed to creep up to a figure sufficient to give surplus lift on the top aircraft, so that it was in fact carrying some of the weight of the lower aircraft. When this state had been achieved, and the balance of the elevators arranged as indicated by the lights provided, then the release was pulled by both the upper and the lower pilots, and the separation would take place, resulting in a clear jump apart, usually of the order of ten to fifteen feet. Each aircraft then flew off under its own control, and the separation was complete. By this means the pay-load lifted by the upper half was far, far greater than could be achieved otherwise for the size of the aircraft.

Bob Mayo himself was the typical scientist, tall and thin, slightly drooping—he had the most meek voice and mild manner of any relatively senior official I have ever known. In fact, his position in Imperial Airways was only one stage from the top, yet his manner was that of a shy schoolboy. Behind his quiet exterior, however, he packed a very fine intellect, and indeed quite a strong character which he only showed when really necessary. His work technically was of a high order, and his contribution to Imperial Airways' success was undoubtedly great. His only weakness was that often he would not stand up, particularly against the commercial interests of the company, in a manner which we pilots would have liked to have seen. He was certainly one of the kindest people for whom I have ever worked.

Unfortunately, the official testing of the Mayo composite aircraft had to be done by the approved Experimental Establishment, which for marine aircraft was Felixstowe. Its laborious processes were unbelievable, and I really think that if

I had not been present during the whole of the tests the Felixstowe staff would have taken at least two years to complete them. Fortunately, their governmental inefficiency was somewhat offset by the fact that a very good friend of mine, tall and cheerful Percy Pickles, was the pilot allotted to the aircraft. We had been fellow instructors together at Calshot, and therefore our liaison was of the friendliest and closest. Finally, with summer well advanced, we managed to wrest *Mercury* and *Maia* away from Felixstowe, and soon they were riding at our moorings at Hythe in Southampton Water. We carried out a few test flights, one of which was of one day's duration, and each had its moments. On the first long test, when climbing on board the aircraft at about five o'clock in the morning, I hurried from the tender, through the lower deck of *Maia*, up on to her flight deck and through the top hatch, preparatory to climbing up into *Mercury* above. As I stepped on to the smooth upper surface, carrying headset and microphone, my sextant, chronometer and a bundle of books, I suddenly found myself slithering on a mixture of water and hydraulic fluid which had been spilled. Before I knew where I was, my feet were in the air and I had gone over the side head-first backwards. I had nasty thoughts about coming to a ridiculous end, for I realised that the motor-boat was vertically below the place where I was falling. Happily, it had just pulled away from the side of *Maia*, and I therefore suffered nothing more than a good ducking. Holding all the things which were in my arms took a little will-power, but eventually I came to the surface and lost nothing. I quickly stripped, borrowed some overalls from Munro, *Mercury's* ground engineer, and carried on with the test flight as arranged. On the second of these test flights the intercommunication between the lower half and the upper half failed, and I regret to say, so did our intended drill, covering such an eventuality. It speaks volumes for the care which Major Mayo had put into the design that in spite of this we separated without trouble. The sensation of separating a composite aircraft is exactly the same as that of dropping a heavy bomb.

A meeting was called by the Air Ministry and the A.I.D., which I attended with Major Mayo and Captain A. S. Wilcockson, the pilot of the lower half. To me it was a new experience, the pattern of which repeated itself in my life many times in the years that followed. Lashings of civil servants, some said to be scientific and some admittedly not, sat around and solemnly and formally told us that *Mercury* with a full load of petrol could barely do the trip from Foynes (on the Shannon) to Botwood in Newfoundland, and that its return flight without *Maia* to help it off the ground was quite impossible. They based their opinion on the Felixstowe test figures, and it seemed to me that dear old Bob Mayo, a somewhat sensitive man, was going to shrivel up and disappear. Fortunately, my close liaison with Percy Pickles provided me with the knowledge that Felixstowe, somewhat ignorant of the peculiarities of Exactor hydraulic controls, had carried out all the fuel consumption tests on rich mixture. Fortunately, Imperial Airways were themselves responsible, and although the Air Ministry still had most serious doubts about what I said, they gracefully stood aside and let us continue the projected flights.

On 20th July 1938 we loaded our newspapers, cinema films and the like, a half-ton in all, the first commercial load ever to be carried across the North Atlantic, into the floats of *Mercury*. Some three days earlier, we had already lifted *Mercury* up on to the top of *Maia*, with the hand-crane on the little wharf at Foynes, and had made full preparations. At 18.49 hours we started up four engines on *Mercury* and four engines on *Maia*, and in due course took off in fine weather ready for the separation. As unhitches go, this went off without a hitch. The first half-ton of commercial pay-load was on its way by air across the North Atlantic.

Head-winds were forecast, and therefore immediately after the separation I dropped down from 2,000 feet to cross the last little piece of Ireland at 200 feet. Thereafter, whilst daylight lasted I cruised at about 50 feet above the surface, avoiding as far as possible the effect of the head-winds. There was an automatic pilot on *Mercury*, and fortunately it was a good one. With a compass excellently sited and very accurately swung, I found *Mercury* a wonderful aircraft to navigate. I had an old Bigsworth chart-board in my knees, my sextant was in a "bed" behind me, my Bygrave slide-rule in a container by my side, with a place for almanac, pencils, etc., conveniently at hand. Never before nor since have I experienced such an excellent navigational arrangement, nor have I ever achieved more accurate results. When darkness fell I climbed to 500 feet and held that height right through a very turbulent warm front with heavy rain. "Faithful" Coster (Radio Officer A. J. Coster) at the radio was regularly sending out the position reports which I gave him every hour, and also trying to communicate with ships. In the middle of the crossing I passed dead over a ship with all its lights on, a coincidence which gave me quite a thrill. I often wonder what ship it was, and whether they knew that their first air-borne competitor, complete with pay-load, was passing over-head.

I followed a great circle track from Foynes direct to Montreal, though with prevailing winds I was in considerable doubts as to whether I would make the distance direct. By three-quarters of the way across the ocean the winds had gone round to the north-west, and I was able to climb up to a more economical height without undue wind disadvantage. I was getting my astro sights again after the bad weather, and all was well. I passed over the small island in the centre of the Strait of Belle Isle exactly on track and on time as the first light made it possible for me to see my landfall through the broken cloud below. At that point I had to take the decision as to whether or not I would re-fuel at Botwood. I went on. By now, Coster was working overtime. The radio at Montreal was working us direct, and wanted to know all our plans, etc. By the time we passed Quebec the weather was sunny and fine, and I saw where Wolfe had climbed the Heights of Abraham as described in my history book. At Montreal I simply landed at the place provided at Boucherville, and tied up to the mooring buoy.

Coster and I got into a small boat and went ashore, and then things started! Never before had I experienced the American press. We were met by Mr. Howe, the Minister for Transport, and officially welcomed. The press, however, considered that both Mr. Howe and also the customs and port officials were far less important than themselves. I made myself very unpopular by ordering all the press out of the customs shelter until I had completed the required formalities. This apparently was a heinous offence for which there could be no forgiveness. We took on fuel, and carried on immediately to New York in fairly murky weather, landing at Port Washington amongst white sails which looked so peaceful compared with the bustling press-boats bristling with photographers.

As a small boy I had seen displays by Australian Aborigines in which they reached a climax of frenzy by rushing at you, shaking spears, woomeras and shields violently. As Coster and I came ashore, exactly such an onslaught took place, but instead of Abos we had camera men, and instead of spears we had cameras with flash-bulbs. Never have I seen anything like it, and never have I seen such results. Even the full size New York papers carried photographs of *Mercury* over the whole width of the front page. The "pick-a-back plane" apparently appealed to their news sense in quite a big way. The fact that we carried the first commercial load across the North Atlantic by air was relatively unimportant. We had also flown not only the Atlantic itself, but without re-fuelling had gone on to Montreal, a further 800 nautical miles which was about 46 per cent. more than the ocean distance itself.

In New York Paul Bewshea, the Imperial Airways représentative, looked after us magnificently, and we had a wonderful time. Queerly enough Pan-American Airways gave us a dinner at which the crew of one of the German catapult planes was also entertained. This plane had catapulted from its mother ship off the Azores and flown to New York. This catapulting method of assisted take-off was in direct competition with Major Mayo's method of the composite aircraft. One such plane had, only 6 months before, been catapulted from its ship off the south coast of England and had established the world's long-distance seaplane record of about 4,500 statute miles. Although I had said nothing, I was determined that after the Atlantic flights were over I would endeavour to give this matter a little attention—the "powers-that-be" permitting.

The return flight, owing to the absence of *Maia*, presented some difficulties. When taking off under its own power, *Mercury*, even without any payload, could lift only somewhat less than one-third of its maximum fuel load. This was not sufficient to make a direct flight from Botwood to Foynes, even with favourable winds. I therefore planned to fly from Botwood to Horta in the Azores. We night-stopped in Botwood, and with a fairly favourable forecast took off at daylight the next morning, with the knowledge that the island landfall had to be made solely on the accuracy of sights abeam (of the sun) giving me the position lines parallel with my track. I flew at 8,000 feet all the way, and got steady drift sights which, coupled with my accurate compass, gave a track which even on my final sunsight required no change of course to hit the first of the islands, which came up very nicely a few minutes before E.T.A. From there we only had to cover about 100 miles to Horta, and we did so uneventfully. At no time did we manage to raise the marine radio station at Horta, even though Coster tried persistently. The landing area at Horta was virtually in the open sea, being a wide sweeping bay unprotected to the south and east. However, there was little swell, and both the arrival and departure the next morning were uneventful. At Lisbon we were given a wonderful welcome, but we pressed on quickly to Southampton, where I had an even more important welcome awaiting me—from my wife.

Immediately after my return from the Atlantic trip, I had the pleasure of meeting Sir Kingsley Wood, who was then Secretary of State for Air and as such was responsible not only for the Royal Air Force and all its supplies but also for civil aviation. Even although I had not at that time had a chance of putting the proposition to my superiors in Imperial Airways, I grasped the opportunity to ask the Secretary of State for Air whether he would approve of an attempt on the world's long-distance seaplane record using the Mayo Composite. His attitude was favourable from the outset, and I immediately took up the subject with Major Mayo, who in turn talked to George Woods Humphreys, the managing director of Imperial Airways. I am glad to say that the Government gave their approval, thanks, I think, mainly to Sir Kingsley Wood himself, and it was arranged that we should attempt flying at least a distance sufficient for the seaplane record then held by Germany.

My own plan was to fly from Southampton to Capetown. This would have given us the world seaplane record quite comfortably, and was, in my view, within the ability of the aircraft. The success on the Atlantic had, however, caused many previous pessimists to somersault into the most unyielding optimists. The plans were therefore changed, and it was agreed that I should start from Dundee in Scotland in order to permit me to break the world's absolute record and not merely the seaplane record should I find that everything went as well as we hoped. This was a wise policy, because it would have been a wonderful thing to have achieved the absolute record, even although we knew at the time that pilots of the Royal Air Force were in training in order to attempt to break the absolute record themselves, and that the figure which they hoped to set up would be in excess of what *Mercury* could achieve. Changes to *Mercury* involved considerable work at Short Bros., and this meant that we could do no further Atlantic flights that summer. The floats were treated internally so as to make them petrol-proof, and electric petrol pumps were fitted in order to pump the petrol up from the floats into the wing tank when sufficient space became available in that tank to receive it. By using both floats as well as the 1,200 gallon wing tank, we hoped to accommodate over double the normal maximum load of fuel. In addition, a hand pump was fitted just in case the electric pumps failed. I planned to set course with an overload of about 45 per cent. in excess of the normal maximum.

In due course all was ready, and we proceeded to Dundee independently, Wilkie flying *Maia* and I flying *Mercury*, accompanied not by Coster, my faithful radio operator, but by Ian Harvey, who had been a radio operator but had recently qualified for his "B" Pilot's Licence and as such had just been appointed as a first officer in the company. The idea was that owing to the very long duration of the flight (two days) it was essential that I should have another pilot on board to take over when necessary. At Dundee we loaded *Mercury* on to *Maia*, and refuelled the main tanks of both aircraft, as well as the tanks in the floats. Unfortunately, however, at this point in the proceedings Adolf Hitler took a hand in the proceedings and created a grave international situation. His territorial ambitions were beginning to take shape. The British Prime Minister rushed off to Munich, and did a certain amount of umbrella waving, but virtually surrendered to Hitler, much to my dismay. I was one of the few who at that time were sick with shame—and said so. In the meantime, we had been ordered by the Air Ministry to delay the flight until the world situation was clarified. We were staying in the R.A.F. Mess at Leuchars, and I must say I was not particularly proud of the reactions of many R.A.F. officers at that time. Admittedly, they had obsolete aircraft, and very few of them. Germany, on the other hand, was relatively weak compared with ourselves, and yet the reaction of most officers in the Mess was one of "peace at any price", which was precisely the policy of the British Prime Minister. The great day arrived when Neville Chamberlain returned from his visit to Germany and waved a piece of paper muttering something about "Peace in our time". Of all those present in the Mess when this news came over the radio, I was the only one who expressed any disgust at what we subsequently called "appeasement". I said that for the first time in my life I was thoroughly ashamed of a British action.

However, Munich gave us the "all clear" to proceed with the flight, and I was anxious to get going. Unfortunately, however, the winds refused to blow favourably, and for days and days we had a considerable head-wind over the first thousand miles. It was my policy to wait until we got at least some help at the beginning of the flight, even though we could hardly guarantee what would happen thereafter. The season was, however, moving on, and adverse weather in the first thousand miles when we were heavily loaded might prove extremely serious. Thus I was eventually forced to take the decision to go ahead, on 6th October 1938. We were bade farewell by various civil dignitaries from Dundee, and B. E. Baker, the station commander at Leuchars, acted as official observer for our departure. At noon, Harvey and I climbed up into *Mercury* and closed the doors; whilst we started our four engines, *Maia* down below started up likewise, under Wilkie's control, and off we taxied. We had never done a full-loaded take off at the weight at which we were then flying, and there was therefore something of an element of doubt in the proceedings. As Wilkie opened up I tended to lead him with my throttles somewhat more than I had previously done, owing to the additional weight up top. Everything went well, however, and in due course, over the centre of "the Law" we did the release. It was the first and only time in my life that I was "above the Law". ("The Law" is the name of a prominent hill in Dundee.) Wilkie said a cheerful

"Good Luck", and then we proceeded with the release and away I went. The power required to maintain flight when we were separated from *Maia* was, I found, somewhat more than I had calculated. This meant additional fuel consumption and, what was worse, it meant that I could not bring weak mixture into play immediately I had set course, as I had intended. The cause of this was mainly that in the process of the separation, which was of course done at a higher speed than any previous separations, one of the main engine cowlings had become loose and torn completely away, thus upsetting the streamlining of that nacelle. This probably added 3 to 4 per cent. to the overall drag of the aircraft, and reduced my range in proportion. I did not discover the cause of this lowering of performance for some considerable time, as I was fully occupied with the process of trying to maintain the optimum air speed and to reduce my power to the pre-calculated requirements. When eventually I did discover it, I was faced with a decision of considerable difficulty. Owing to the long delay we had had before the start of the flight, there were many people in London who were all for calling it off, and I realised that if I were to turn back I could be sure that I would face considerable pressure to give up the project altogether. Moreover, I could not in any case land back for very nearly twenty-four hours, if I were to use up my fuel; or if I were to jettison it, I would still need to fly for over twelve hours to get down to my landing weight. Thus I felt that the best thing to do was to proceed, at least for the early part of the flight, and to make the decision later.

With full throttle I was able to get into weak mixture, and with a slight climb, after about an hour's flying; I felt slightly more optimistic when I had achieved this. Owing to my additional drag I was, of course, lower than my intended critical cruising height by this stage, but I continued hopefully. Unfortunately, over Southern England I ran into an old cold front, which caused some icing, and as I was only at about

5,500 feet at that time as against my planned 7,000 to 8,000 feet, I was loath to lose height, which this front caused me to do. There was, however, no alternative, as I was unable to climb, and to sit at the icing level would have been even more disadvantageous. I therefore deliberately lost height quickly to below freezing level, and then continued. This meant that I had to recover the lost height, and indeed by the time I got to the Atlas Mountains in North Africa I only had just sufficient height for safe clearance.

The first twelve hours of the flight were continuously at full throttle, which speaks well for the engines. Every half-hour I logged my fuel consumption and my true air speed, and calculated my air miles per gallon, plotting a graph as I went along. On this same graph I also plotted my ground miles per gallon, which was, after all, the thing that mattered. My navigation consisted of both map reading and astro, and every hour I transferred my position from my local maps or charts on to an overall planning map of the whole route. This showed me my general progress at a glance, and gave me an estimate of my chances of success. I was not entirely depressed by the bad early start, for I realised that as soon as my weight came down a little I had a fairly definite knowledge of the performance of the aircraft, and I felt confident that I would still reach a figure in excess of the world's Long-Distance Seaplane record, though naturally I was fairly certain that I would not achieve the Absolute record. Harvey sent off the signals which I gave him every hour, and in addition to our position reports we added to each message a code group indicating our estimate of progress and chances of success. For about the first eight to ten hours I was sending out very pessimistic code words, owing to the obviously adverse situation which then prevailed. This apparently caused no end of panic in London, and Bob Mayo and Wilkie rushed back to Headquarters, Imperial Airways, and had in mind sending me a signal ordering me to return. By morning, however, my reports were fortunately much more favourable.

We had had a fair bit of thunder cloud over France, which had not helped performance much but was not anything serious. Again approaching the Atlas Mountains we had a little adverse weather just as we crossed the North African coast near Bône, but thereafter the weather was perfect, and we crossed the Sahara—which is about the same size as the Atlantic Ocean—in perfect weather. As the first sunrise came up, we were over the picture-book version of the Sahara, with its undulating sand dunes stretching as far as the eye could see. It was the true genuine "Beau Geste" stuff. We maintained the Constant Course which I had decided to hold, and very soon we were into Northern Nigeria. This Constant Course, by the way, is a theoretical optimum for long-distance flights. I had simply calculated my mean forecast winds for the whole of the journey and set course true on this basis, and maintained this heading throughout the entire flight without any change due to local wind variations. I then plotted my actual ground position as I went along, but did not make any alterations until the last few hundred miles. The forecast winds were an average westerly in the north and in the south, with an easterly drift in the equatorial regions and the two left a residual westerly component for which I had allowed. In the event the Constant Course steered turned out to be almost exactly correct.

As we crossed the railway quite close to Kano, I was able to pick it up visually, and in addition I had radio bearings from that station. Thereafter the rest of that day would have been fairly straightforward flying but for two things. The first of these was that the petrol pumps refused to function. This we had discovered as soon as we had started to transfer petrol during the first night, and Harvey spent about 60 per cent. of his time trying to get the pumps to work, the remainder of his time being spent working at the radio. He tried every connection, and did everything he could, but unfortunately the electric pumps would not lift the fuel at all. We were, therefore, faced with the problem of pumping about

1,400 gallons by hand from the floats up to the main wing tank—a lift of about ten to twelve feet. The little wobble pump provided for emergency hand operation was far from adequate for the purpose, but between efforts at the radio and his attempts to get the electric pumps working, Harvey battled away gallantly on this hand pump. By this time we were flying at about 12,000 to 13,000 feet, which in the tropics is fairly short of oxygen. Thus the pumping at this level was quite strenuous work. Harvey got more and more tired; eventually I realised that the situation was critical, and had him come and stand by in the cockpit occasionally while I myself did bouts on the pump down in the tail. This, however, was seriously interfered with owing to the fact that, as the day progressed, we kept running into thunderstorms, and in fact by mid-afternoon we were having quite a bad time with very heavy turbulence and torrential rain. We were, however, now much lighter, and from a performance point of view the situation was not so critical, as we could adjust our power requirements to suit our height without any great loss of efficiency.

The interference with the aerodynamics was unfortunate, as it probably lost us another 2 to 3 per cent. during this period. What was more serious, however, was that unless we could get the remaining petrol up into the main tank, I realised that we might not have sufficient fuel to stay in the air for the period of darkness of the second night. We were over land, and although we would be fairly close to the coast, it was obviously impossible to continue through the second night unless I could be assured that I would stay in the air till dawn. There were no seaplane stations down the whole of that coast, and therefore it was impossible to arrange any night landing facilities. This was my second rather awkward decision. For the last few hours of daylight—come thunderstorms or anything else—I stuck to the pump in turn with Harvey, and we worked like slaves trying to get up sufficient fuel to ensure that we would be able to stay air-borne during the night. When darkness fell we still had not got sufficient up into the top tank to keep going during the whole of the night, but from the progress we had made I could see that by keeping pumping whenever possible we would between us manage to remain air-borne at least till dawn. Nevertheless, it was an extremely worrying situation, for before dark I had either to give up my attempt on the world's long-distance seaplane record, or else risk the possibility of running short and having to force-land in the dark. The fact that we were able to get up enough fuel and to calculate that we would get the remainder up before it was needed, was a great comfort—and one which I enjoyed only in the nick of time.

Harvey, owing to the continuous pumping at relatively high altitude without oxygen, was getting a little light-headed. I discovered that when I went aft to do my pumping he was taking little or no notice of the aircraft, and in fact on one occasion I found, when I came back to the cockpit, that he was not even there, but was at his radio table behind it. Fortunately the auto pilot was good, and all was well, and thereafter I, on a number of occasions, quite deliberately left the aircraft entirely unattended while I went aft to do my pumping. One interesting little hallucination which occurred during the night was that as I went past Harvey he said to me, "Where is he?" I asked him who he meant, and he replied, "Where is the other chap? He's gone, I know he's gone." This was presumably some peculiarity of fatigue; when we talked about it afterwards he said that for a period he imagined that there was somebody else on board the aircraft, and that this worried him considerably.

During the night, as there were no radio aids whatever, I had to pick up my positions entirely by astro, and this I did at regular intervals once an hour so as to ensure my exact position, so that when our fuel was exhausted I would know where to land. As the night wore on and dawn approached, I kept very accurate readings of the fuel gauge, and it was clear that I was not going to be able to make Cape Town, which was our ultimate optimistic destination. I could see, however, that I was well past the world's seaplane record, and there-fore that I had at least achieved our main objective. What re-mained to be done was to achieve the best possible figure for distance, and bring the aircraft down in a place which was relatively safe, even although the coastline was peculiarly devoid of suitable seaplane alighting areas. As the second dawn broke we were over South-West Africa, and inland from the coast a matter of some 80 miles. As we passed Walvis Bay there was very little reading on the fuel gauge, but I cal-culated that at least we could get to the border of South Africa, and this we struggled on to do. The wobble pump was sucking air now, but we kept wobbling it in the hope that more fuel might be brought up from the floats. On we pressed, and fortunately the weather was good. As we closed with the coast heading for Alexander Bay on the Orange River, I realised that it would be absurd to carry on beyond that point. We might just have made Port Nolloth, but I real-ised that there was no shelter there, and it would mean virtually an open sea landing—and the swell coming in from the South Atlantic was quite considerable for a small float seaplane. We had broken the world's long-distance seaplane record, we were at the South African border, and there seemed little justification for risking danger to the aircraft by landing in the open sea for a mere extra 50 miles. There-fore I circled Alexander Bay, and in the broad estuary of that river mouth I set *Mercury* down at the end of the forty-two and a half hours' flight, the new holder of the world's long-distance seaplane record. *Mercury* still holds that record eighteen years later.

I was innocent of the fact that I had landed in the most highly policed piece of desert in the world—namely, the Orange River Diamond Mine. I taxied towards the Mine Settlement where I had seen a small aerodrome, and as I did so I saw great commotion ashore and boats putting out to meet me. The river mouth was full of sandbanks, and I was soon aground at a fairly considerable distance from the shore. The men in boats came out, most of them bearded and rather wild looking, and greatly excited at my arrival. They knew all about the flight, and were delighted that I had landed there. Their co-operation and their welcomes were wonderful. We were extremely tired and hungry, but I felt that the essential thing was to get on to Cape Town, where we were, after all, expected. I, therefore, asked them whether they could let us have fuel, and this they did. The procedure for re-fuelling was that they pushed a 40-gallon drum of petrol into the water and floated it out to the aircraft, where we received it by heaving it up on to one of the floats, cleaning the water away from the bung, opening it and then pumping the petrol up into the wing tank with a hand pump which they fortunately had available. By this means we uplifted about two hundred gallons, and then, with a few words of thanks and a wave, we started up our four engines and took off.

The take-off was an extremely doubtful and dangerous proposition, for I had no idea where the sandbanks were, and neither in fact had the people from the mine, for the river was apparently little used for fishing purposes because of the security restrictions. Just as we took off I was amused to see an aircraft flying over us; it had come up all the way from Cape Town to get photos of us. We were airborne again and on our way in about three hours, which was very good at a place where we were hardly expected and where no marine facilities existed at all. The flight down to Cape Town was uneventful, but we had mixed feelings, for in seeing the rest of that coast-line we felt great remorse that we had not managed to do that relatively short extra distance with the fuel which we had taken on board in Scotland. It seemed so little in relation to the main effort, and yet it made such a difference to the satisfaction of the achievement. In fact, we had flown just on six thousand miles against the previous existing record of just over four thousand miles.

By the time we reached Cape Town it was mid-afternoon, and we landed in the harbour and started to taxi in. We were soon surrounded by welcoming craft of all sorts and sizes, in one of which was the mayor. We moored up, and from our aircraft we were taken ashore in company with the mayor and were given an official reception. It was journey's end, and we were delighted to be there. We were even happier at the grand way everybody looked after us and made us feel reasonably satisfied with our performance, though some of them were openly disappointed that we had failed to reach Cape Town direct. I could not help feeling sorry that we had not started from Southampton and had thus been able to satisfy the good citizens of Cape Town by a direct flight from England to Cape Town instead of failing to do Scotland to Cape Town! That evening I was called upon to do an impromptu broadcast over the South African radio stations, and I must admit that after more than sixty hours without any sleep I was somewhat light-headed. I was told by some people I met the next day that they were extremely disappointed with my broadcast! We stayed two days in Cape Town and enjoyed every minute of it. We then flew across to Durban, which was the Imperial Airways terminal base on the East Coast flying boat route. There we were amongst people we knew once again, and we had proper engineers to service us and look after us. There again we had a wonderful welcome, not only from Imperial Airways but also from many locals with whom I was friendly.

The flight home to England was a real pleasure jaunt. We flew up to Beira, put on a big load of fuel—as much as we could carry on the buoyancy of our floats—and managed to do a direct flight to Kisumu on Lake Victoria. It was a most interesting flight, up to the length of Lake Nyasa and then directly across Central Tanganyika to the southern shores of Lake Victoria. From Kisumu we went direct to Khartoum and thence to Alexandria, Brindizi, Marseilles and home to Southampton. The outward-bound flight had taken us 42 hours and

26 minutes, and the homeward flight from Durban had taken us 6 days.

After this flight, which was one of the major world air records, I received no official reception, no trace of recognition of any sort from the Government and no celebrations from Imperial Airways, from Short Bros., the makers of the aircraft, or from Napiers, the makers of the engine. I wonder if such a flight could have occurred in any other country without at least some form of celebration on the return?

Our next job was to get *Mercury* back ready for ordinary freight carrying service, and by the end of November she was ready for this purpose. The first duty was to undertake direct mail flights to Egypt to ease the burden of the Christmas mail on the main routes. In those days all first-class mail to the Empire went by air without surcharge. Thus, the Christmas rush was something of a burden on the relatively small fleet of flying boats. There were two services a week to Australia and two to South Africa. This kept the fleet fairly busy. The "bottle-neck" was the early part of the flight from England, as we dropped off load as we went along and never picked up as much as we dropped off. Thus it was decided that *Mercury* should help on the England to Egypt section of the route. We loaded up with one ton of mail, which was a goodly payload for an aircraft of only 20,000 pounds all-up weight, and the first flight took place on the last day of November, 1938. After an uneventful separation from *Maia* over Southampton Water, I proceeded direct non-stop to Alexandria, and delivered the mail. The homeward flight was virtually without load in the easy stages, as we had no "parent" aircraft to give us an "assisted take-off" at that end. The second flight was on 12th December, and once again I carried a ton of mail. These flights, incidentally, were relatively simple, taking just over fourteen hours each. They were the first commercial non-stop flights ever made to Egypt.

During the winter, when there were no Atlantic flights, I

did a few trips on the Imperial Airways routes which were always quite a pleasure and most interesting. Interspersed with these flights I carried out development work, for I was still officially the development pilot for the company, and as such I had a good deal of testing of various sorts to do. Incidentally, I was in Bob Mayo's department (General Manager Technical).

During 1939 the British Overseas Airways Corporation Act came into force. This Act, in my view, was one of the most remarkable pieces of political nonsense that I have seen. Imperial Airways had been created as part of government policy to run the overseas routes of the Empire. It was a public limited company formed from five small companies, and was technically and operationally most successful. For the Empire all-up mail scheme it received a small subsidy, but otherwise had practically no government aid. It did, in fact, pay a small dividend when it was receiving government aid, and that apparently was an offence in the eyes of some people! Beside Imperial Airways, there had also grown up a small company in England, operated principally by people who were critics of Imperial Airways mainly through personal animosity of one sort or another. As I understand their history, they had not been financially successful and it seemed to me that they used almost entirely foreign aircraft—Dutch, German and American—without ever operating British aircraft on a regular basis. They managed to get a Conservative government to nationalise the International Civil Aviation of Great Britain under one head—British Overseas Airways Corporation. Imperial Airways shareholders received somewhat less than the market value of their shares, whilst those of the small company with such a *distinguished record* were paid most generously for shares. What was more serious, however, was that the technical heads of the small company were given the key positions in the new corporation and complete control of the new airline. Moreover, the pioneers of the Empire air routes were given no recognition whatever. Admittedly George Woods Humphreys, the managing director, was given a grant by the company, but otherwise he received nothing. In fact, he left Great Britain and went to live abroad, as a direct result of this unhappy political viciousness, and never returned. Neither he nor Colonel Burchall, the General Manager Administration, nor Major Bob Mayo, the General Manager Technical, ever received any honours for the grand pioneering work they had done. Imperial Airways at that time was the major airline of the world; its machines were almost entirely the four-engined aircraft which it had itself pioneered; it covered half the world with its routes. The merry men of Major Brackley, the Air Superintendent, had seared their way through darkest Africa and across the deserts of the world, and had brought civilisation and good communications to all sorts of outposts of the Empire. In fact, the heads of Imperial Airways had done great things, not only for all British people but also for world civil aviation. It is as deplorable as it is typical that the country of their birth gave them no honour.

In the late spring of 1939 we got our first S 30 flying boat modified for flight re-fuelling. The method was to let out a line from the tail, which was picked up by the re-fuelling aircraft, winched on board and connected to their supply. Then the tanker aircraft passed its fuel through the pipe into the tail of our flying boat, thus filling our tanks. We carried out a number of tests of this system during the spring. There was no doubt that Alan Cobham and the staff of Flight Re-Fuelling Limited had done a wonderful job, and everything worked smoothly. Dear old Wilkie was in charge of the operations, and two additional pilots were brought in to complete the programme. These were Gordon Store, a South African of excellent technical and navigational qualifications, and also Jack Kelly-Rogers, a Southern Irishman (who is now the Operations Manager of Aer Lingus). S 30 boats were used for other than flight re-fuelling operations, and for general use were to be flown by all the pilots on the line.

During the spring I did a considerable amount of instructional work, converting the captains from the ordinary S 23 Empire boats to the S 30s, which were, incidentally, fitted with Bristol Perseus sleeve-valve engines. In the late spring it was suddenly decided that the S 30 engines had not been tested sufficiently to be considered entirely proven for Atlantic use. It was decided, therefore, that one of the boats to be used on the Atlantic should be given intensive flying tests, and then the engines stripped for examination. This intensive flying was done by three crews, of which mine was one, the others being Gordon Store's and Jack Kelly-Rogers'. The boat selected for the job was *Connemara*, a good old Irish name, which, of course, appealed no end to Rogers and consequently to the propaganda boys who naturally connected the Southern Irishman with a flying boat of that name—to the great amusement of Gordon Store and myself. This intensive flying was a most wasteful procedure, as we achieved nothing useful; the process was quite unnecessary, as we could have carried freight or the like all over the world and thus have lightened the burden of the main route aircraft. Instead we simply flew round and round the British Isles, each doing about twelve hours at a time. We changed crews at night and morning, re-fuelled and went off again.

These flights were quite amusing—up round the Shetlands, over towards Norway, all round Ireland and the like. But unfortunately things went slightly wrong. I was just walking down the long slipway at Hythe to go on board one evening when half a mile away, out on the water, I saw a burst of flames, and *Connemara* went up in smoke. The re-fuelling barge had apparently had some small back-fire or explosion on board, and had burst into flames immediately below the wing of *Connemara*. One of the men on the re-fuelling barge had been killed and blown into the water by the initial burst, and panic reigned immediately. Apparently it was not practical to get the barge away from the aircraft, and the flames burnt through the wing, burst the main fuel tanks just above it, and flooded the entire deck of the steel barge with petrol to a depth of about six inches. The resultant fire was enormous, and it was quite impossible to get anywhere near the aircraft. In due course the spars burnt through, and *Connemara* rolled over and sank. Thus came a premature end to an expensive piece of testing. The engines were, however, retrieved from the water, and the examination of the main parts worked out reasonably satisfactorily, in spite of the mishap.

When the flames had subsided somewhat I went alongside in a motor-boat, got a line on board the still-burning barge, towed it into shallow water away from the other aircraft at moorings, and dropped an anchor in this relatively safe position. I discovered afterwards that the petrol still burning on the decks of the barge was relatively of no importance— the main re-fuelling tanks on board the barge were still full!

In August, 1939, I set out from Southampton and Jack Kelly-Rogers set out from New York on the inaugural two-way regular service of the Atlantic, which Imperial Airways (now B.O.A.C.) had laid on for that summer. Flight Re-Fuelling had stationed an aircraft at Gander, near Botwood, and in Rineanna on the Shannon, to re-fuel us at Foynes. On the first flight I carried Captain Lorraine as my first officer, plus a full crew. We circled Bristol on the way over to Foynes, for the name of the craft I was flying was *Cabot*, of historic connection with that city. After take-off from Foynes we were met by the re-fuelling aircraft, and heading out into the Atlantic on our course, we did our connecting-up procedure and received the full compliment of fuel as planned. After disconnecting, we proceeded on our way happy and contented. It was a straightforward flight of sixteen and a half hours.

We landed at Botwood, and then so on to Montreal and to New York. We had a three-day rest in New York, and then proceeded on the homeward flight. The flight re-fuelling only took place at Botwood on the homeward flight, and the tanker aircraft used Gander Airport, which was then being built about forty miles south-east of Botwood. We carried out a series of these flights during the summer, and they all went well. They were the first regular scheduled flights.

4

RELENTLESS SKIES

ON 3rd September 1939 my wife drove me from our home at Dibden Purlieu, in the New Forest, down to the flying boat base at Hythe on Southampton Water. I received the weather reports from my route, signed the ship's papers and then went to the car, where with my wife I listened on the radio to Mr. Neville Chamberlain, the Prime Minister of Great Britain. He told us, in words sombre and dull and completely uninspiring, that Great Britain had just declared war on Germany. He told us of the circumstances, of our obligations to Poland and of our declaration of war. In this grave hour he made no soul-stirring appeal to the people of Great Britain. He simply declared war.

As I looked at my wife after the broadcast was over, I knew that she had the same thoughts as I: would we survive? With a heart full of feelings and of doubts, I boarded the motor-launch, went on board my flying boat and took off. It was a flight to America, as planned, and there seemed to be no reason why it should not proceed. I landed at Foynes, where we re-fuelled; after take-off we flight re-fuelled once again, and set course out into the Atlantic. As darkness came on, we of the crew had considerable misgivings in leaving our relatives in a country at war against a nation which was in the process of demonstrating the "blitzkrieg" technique and which might unleash almighty powers against us overnight. It seemed, however, that it was our duty to continue our job.

As darkness fell I was given an abrupt and urgent message

from the radio operator. It was the first S.O.S. of the war, from the *Athenia*, a ship carrying nearly a thousand passengers, mainly women and children on their way to North America in anticipation of the European conflagration. She had been torpedoed at a position only about a hundred and fifty miles from us, and my immediate thought was to go to the scene of the disaster. I realised, however, that in the darkness we could do nothing, and I therefore decided to continue towards Newfoundland. We relayed her messages and tried to be useful, but in fact we were relatively impotent in this calamity.

The receipt of this S.O.S. sharply struck home the reality of war, like cold steel through the heart. Then, and not before, did we realise fully that we were in fact at war.

The flight onward to Newfoundland and down to Montreal and New York, and thence homeward bound, was uneventful enough. The newspapers on the other side of the ocean, however, were anything but comforting to us who had left our families behind us. On arrival back in the U.K. we were not allowed to go straight to Southampton, but had to use Poole, the new base which the company was going to use for the rest of the war in order to keep out of the balloons and the defence complications of Southampton. We did, however, have to ferry onward to Southampton after landing at Poole Harbour, and in doing so all the defences were given due warning of our movements. As we were about to go, we were told that Bill Bailey had been shot at unmercifully by our dear friends the Royal Navy, when flying at about a thousand feet up the Solent only the day before. This was cheerful news. We were, however, given the colours for the day, the code method of identification for aircraft. This was a comfort, for in those innocent days we really thought that the "colours of the day" fired from the Verey pistol would stop the guns firing at us. It was only later that we came to realise that this was, in fact, a farce.

The war meant that the whole of the routes had to be

reorganised to suit the war conditions, and the loads which the Government required us to carry. Plans were made and remade, and we were all moved to various places overseas. For my part, I was relatively immune from all this great excitement, for I was put on special duties in connection with unfriendly submarines, and this carried on from the end of September right through the winter and into the spring. The way I would meet the "cloak and dagger" people in London in odd meeting-places of their own choosing was real "story-book stuff". Moreover, the job was itself quite thrilling at times. In late spring I came back to the company proper, and having nothing to do, I flew a couple of trips on the line—one to South Africa and one to Singapore. On return from the latter, I passed through Rome on the day that Italy entered the war. At Brindisi there was great excitement as to whether I would be safe to land at Rome, but it was decided after much conference on the telephone with the manager in Rome that I should do so, pick up such English staff as possible and take them with me. This I did; it was a little sad to say good-bye to various Italian employees of the company, since they seemed genuinely sorry to be on the wrong side, and said so quite openly. That night, 9th June, 1940, we night stopped at St. Nazaire, and the place was full of dispute and despondency. Hitler was indeed on the rampage, and Italy was joining him in order to be in before "the kill" It was, incidentally, the last time I saw St. Nazaire intact.

A few days later, back at Hythe, I had the sad duty of delivering my beloved *Mercury* from Hythe up to Felixstowe, the place from which she had come after her tests there two years before. On arrival at Felixstowe I handed *Mercury* over to a Dutch Float seaplane unit, who were going to use her for reconnaissance work. It was a sad good-bye, for *Mercury* was very much a part of me in many ways. I had been her only operating pilot.

Two days later, on 20th June 1940 General Sikorski was brought over from France, and immediately saw our new

Prime Minister Winston Churchill. He explained that the Polish general staff and members of his cabinet had made their way down towards the south of France, and had reached a place near Bordeaux; he wanted to bring them out. The French had capitulated two days earlier, and, of course, theoretically, France was occupied territory However, we were still getting troops out through Bordeaux, and apparently it was considered worth the risk. I was given the job, with one of the S 30 boats, of taking General Sikorski with one aide, landing at Biscarosse just south of Bordeaux. We also carried a French colonel who was anxious to search for his family. On arrival, General Sikorski and his aide, each armed only with a pistol, commandeered motor-cars on the French roads and set off in the direction of the approaching enemy. Quite cold-bloodedly and in broad daylight they drove some fifty miles to the place where they knew their colleagues would be. I, on my part, had strict orders that I was to do everything possible to assist General Sikorski and his colleagues, but that I was not to lose the boat under any circumstances. It was one of those very convenient orders with two conflicting requirements.

Before General Sikorski left me, I conveyed to his aide the decision which I had made that I would remain in the vicinity of the point where I had dropped him until dawn the next day, but that if he had not arrived by first light I would take off and proceed to England without him. He accepted the condition, and off he went. I immediately contacted the local French people, particularly in the met. office at the seaplane station at Biscarosse. From what they told me there were already considerable numbers of Germans in the district, mostly mobile columns which were roaming round picking up the French troops. Quite frankly, I did not expect to see General Sikorski again. During the afternoon I had one or two scares when German aircraft came over, but we had drawn the big flying boat close in to the shore and actually aground, so that she was partly hidden by trees. I was never-theless extremely grateful when darkness fell and we had relative security, at least from the air. We tried to sleep on board that night with one person on watch all the time. We could hear the tracked vehicles of the Germans on the roads not very far away.

As the first light appeared next morning I was restless to go, and there was still no sign of General Sikorski. We rowed ashore for one final look; as we approached lights appeared, and there in four cars, loaded to the brim, were the Poles, with General Sikorski himself at the head of them. Without any further ado they came on board, we started up our en-gines and took off. Everything seemed peaceful and quiet, and we headed out west clear of the coast as soon as possible. The only thing that shot at us was a British cruiser just off the Estuary. I presume she was there for the evacuation of British personnel. Fortunately their shooting was more or less of the usual standard, and we were not hit. When we were off the coast I turned homeward and soon found plenty to occupy our attention. We saw aircraft flying well over to starboard over the land, some of which we recognised as Ger-mans and all of which we assumed were Germans. Moreover, we also found the unhappy evidence of warfare on the sur-face of the sea below us. We found two ships damaged and deserted, and at one stage we found three lifeboats, in one of which were the bodies of men. As we passed to the west of Ushant there was a vast column of black smoke reaching 20,000 feet at least. This was obviously coming from oil storage which the French had fired to prevent it from falling into the hands of the Germans. On we went, very depressed at the fall of France and at the gruesome things which we had seen. I was then, as much as at any time in the war, thoroughly sick at the principle of international massacre which this world apparently regards as normal policy. When we got back to Poole Harbour we dropped our distinguished passengers and all was well. Nobody there, of course, knew exactly what our job had been, but they seemed reasonably surprised that we had returned!

I had to report to headquarters of B.O.A.C. after I got back, and I therefore drove to London. On the way a hitch-hiker stopped me, and I gave her a lift; she was a Church Army lady. My whole being at that time was filled with disgust at warfare, and it was not long before I let her hear my views. The good lady said to me that she quite agreed, and that the only way of preventing warfare was Christianity. Now, I have myself been brought up by a most religious mother, and I have tried to be Christian, but I have also tried to be a practical man, and I am afraid I turned on the good Church Army lady very harshly indeed. "Would you sack that policeman over there and rely entirely on Christianity to prevent crime?". I asked, and then I went on with my idea that only by suppressing evil compulsorily could we achieve this last final step in the evolution of law and order, the permanent prohibition of wars. I believe that the complete prohibition of the use of force, simply by creating an international policeman strong enough to prevent it, is the only practical way in which mankind can be saved from another world war far more murderous and destructive than either of the last two. I am opposed to too much government and, therefore, I am opposed to too much world government. I do, however, believe that a sensible international organisation, within which the voting power is properly balanced in proportion to the status and strength of nations, could undertake this simple duty of the prevention of international murder, and do so effectively and well. The natural corollary of such an application of compulsory peace is, of course, that there should be compulsory justice, and I admit that there is difficulty in this connection. It seems, however, that if peace were established and all nations knew that it was permanent, then there would be some chance of getting a fair and equitable approach to the problems of justice wherever they might occur.

A week after the Sikorski episode I was called upon to do another special flight, but this time much more peaceful. I had the privilege of carrying the Duke of Kent from Poole to Lisbon, to an international exhibition in that city; Britain felt she should be represented in spite of the war, to show that she was completely undisturbed by the trend of events and that she was still strong enough and able enough to send one of her own royal family. Whilst waiting in Lisbon for the royal party, we were accommodated in a rather doubtful hotel, and in the same building—in fact, on the same floor— were the crew of a German aircraft of Luft Hansa. After what I had seen in France and the Bay of Biscay, I was hardly on friendly terms!

Our departure from Lisbon was wrapped up in all the usual war-time security. We gave our destination as West Africa, and we left on a south-westerly course out of Lisbon. Our departure was at night, and, of course, we were seen off in the general direction in which we had said we were going. Whether anybody was fooled by this subterfuge or not, I very much doubt! In fact, we altered course first to the north-west and then to the north, when clear of the coast, and flew during the night through the danger area of the Bay of Biscay, approaching the English coast just about dawn. Once again we landed at Poole, and the Duke of Kent, Lord Birdwood, etc., proceeded to London. That was the last flight which I ever made in British Overseas Airways Corporation; it was on 2nd July 1940.

5

WINTER CONQUEST

SHORTLY after my return from the brief visits to France and Portugal, I was called to the Ministry of Aircraft Production to be told that I was to go to America in order to ferry American aircraft across the Atlantic to Great Britain. This was very exciting news and exactly what I wanted, because at that time Dunkirk was over and Britain was in a position of extreme danger. It was obviously a most uncomfortable position, in such circumstances, to have virtually no important work to do.

Two other Imperial Airways pilots were also called upon, Ian Ross and Humphrey Page. These two were to go with me to America. In the first instance I was under the impression that we were the entire team, and would call on American pilots and local engineers and the like to build up the necessary organisation on the other side of the ocean. Subsequently it transpired that Captain Wilcockson was already on his way to Canada, and that the arrangements would be under Mr. George Woods Humphreys, my previous chief in Imperial Airways and one for whom I had great respect. I had the pleasure of meeting Lord Beaverbrook, the Minister, and, of course, was duly impressed by his studied dynamic activities at all times, which I rather felt were somewhat ostentatiously intended to impress! Undoubtedly he was a man who was getting things done, and that was precisely the type of man for whom I wanted to work. For indeed, at this stage of the war, I was more than disgruntled at the indolence and general fatuity displayed by so many in the Civil Service and, indeed, in the fighting services. Dunkirk had at last woken us up. With men like Beaverbrook I hoped that our future would be safe.

Ian Ross, Humphrey Page and I sailed from Liverpool a few days later. The experience of an Atlantic crossing in wartime was very impressive. The ship, one of the *Duchess* class, was packed with people, including a large number of women and children evacuees. The rule was to carry one's lifebelt at all times, and the ship was very strictly "blacked out" during the hours of darkness. To my considerable surprise we went without escort on this trip, as the ship was fast and as there was, apparently, neither escort nor convoy ready for departure at the time we were.

On arrival in Canada we reported to Morris Wilson, the President of the Royal Bank of Canada, in whom had been vested the Beaverbrook dictatorial powers for the whole of the North American continent. No doubt he must have been a very capable man—but so far as I was concerned I can only say that I have never met anyone so devoid of qualities either good or bad. He sent us to the Canadian Pacific Railway, where we were welcomed and looked after in a most delightful manner by everybody from their Chairman, Sir Edward Beatty, downwards. Sir Edward was old, but obviously powerful of character, and by nature kindly. We understood that the arrangement was that Mr. Woods Humphreys, who lived near New York, would keep a general supervisory eye on the proceedings and that the Canadian Pacific Railways would provide all administrative facilities such as we might need. Captain Wilcockson was already there, and to my surprise another of the old company, Colonel Burchell, was already installed in administrative charge of the organisation. It was decided to call the concern the Canadian Pacific Air Service. Colonel Burchell was General Manager, with "Wilkie" his assistant. I was the Flying Superintendent, with Humphrey Page and Ian Ross as my immediate assistants. The C.P.R. provided us with offices in the Windsor Street Station, and we began to formulate plans. The first responsibility was to deliver the Hudson, which was to be followed quickly by the Catalina and other types of aircraft.

I left for California almost immediately, accompanied by Page, and we were welcomed at the Lockheed Works by Jimmy Adams (Wing Commander), who was the R.A.F. representative on the West Coast. Jimmy Adams was a most colourful character, dark and handsome, and as glamorous as any film star. In fact, he was a personal friend of the majority of the stars, and it was one of his particular qualities that he entertained people from England by introducing them to the film community in quite a big way. On this occasion Lockheeds acted as our hosts by putting us up at one of the most expensive hotels in Los Angeles, the Beverley Wiltshire. Lockheeds were a little surprised when the question of testing was discussed, and I asked them for an immediate flight test with myself at the controls and in charge of the actual readings. This caused considerable consternation, as they had anticipated that I would be happy to sit and watch and accept the figures which they themselves produced. However, arrangements were in due course made, and the aircraft to be tested was eventually ready one evening a few days later.

I demanded a test flight first thing in the morning. By "first thing" I meant first light, and this again caused a little consternation. However, the flying was laid on, and we took off in spite of considerable protests by the Lockheed safety pilot at the existence of a little light ground mist, which he seemed to regard as bad weather. We eventually did our test of five hours' duration, and had the benefit of excellent instrumentation, including torque meters on the engines. On the hourly readings, I did my analysis as we went along, and at the end of the flight I was able to present a complete picture of the results obtained. The aircraft was inferior to estimated performance by approximately 8 per cent.; and this, of course, meant extra fuel for the Atlantic crossing.

On landing, Lockheed technicians immediately checked my results. They were inclined to doubt them at the first hearing, but after investigation they had the very good grace to agree not only with the figures obtained but also my analysis of the causes: partly air frame, partly engines and partly propellers. The provision of torque meters was a vital factor in this analysis, which would not have been possible otherwise. It was the first occasion on which I had ever been provided with an aircraft to test in which torque meters had been fitted. My demand for extra fuel was not only agreed to, but it was provided by the next morning! In fact, on arrival at work next morning I found that the test aircraft was already fitted with an additional fuel tank in the fuselage. The speed with which American manufacturers implemented the demands made on them was an object lesson I shall never forget. Their spirit of co-operation was simply wonderful, and I wish some British manufacturers could get the same idea into their heads that the customer is sometimes right. Admittedly, the Americans were inclined to be a little complacent technically, as, indeed, I believe they still are, but once one had convinced them on a particular point the speed with which they acted was simply fantastic.

On the way back to Montreal we hitched a ride with the first two Hudsons to be delivered to us. We were not allowed to fly them away ourselves, owing to legal and diplomatic considerations, but were allowed to ride as passengers, myself in one aircraft and Humphrey Page in the other. We went up through the States, sticking always strictly to "airways", which added considerably to the distance and nothing to safety—in fact, to the contrary. These two American pilots would not leave the beam for any reason whatever. Thus we unnecessarily went through heavy thunderstorms to our great discomfort, and remained in the thick of the airline traffic, to our considerable danger—but that was, and is,

American aviation. We night-stopped at Omaha, and the next day we landed at Pembina on the Canadian border just south of Winnipeg. We solemnly stopped the engines, and had a horse hitched on to the front to pull the aircraft across the border, which was, in fact, in the middle of a piece of farmland and was hard to define in any case. This most vital formality having been completed, we took off and flew on to Winnipeg, where we night-stopped.

That night I had the opportunity of seeing some of the Trans-Canada Airways people whom I had met before, and also of seeing something of their base in Winnipeg. The next day we pottered along, but slowly! Our two American pilots were obviously in no hurry to get the job done, and so we had the opportunity of seeing a little of Canadian life by night-stopping at Kapuskasing. It was a colourful little place built on the timber trade and right in the heart of water and the woods, and it would certainly satisfy anyone who appreciated scenic beauty. To me it was simply another insight into the life of the country, full of interest in every possible way. At Montreal we landed at St. Hubert and were met by Gilmour, who turned out to be such a pillar of strength on the engineering side in that first year of the Atlantic Ferry. He had been with Imperial Airways Atlantic division. He knew his job, and did it.

In our absence, dear old Wilkie had been busily engaged in interviewing all sorts and sizes of American pilots, most of whom were throw-outs from the American airlines. He said that one proudly sat on his desk and said: "I'll show you how to fly the Atlantic—I've been thrown out of every airline in America for drunkenness. I'll show you how to fly the Atlantic!"

Seriously, however, the question of engaging pilots was a somewhat difficult one. The authorities in Washington had, on the instructions of Beaverbrook, already offered extremely high rates of pay for any pilots who would come and fly the Atlantic for us. This caused no end of friction, as it meant that those of us from England were working for a fraction of the money which the American "rejects" were to receive. Admittedly, those of us already in executive positions in Montreal were not unduly worried about this, but there were others, some of whom were the pilots from the U.K. who arrived subsequently. We also ran into the rather difficult comparison when British subjects from Canada and Newfoundland, or even from Australia, turned up for engagement in Montreal as ordinary civilian ferry pilots. They had heard of the rates of pay that were offered, and naturally resented any suggestion of unfair discrimination against themselves. This situation was one of the greatest causes of friction in the Atlantic Ferry and became worse as more and more outside authorities pushed their noses into our affairs. In fact, we could have got all the pilots we wanted and, probably, some better ones, had we not attempted this pathetic piece of bribery.

With the two Hudsons now in our possession, we immediately got busy on the question of training pilots on to the type of aircraft. The procedure was that I was the authority to whom difficult cases were referred, but Humphrey Page and Ian Ross did the donkey work of instruction. They certainly worked. Day after day, for all hours, they carried out dual instruction on an aircraft which had some very tricky characteristics, including an ability to drop a wing if bounced and quite a nasty stall if one was so stupid as to get too slow. It is not being unduly rude to say that the Hudson was a fine performer, but a handful, which could be extremely dangerous if one were careless.

With this training programme under way, I soon slipped back to California to see Consolidated about the B 24, which was then going into production. Consolidated had done the most amazing job in getting a four-engined bomber from the drawing board to production in eleven months, and the prototype was already flying with good results. Its main feature was its amazing range with an appreciable pay-load, and I already had my eye on some of these aircraft as a means of bringing my crews back across the Atlantic after deliveries. It eventually turned out to be the way we did it—with good results. I flew the PBY (subsequently called the Catalina), and did some performance figures on it from the point of view of endurance and range for the Atlantic crossing.

The first boat was soon delivered to us at Montreal, and we used the same base and moorings as on the first occasion I had landed with *Mercury* on the St. Lawrence River, not far from St. Hubert just downstream from Montreal and across the river. The PBY was a twin-engined boat of monoplane construction, with its two propellers immediately behind the cockpit, making the most infernal din of any aircraft I have ever experienced. It was a far smaller flying boat than any I had previously flown except the Saunders-Roe Cloud, and I was not any too happy about it from a forced-landing point of view. It did, however, have reasonable one-engine performance, and so there seemed to be no reason to worry unduly. With the first of these boats in Montreal, the onset of winter was getting close, and I sent Ross down to California for the second boat. As I was extremely worried about his getting iced up if he came north, it was arranged that he should go direct from the Southern States across to Bermuda, and thence direct to the U.K. This he did, and he, in fact, was the first person in the Atlantic Ferry organisation to make the delivery of an American aircraft by air direct to the U.K. I do not remember the exact duration of the flight, but I seem to recall that it was somewhere in the vicinity of nineteen or twenty hours, which was a fine effort and a successful one in spite of quite a few difficulties.

A few weeks later we were assembling our first formation flight up at Gander in Newfoundland preparatory to the first formation crossing. Without navigators, we were in the position of having to rely entirely on the leader. Although I did not like this proceeding, it was unavoidable, and therefore every effort was made to make it work. We had station-keeping lights on each aircraft clearly visible from behind, and quite bright. We had already given lectures to the crew on the procedure to be adopted both navigationally and from a flying point of view. I laid down rules of procedure for divergence and subsequent continuation on the courses laid out in the flight plan, in the unhappy event of being separated by bad weather. Our aircraft had de-icing shoes on them, but to this we had managed to add "Kilfrost" where no de-icer shoes were provided, and put Kilfrost on various other vital parts of the aircraft, such as aerials. This Kilfrost de-icing paste was something in which I had, with some reason, quite considerable confidence; but the Americans were not familiar with it, and had to be convinced.

Just before this time we had the very good fortune to have our air crew strengthened by the addition of eight B.O.A.C. pilots and nine radio operators. None of the pilots had ever flown the Atlantic, and unlike Ian Ross and Humphrey Page, were not themselves navigators at the time. Moreover, quite a number of them had not been in command in Imperial Airways and B.O.A.C., and were, therefore, apparently immature from the Atlantic point of view. Comparatively, however, they were generally of a higher calibre than those already in the organisation, and I arranged that one B.O.A.C. pilot should be in each formation behind the leader and to be deputy to him in the event of emergency.

It was early November before we got our first formation ready to go, and the aircraft moved up one by one independently to Gander. On 9th November I took off in a Hudson Mark III, and flew to Gander. On route I signalled for all aircraft to be prepared for immediate departure. On arrival, however, I found that the order was more than too much for them. All the aircraft on the ground were heavily iced up. The top surfaces of the wings and the fuselage and tail plane were coated with half an inch of clear steel-like ice which took a great deal of removing. We immediately started work with every type of tool, but within an hour or two it was clear that we could not achieve a take-off that night. In fact, even if we had got all the ice off the wings sufficiently for a safe take-off with a full load, all the crews would have been relatively tired out before the start, which was hardly advisable on their first Atlantic crossing. I therefore postponed the departure for twenty-four hours. Fortunately no further icing conditions occurred, making it possible for us to finish the cleaning off of the top surfaces the following day and to prepare for our flight with reasonable time at our disposal.

I kept a thorough eye on the weather, with the help and guidance of McTaggert-Cowan, who was the met. officer in charge at Gander. I had known him before, when he had provided me with a forecast at Botwood during the return flight of *Mercury*, and he certainly had an excellent grip on Atlantic weather at that relatively early stage of Atlantic aviation. In fact, he gave us forecasts for the first crossing with practically no ocean information at all at his disposal; and the result, although not perfect, was extremely valuable. I briefed all crews after I had prepared the flight plan, and I gave them all detailed instructions on a card which we had prepared of courses to be steered and times for alteration of course, so that, in the event of separation due to bad weather, each aircraft was fully instructed on what to do thereafter. On the opposite side of the card were full cruising instructions, the use of which had previously been explained to all pilots.

On each aircraft we carried a captain, second pilot and a radio operator; the latter was not intended to function except in real emergency, but was simply to keep a listening watch.

After briefing, Mrs. Patterson, the wife of the airport manager (and the only woman on the aerodrome at Gander), kindly came in and distributed poppies—for the next day was 11th November, Armistice Day.

We taxied out in the dark a few hours after sunset, in reasonably good weather, and took station as planned on the runway ready for take-off. We did not in fact take off in formation, but in quick succession, one after the other, and I circled the aerodrome in a gentle turn so that each could pick up his position in the formation quickly, ready for setting course in a compact body. All went well, and we set out for the long dark crossing which was for the six crews behind me a complete novelty, and for me a considerable responsibility.

Never before had the Atlantic been attempted so late as the middle of November, and, indeed, all previous attempts made later than September had ended catastrophically. This flight so late in the season was a direct challenge to the "Winter Barrier".

As soon as we had settled on the climb, I handed over to the second pilot and took over the navigation. The whole navigation depended upon me, and I was aware of the fact that with practically no radio aids available, my sextant and myself were rather vital to the proceedings. The sense of heavy responsibility was somewhat peculiarly relieved by the knowledge that on this occasion, at least, one was appreciated.

I will not labour the details of the flight. In fact, one of the things which remain most clearly in my memory was that at one particular stage when the weather was beginning to deteriorate and I had a number of worries on my mind, I glanced from my seat at the navigators' table, to note with considerable surprise that my second pilot, Clauswitz, was wearing Texas cowboy boots with fancy leather-work and high heels! For luck, I believe!

Unfortunately, about three-quarters of the way over a front which had been forecast as being expected somewhat earlier in the flight was in fact also higher than anticipated. I endeavoured to climb over it, but it soon was obvious that this was not possible, and as soon as we were in really dense cloud I had to give the signal to separate. We were already well on our way and on the intended track, and therefore I had no particular worry about the navigational side of the flight for the other aircraft. The icing, however, was fairly severe, particularly as I endeavoured to climb over the front, and was still in the "thick" at 22,000 feet. I only hoped that the others had sufficient knowledge of icing and that their de-icing facilities all worked satisfactorily. We ourselves proceeded quite happily, and daylight broke just before we reached the coast of Ireland.

We descended through a fairly low cloud base with beautiful clear visibility below, and steamed round the north coast of Ireland at low level and on into Aldergrove. Another Hudson had joined the circuit just ahead of us, and very soon there were five of the seven of us on the ground, and all well. The other two, however, gave me a considerable amount of worry as I stood watching and waiting. One of them finally turned up, landed, and taxied in, without any particular reason for his delay other than that he had misread his map somewhat on his first landfall and had turned up north amongst the Scottish islands. The other one did not arrive, and in due course landed at another aerodrome, which was quickly signalled through to us and gave me peace of mind once again. Incidentally, in the latter part of the flight some of the formation had panicked a little and broke radio silence with a bang. My own W/T operator, Radio Officer J. Giles (ex-Imperial Airways) tried to cope with the resultant bedlam and to shut them up. I often wondered whether any German monitoring service picked up the signals!

The flight had been completed 100 per cent. successfully; even in spite of our lack of navigators and a slight error in the forecast. The first mid-winter flight was over.

That night we stayed in Belfast, and it was indeed ridiculous trying to make the hotel people believe that we were something which we were not. With about 80 per cent. American personnel, it was naturally hard to convince them that we had purely local interests.

The next day we flew on to Blackpool, where we landed at

the base which was to service the aircraft before they were sent to squadrons. Most of the crews immediately were put back on a ship for Canada, much to their annoyance. There was a very considerable temptation amongst some of them to try to be difficult over the proceedings, but I explained the situation to them, and in the main they took it extremely well. It was, however, a very great disappointment to some of them that they did not have a chance of at least having one or two bombs dropped on their heads whilst they were in war-scarred England of which they had heard so much. In fact, I believe they did get some slight experience of bombing that night whilst in Liverpool.

I myself reported to Beaverbrook in London, and he was smiles from ear to ear. And how the Beaver can smile! In fact, nothing that I could tell him about the unsatisfactory nature of flying without navigators would convince him that there was anything wrong. Seven aircraft had set out, and seven aircraft had arrived; what more could I ask? Indeed, it was not until a later visit to Beaverbrook that I was able to deal with the situation. Certainly the success of this, the first flight, was not a good argument to try to convince the Beaver that I should change the policy. I stayed in London during my visit, and had the experience of a few raids during this period.

The return journey to Canada was fairly straightforward. We sailed in convoy this time, a somewhat slower process, and, if anything, more nerve-racking. For security reasons we were supposed to keep quiet about what our real job was, and I therefore somewhat facetiously said that I was simply a young man going to Canada for winter sports. To my surprise, the story was accepted completely, and how the passengers on that ship despised me! But I stuck to the story.

On my arrival back in Canada I regret to say that there was a little matter of friction. In London, Beaverbrook had at one stage summoned me and showed me a signal from Ottawa saying that the Canadian Pacific Air Services were bungling the affairs of delivery, and had been stupid enough to have put a PBY flying boat into Halifax in November. For the benefit of innocent Englishmen who do not know the Canadian winter, I should explain that the cold is so severe at times that even the sea-water freezes around the Canadian coast, and to put a flying boat into Halifax at that time of the year was indeed asking for trouble. I had explained to the Beaver that before I had left, I had arranged that this boat should fly from Montreal direct to Bermuda, and that it should have reached there without any trouble. If somebody had sent it to Halifax, it had been contrary to the arrangements which had been made before I had left. On arrival back at Montreal I was summoned to the office of Sir Edward Beatty, the President of the Canadian Pacific. He wanted to investigate the same matter. I simply told him what had happened. The net result was something of a blow-up between Beatty on the one hand and Woods Humphreys and Burchell on the other. I am sorry to say that Burchell, at least, put the blame on me, and tried to infer that I had let him down. This was not true, but nothing I could say could convince him otherwise. In any case, it resulted in the breaking up of the initial team, and although Woods Humphreys had been disappointing in that he had apparently, as far as I could see, rendered us very little practical support. Burchell, who had been active, was, of course, a considerable loss.

This meant a re-organisation, and a Canadian was brought in to take charge of the department as such. It was a little awkward for "Punch" Dickens, the newcomer, as he had very little to justify the appointment other than that he was a very nice chap. He had never had experience of any major airline operation, nor of the Atlantic, and he was not a navigator. As an honest "bush pilot", however, he had every bit of common sense, and we soon were on the best of terms. I accepted him happily as the boss of the department, and he, on his side, gave me the assurance that he knew his own limitations and that he would let me get on with my part of the job without any interference, and that I had his complete support. In fact, it worked perfectly—he looked after Ottawa and Washington whilst I looked after the technical and operational sides. "Wilkie" was appointed to be in charge of training, a post which he filled extremely successfully from then onward.

Two most valuable members had joined the organisation a month or two earlier, Gordon Store and Taffy Powell, both ex-B.O.A.C. pilots, both having first-class navigators' licences and with Atlantic experience in command. Taffy had been discovered as a squadron-leader up at Dartmouth in the R.C.A.F. teaching navigation; and Gordon Store had become available, having been shot in the foot when the Germans picked on his S 30 flying boat in Narvik whilst he was trying to assist the British forces there. He had been lucky to get out of that one. He was now recovered, and helped us in the training at St. Hubert, whilst Taffy Powell went to Bermuda as Station Manager. I gave the second flight to Humphrey Page, and he led it like a veteran, even though it was, in fact, his first flight in command across the Atlantic. Gordon Store took the third flight equally successfully, but winter conditions were obviously far too severe on the North Atlantic crossing to make formation flying a practical arrangement with any degree of certainty. I therefore took the fourth formation myself, in December, and that was the last formation flight which ever took place. I went down to London and, perhaps fortunately, was able to report that the flight had not gone too well. One aircraft had swung at take-off and had crashed; another had had technical trouble and had turned back early; the rest of the formation had crossed successfully. By this time I had learned to speak to Beaverbrook in his own language, and was able to tell him that I was proposing to run the show as I thought best. He acceded to my request, therefore, that we should use R.A.F. navigators trained in Canada, and this decision was signalled immediately to Montreal and the arrangements made accordingly. In fact, by the time I got back to Montreal, our first navigators had already arrived for their training with us.

The system was that, although our pilots remained with us permanently, the navigators would be ours for one trip only. In order to get them settled down to the job—and most of them were only half-baked navigators, having merely been trained and never having had any practical operational experience—we gave them two long trips for navigational experience with their own captain. On these flights the captain checked the fuel consumption of his aircraft, and generally got it serviceable as well as training his navigator. He then went up to Gander, which was a further navigational trip for the youngster behind him, and they then set off across the Atlantic. In general, the system seemed to work excellently, and we had no failure in navigation with any serious result during the whole of the rest of the period I remained in charge of the operations of the Atlantic Ferry.

We had also recruited a few direct-entry civilian navigators to the organisation, and on one occasion one of these particularly impressed me. He had been put up for dismissal on the grounds that he was quite unable to navigate. In fact, he was a marine navigator, and really had no idea of air navigation. I therefore gave him a test. I took him one night in a Hudson which I flew myself, and we did a three-hour trip due north from Montreal, which took us up near Hudson Bay, after which we returned to Montreal. It was midwinter, and Canadian winter at that. His efforts at navigation were almost nil, though he tried extremely hard. Suddenly, about half-way through the flight, he opened the cockpit window on to the starboard side and put his hand out into the icy blast. This was a really dangerous thing to do, because the temperature was minus 40° Centigrade, and if he persisted it was likely that he would lose his fingers, if not his whole hand, in a very short time. I grabbed his arm, pulled it back and closed the window. Then on the intercom. I asked him what he thought he was doing. Apparently it was all very simple—he had heard that when you got frost-bite you rubbed snow on your fingers. He apparently thought that as his fingers were extremely cold the procedure for recovery was to put them out into a minus 40° Centigrade, 170-knot breeze. He came from California—and back he went!

Whilst these first mid-winter flights across the North Atlantic were taking place, an entirely extraneous subject suddenly insinuated itself into my affairs. A signal arrived from the Air Ministry via Ottawa asking that I should call on the Directorate of Bomber Operations on my next visit to London. This I did, and discovered that they required a little advice from a navigator. The director at that time was John Baker, and his deputy was Aubrey Ellwood. A little bit further down the line, however, was an old friend of mine, Ralph Cleland, then a wing-commander. He had apparently reminded his seniors in the directorate that I was a navigator, and that in their difficulties they might do well to discuss with me the subject of bomber operations and the results obtained. At this time the "phoney war" was over; France had been invaded and conquered, and we stood alone in the world against Hitler. In these circumstances the British Government had at last given Bomber Command permission to retaliate, and to the horror of everybody concerned the retaliation was a ghastly failure. It gradually dawned on those in authority that crews were not able to do the job of going out over Germany in pitch-black darkness and finding difficult aiming points. The Directorate of Bomber Operations showed me raid reports which described excellent raids, and then showed me P.R.U. photos of the target taken the following day, which showed not the slightest sign of damage of any sort. They told me that Sir Richard Pierse, the C.-in-C. of Bomber Command, refused to believe that the results were so poor, but that they themselves were convinced that the majority of crews were getting nowhere near anything and certainly not the target. They quoted examples of experienced crews claiming to have bombed targets, though they were subsequently proved to have been sixty to eighty miles away at the time. They wanted my views as a navigator.

I looked at the assembled company and I simply asked a question. "You are all experienced general duties officers; you have been flying a lifetime. Could you get into an aircraft on a pitch-black night, fly for three or four hours on a compass and an air-speed indicator, find a pinpoint in central Germany, avoid spoofs and dummies, not be put off by night fighters, flak and searchlights, and guarantee success?" They looked at each other and then looked at me and replied, "Of course not; we are pilots, not navigators." I pointed out that they had had twenty years or more in the air, whereas those boys they were sending out over Germany had had no practical experience whatever of genuine operational flying. They had only had the aircrew training which was carried out in distant and peaceful parts of the world, and in the circumstances their chances of success were remote. I pointed out, however, that if a force of experienced navigators were to lead the crews, and if such navigators were to be given somewhat better equipment than that available in ordinary bomber aircraft, the chances of success were relatively high, and if they were then given fireworks of some description with which to attract the main force to the target it should be possible for them to act effectively as leaders and to get the whole of bomber effort on to at least some targets. We discussed the scheme in considerable detail before I returned to Montreal. It was the first seed which I sowed on the subject of the Path Finder Force which was subsequently to turn Bomber Command from failure to success.

The personnel in D.B. Ops. came and went. The C.-in-C. of Bomber Command was changed; the Pathfinder idea grew, and although opposed bitterly by some it eventually came out on top as the only means of saving our bomber offensive. Few people knew, either during the war or after, that I had sowed the seed of the idea so early in the proceedings. And to those charming and generous Air Force officers who so bitterly criticised my subsequent rapid promotion when the Path Finder Force was formed, I would like to suggest that it was no fault of mine that the Royal Air Force, due to peacetime economies and restrictions, should, at the critical moment, have been unable to produce a more senior Regular officer with the necessary combination of flying, navigation, radio, engineering and scientific knowledge suitable for the creation of such a force.

On subsequent trips to the U.K. I called on D.B. Ops. again, and we discussed the subject further. At that time, of course, I had no idea whatever that I should be returning to the Service, or that I should ever be considered for the job of commanding the force if it were created.

Early in the New Year I went down to San Diego to the Consolidated plant to test the new B 24. A very fine aircraft it was, with the longest range of anything then available. I also did some fuel consumption tests on the new Hudson 5, which, with its different engine, might have had a different performance. In fact, the existing tankage was excellent, and the difference between the Hudson 5 and the Hudson 3 had no effect upon us or our operations.

On arriving back at Washington, where I had some business to attend to, I heard that we had lost an aircraft *en route*. This was the only occasion on which this had happened, and naturally it was a shock. I went up to Montreal by air, and arrived there that evening. The aircraft had by that time been missing for forty-eight hours. I immediately got in touch with the pilot's wife on the telephone, as there was no time to spare. I asked her the simple question— whether she believed that her husband was alive or dead. She said that she was convinced that he was alive. I had heard in my various experiences in aviation, of a number of occasions when through telepathic effects, wives had been able to tell when their husbands were alive in doubtful circumstances such as this. It was for this reason that I asked

Mrs. Mackey whether her husband was alive, and on her answer I acted.

The R.C.A.F., which had taken charge of the rescue operations, had decided that the Atlantic Ferry aircraft were not to participate in the search. I immediately signalled to Gander that I was coming up by Hudson. I took off before midnight, and was approaching Gander just before dawn. I sent a signal to say that all the delivery aircraft then on the ground, of which there were about eleven, were to stand by to take part in the search immediately. Naturally I had intended that they should only do so after I had landed. To my surprise and, in fact, delight, I found that many of them were already off the ground before I arrived. They had been more than furious that they had not been permitted to search for their colleague, Captain Mackey, who was missing. As soon as I arrived I began sorting out with the R.C.A.F. officers present, and discussed the whole matter with the airport authorities. As a result of these discussions we decided to carry out a land search and a limited sea search. Before this could be put into effect, however, one of our own aircraft signalled that he had found the crash, which was about three-quarters of the way to the coast. I replied that our aircraft was to remain circling overhead until I arrived.

I took off immediately, carrying all sorts of blankets and supplies in bundles, ready to drop. When we got to the search aircraft we still had great difficulty in seeing the wreck. The camouflaged Hudson had touched down on the edge of a frozen lake, and had swung into trees as its wing tip touched the edge. The only indication of it were the tracks in the snow and a small figure reclining disconsolately also in the snow. He had solemnly plodded out the message "Three dead" in the snow, and then lay there exhausted. We subsequently discovered that he was the pilot, Mackay. We immediately started the supply dropping operation, and sent back the aircraft which had found him, having made arrangements for another aircraft to take over from us. We continued the supply runs carefully and methodically, and dropped all the stuff that we had on board. We saw the lone figure in the snow crawl to the packages and open them, and were delighted that we had at last got help to him. What to do next was the problem, and it was my intention that we should go back to Gander and get parachutes so that we could land. Just as we were due to hand over to the other aircraft, however, I suddenly saw two men with a dog sledge crossing a lake not too far away. We immediately went to them and flew over their heads in the direction of the wreck. We wrote messages on paper, wrapped them up in packages, threw them to the sledge men and got them to go in the direction of the wreckage and finally reach it. This gave us the greatest sense of relief that one can imagine, for we knew that whoever was there was in safe hands.

We then flew back to Gander, and were pleased to find that a DH Moth on skis had arrived there and was ready and willing to take me over to the wreck and land on one of the frozen lakes. I went in this aircraft, and the pilot, whose name I never learned, did a good job of getting us down close to the wreckage. To my surprise, however, there was no sign of life of any sort. In fact, the sledge men had taken the pilot with them on the sledge to their little township on the coast. I had a good look at the wreckage, and spent some time trying to see what had happened. I could do nothing for the dead. Incidentally, the radio operator on board was sitting in his seat apparently uninjured. His neck was broken, for he was wearing a safety belt round his waist!—the best way of cracking one's neck that I know. The reason why there were four people aboard this aircraft was that a V.I.P. had been "wished" on to the flight by Ottawa at the last moment. Even more unhappy was the fact that this V.I.P. was that very great doctor, Dr. Banting, who had discovered insulin. He had not been killed outright, but died of injuries some time later, having first been delirious and thereby giving poor Mackey an even more difficult and trying time.

This was the only aircraft we lost *en route* during the whole of the first eleven months of Atlantic operations, the time in which I was in charge. It had been caused by an engine failure, with a full load coupled with some icing.

As spring passed on, one interesting flight took place which was worthy of note. The first of our B 24s, later called Liberators, had been delivered to us with a view to starting the return service on which to bring back our crews. Before starting this service, however, I took the opportunity of taking one of the aircraft up to Gander, and from there I did a long and extremely interesting flight up to Greenland looking for possible landing-ground sites there. We took off just after midnight (local time) from Gander, and had the aircraft full of photographic apparatus and a great deal of film. A small American ketch was to be up the west coast of Greenland, and the idea was that we should drop messages to this ketch giving such information as we had obtained. I gather that the boys who thought of this idea of dropping the information had in mind not so much to help the ketch, but to ensure that any information that we might have obtained would not be lost in the unhappy event of our not returning to base. Such optimism was a delightful feature of operations in those days. Indeed, during this flight we did have one moment lacking in tranquillity. About fifty miles south of Cape Farewell we were descending slowly just on daybreak. There were some heavy clouds around; conditions were not particularly good, and as we caught occasional glimpses of the surface we saw an iceberg, which is always an impressive sight. Without warning, the flight engineer, who on a B 24 is behind the pilot and therefore somewhat out of his control, decided to change into low super-charger gear. All four engines changed together with an apparent effect as if all four had failed completely. As I say, it was an interesting moment!

The flight up the west coast was most impressive from a

scenic point of view—the dark rock mountains of Greenland, the ice and the icebergs, and, later on in the morning, when we had good weather, the clear water, was something which I shall never forget. Finding aerodrome sites in Greenland was, however, a somewhat difficult proposition. Rising steeply out of the sea, the west coast is not exactly a flying paradise. We searched in and out the fjords and we hunted as best we could, taking photographs as we went. Wherever we could see the slightest piece of flat; we went and investigated and took photos. We found the ketch successfully, as planned, and dropped our messages, and indeed I believe we put them on to the site which is now Bluey West 1. When we had completed our task we turned for home, and flew from there direct to Montreal across the northern end of Labrador and so on down into civilisation. It was an interesting interlude, and one on which I seriously broke security rules by writing home to my mother in Australia that "I had not been to India's Coral Strands". I often wonder if she understood what I meant. She knew her hymns well. Unfortunately, she died before the end of the war, so I was never able to check up.

At about this time we had a visit from Air Chief Marshal Sir Hugh Dowding (now Lord Dowding), who had been relieved of Fighter Command after the Battle of Britain was over. As the Commander-in-Chief of Fighter Command he had, of course, saved us and thereby, I believe, the civilised world. But as I have indicated elsewhere in this book, Britain behaved as it always seems to in such circumstances—it promptly turned round and started criticising the man who had been responsible for our salvation. Petty jealousies amongst senior Air Force officers are unhappily all too frequent, and on this occasion I believe that such jealousies were responsible for one of the most deplorable examples of lack of appreciation for a great Englishman which we have ever displayed. Old "Stuffy" Dowding had not only been the C.-in-C. in the whole of the Battle of Britain proper, but he had also been responsible for the introduction of the 8-gun fighter and many of the developments which made that victory possible. There were very good reasons for his leaving Fighter Command, but outwardly the method of his going was unfortunate, to say the least. He had been doing a tour of the United States, and was then sent up to inspect the Atlantic Ferry organisation.

I should explain that about a month or so earlier we had had the misfortune of another re-organisation. Once the Atlantic Ferry had proved to be a success it immediately became a "political football"—everybody wanted to take it over. The result of this was that considerable pressure was brought to bear to take it away from Canadian-Pacific, who were suspected of getting something out of it—if not at the time, at least for the future. Therefore Morris Wilson, on behalf of Beaverbrook, had taken us away from Canadian-Pacific, who had been so good, and appointed over everybody a man called Harold Long to be in charge. Poor "Punch" Dickens was put down level with me. We were joint Operations Managers, with Harold Long as the "big shot". He was extremely fat, extremely soft, and wore thick-lensed glasses which apparently were not sufficiently effective to prevent him from finding his range from his associates until he had walked up to them so closely that his tummy touched them. In my opinion he was a "dead loss" in every way. He was, however, Morris Wilson's blue-eyed boy, and the latter called him a "human dynamo" and words to that effect. As far as I was concerned, I had never known such a catastrophe at any stage of my career. However, we managed to get along in spite of him, and the operation was growing in strength. Our numbers were increasing in personnel, and the number of aircraft delivered was appreciable. When "Stuffy" Dowding arrived it was clear that something was afoot, and indeed I believe it was largely because of the intrigues that were going on that he was sent to us. The Canadian Air Force was keen to take over, and I know the American Air Force were also keen. By this time, Pearl Harbour had taken place, and America was a different country.

I had the pleasure of taking "Stuffy" Dowding up to Gander for a visit, and then a few weeks later I took him over to England in the first flight east to west of our Return Ferry Service. Jimmy Youel was at the other end with another B 24, and we crossed *en route*. We landed at Prestwick, and in the train to London I accompanied the man who had saved Britain.

An interesting experience of that particular first Return Ferry flight was that in taking off from Montreal we had a condition known as "the frost coming to the ground". I had heard of this before, but never had I seen it so marked. The runways were, of course, bitumen surface, but owing to the water beneath the surface freezing during the winter and then thawing, a virtual river occurred some foot or two beneath the surface. This was the state of affairs at Montreal when the date arrived on which we wished to take-off a heavy four-engined bomber for the long flight to England. Tests of the runways proved that it was dangerous, but the flight was important from many points of view, and eventually I decided that we would go. I had wooden strips built on the end of the runway long enough for the aircraft to get rolling fairly rapidly. With no fuel on board and no load, we towed the aircraft on to these wooden stands. I was disturbed at the way the tarmac rippled ahead of the aircraft wheels, just like an ocean swell crossed with a piece of sponge cake. However, we got the aircraft safely on to the three-inch thick boards, and refuelled ready for the take-off. I am pleased to say that we eventually got off the ground without going through the tarmac. Unfortunately, on arrival at Gander, the nose wheel would not extend because it was jamming on its doors. Whilst the aircraft circled, under the control of the second pilot, I had therefore to climb down into the nose and have him retract and then extend the undercarriage a number of times whilst I tried to hold the doors clear for the nose wheel to go down. Needless to say, the nose wheel eventually did go down, but caught my hand and badly gashed two fingers.

On the return flight I carried twenty-four of our pilots in the bomb bay, with heavy bed mattresses to keep them warm. Warmth was the greatest problem in the arrangement of this ferry service, as the heaters provided in the B 24 either blew up with violent heat or completely failed to function. The flight back was, in a way, historical, as I believe it was the first land plane flight from the U.K. direct to Montreal. It took place on 8th May 1941. I had, of course, done the first direct flight from the British Isles to Montreal in a seaplane some three years earlier, on 20th-21st July 1938. That flight had taken me twenty hours thirty-five minutes, but this one took only sixteen hours fifty-five minutes.

A few months later my association with the Atlantic Ferry came to an end. America was in the war, and the U.S.A. Air Force took over responsibility for the delivery of aircraft to Montreal. It was decided that it was proper that they should hand over to their "opposite numbers" the R.A.F. In late July, "Ginger" Bowhill came out with a handful of R.A.F. officers to take over from us. At the same time, Beaverbrook was given the push because he was unpopular with senior Air Force officers. So far as I was concerned I was only an ex-Air Force officer acting as a civilian in the Atlantic Ferry. "Ginger" arrived, and was well aware of the fact that I did not get along with Harold Long. He told me he had instructions that he was not, under any circumstances, to dispose of any Canadian personnel, and as I declared that I did not get along with Harold Long it would be better if I went. In any case, he himself would take charge of operations, and there was really no room for me. He was extremely nice about it, but, of course, the position was an impossible one from my point of view. He said that he had arranged with the Air Member for Training (Sir Guy Garrod) that I should be given the rank of Group Captain and be found a job in the U.K. as soon as I returned—back in uniform. It was a little strange that I should be virtually handing over my responsibilities to an Air Chief Marshal, when I should go back and, as a very great act of grace, be made an Acting Group Captain. It was, perhaps, even more quaint to remember that when dear old Ginger had been C.-in-C. Coastal, he had been emphatic in denouncing the idea of the creation of the Atlantic Ferry Organisation—before it was formed. In fact, at one meeting Coastal Command maintained that it would be absolute suicide to attempt to fly aircraft across the North Atlantic from the American continent in winter, and, indeed, he was one of the more important influences in the R.A.F. which were opposed to the idea. It must be remembered that the Air Ministry and the R.A.F. consistently fought against the creation of the Atlantic Ferry. It was the Beaver and M.A.P. who established it. In saying this, I do not hold it against those who were of that opinion—at that time they knew no better.

Ginger very kindly allowed me to fly a Hudson on delivery as a means of getting back to England, and arranged for my wife and two children, who had come over by sea to join me in Canada, to go back by air so that they could be with me in England. They flew on a B.O.A.C. flight, and were the first children to cross the North Atlantic by air.

Thus ended a chapter in my innocent young life in which I could feel an inner satisfaction.

When I arrived in London I went straight to the Ministry of Aircraft Production. Although it was very early in the morning the Beaver, typically, was there. I saw him—but, oh, so briefly! In fact, he was in the act of leaving. He simply said in effect, "I'm sacked, so you're sacked; but you've done well and if I am ever again in a position to do so I'll see that you're rewarded." He then told me he was going to Canada, and was going to get a lift on the Return Ferry Service. I told him that of the two aircraft then at Prestwick he should endeavour to get on the one with the better heater! I believe that when he got up there, because of what I had said, he insisted on changing aircraft—and this by chance saved his life, for the aircraft on which he was to have flown crashed and killed all on board.

Unhappily, in the first six weeks after I left the Atlantic Ferry there was one crash after another, from various causes. Three B 24s were lost in this period. One was piloted by E. R. B. White, an experienced Imperial Airways captain who took off from Prestwick and climbed with a following wind into cloud straight on course. He just failed to clear a mountain on the first island *en route* (Arran) and all on board were lost. Another crash was Stafford's, at Ayr. He was taking off on a runway which was too short for the load which he carried, and although, admittedly, he is said to have swung, in fact he would not, in my opinion, have got off the ground in any case. The all-up weight of the B 24 had been increased by some 3,000 lb. after I had left the organisation, and certainly no opportunity had been given to the captains concerned to test out this new increased take-off weight before they were asked without warning to do it on service. Whether or not these two B 24 crashes would have occurred at the lighter all-up weight is a debatable point.

The third B 24 crash was my very good friend Ken Garden, a fellow Australian, with a face of a boy of sixteen and a permanent grin from ear to ear. He was coming from Canada to the U.K. and, on approaching the coast, became subject to Flying Control orders. This, of course, was a change for him, as I had always been, and still am, most insistent that under no circumstances should any Flying Control officer ever give a direct order to a captain of an aircraft. In this particular case the R.A.F. bungled things properly; they thought they had him under control in a particular position whereas actually they had misidentified him. They told him to descend on a particular heading, and this took him into the side of the Mull of Kintyre, with the loss of all on board.

These crashes were of a major nature, and I heard of them

very soon in London. What I did not know, however, was that six Hudsons were also lost between Canada and the U.K. My first knowledge of this was some months later at Leeming, when suddenly a communications aircraft came in, taxied up to my hanger, and out stepped a civilian. It was McTaggert-Cowan, the Met. Officer from Gander. He came to see me because apparently those enquiring into the loss of these Hudsons had endeavoured to put the blame on him, suggesting that he had failed to forecast icing conditions and that this was the sole cause of their loss. He produced some written instruction which apparently had been issued by some civilian Canadian who had been employed by Ferry Command after my departure. These instructions had obviously no relation to the nature of the Stromberg carburettors fitted to the Hudsons, nor to their ice-forming characteristics. In short, they were diametrically opposite to the instructions which I had issued whilst I had been there, and it was absolutely certain that they would cause icing in some circumstances. He asked me what I thought of these instructions, and naturally I told him. We put a few things in writing for him to take back, and he left. I have never seen him since, but I only hope that the information which I was able to give him cleared his name completely. From what I know of the war and how it was conducted, I am, however, quite certain that the person responsible for this calamitous ignorance suffered not one jot.

6

WAR WITHOUT AIM

WHILST the Prime Minister of Great Britain repeatedly announced with considerable pride that Great Britain had no war aims, I must say I was a little shaken to find that Bomber Command also had very little "aim" literally. It was, however, not my good fortune to be able to get busy in the bombing business for quite a considerable time. I had immediately reported to Sir Guy Garrod on returning to London on 9th August 1941, and he had been very helpful and courteous. He passed me down the line, and I very expeditiously reached the most junior of junior civil servants, to whom it was quite impossible to bring in an apparent civilian into anything like a senior position in uniform. To cut a very long and tedious story short, I spent no less than six weeks completely idle, yet daily attempting to get back into uniform, as had apparently been arranged for me before my departure from Canada. Originally it was proposed that I should come back as an acting group-captain. This, in due course, dropped down to acting wing-commander, and after six weeks I was very graciously offered as a special favour a job as a squadron leader. I really became annoyed at that, told them what I thought of them with the result that I was up-graded one notch and sent to Eastbourne as an acting wing-commander, second in command of a new elementary air navigation school. This was a new scheme, and it was intended that about 2,000 navigators should get their initial grounding at the establishment. To that extent it was important, but it was a job which anybody could have done without any very great knowledge of navigation—and none of advanced navigation.

Here let me interject a little story which demonstrates admirably the outlook of some civil servants at that time—the most dangerous in modern British history. As an indication of the stubbornness of British bureaucracy, I would like to cite the case of the civil servant connected with the procurement of arms for the defence of British aerodromes at a time when we were expecting invasion any day. There was a group captain in the Air Ministry whose job was Ground Defence. He tried to get some weapons with which to defend our aerodromes against possible enemy attack either by parachutists or by land invasion. It was virtually impossible to find anything in England, and after a very considerable struggle he managed to get the British Purchasing Commission in New York to obtain some Thompson submachine guns. These "tommy" guns were excellent for ground troops defending aerodromes, and they were regarded with great delight by this group-captain, who rushed round obtaining the necessary authority on the minute sheet of the file concerned. In due course all the senior officers involved gave their approval, and signed the appropriate minutes authorising the purchase of these "tommy" guns. Even the highest R.A.F. officer involved in the purchase gave his blessing, and the group-captain concerned sent the file off for the order to be placed firmly with the Purchasing Commission in America. After a moderate lapse of time he started checking shipments into England to find whether his precious "tommy" guns had arrived. Ship after ship arrived, convoy after convoy, but still no "tommy" guns, and eventually he signalled New York to investigate what had happened. The reply was withering. In short it blamed him for spurning the offer which had been made of these valuable guns, and most emphatically denied any knowledge of any order. He sent for the file. On the minute sheet there was written by a junior civil servant, "It is the policy of the Government to give priority to defensive weapons. It is a well-known fact that the 'tommy' gun is an offensive weapon. This order therefore cannot be placed." It was signed by a junior financial civil servant of the Treasury. I only know one enemy greater than Hitler during the war, and that was the British Treasury and its fifth column in the Service Ministries.

Personally I think the British Treasury still is one of our greatest enemies.

My meeting at Eastbourne with Group-Captain Dand, who was to be in command of the school, was an occasion during which I had to exercise considerable self-control. At first meeting, Dand appeared pompous and icy. He did not ask me who I was or what I had been doing or what I had ever done. He simply was furious that I was not wearing at least a few V.C.s, a couple of D.S.O.s and an odd assortment of D.F.C.s, A.F.C.s, etc. In fact, he appeared to require decorations as the sole qualification, and the fact that I had not got them was to him the absolute end.

I stayed with him long enough to play my part in getting the concern going. It was mainly administrative work in organising the school itself, the syllabus, the lay-out of classrooms and such matters as the accommodation in commandeered hotels throughout the town. The classrooms themselves were in Eastbourne College, which was excellent for the purpose. I saw the first course started, and then I went to Dand and said that I felt that I had done my duty to date and that, if he did not mind, I would like to pay a social call on Bomber Command. He was very decent about it, and even gave me the tip to go to see "Daddy" Dawes, the Personnel Officer at Bomber Command, who would surely welcome somebody with a lot of flying experience. I went up to H.Q. B.C. and old "Daddy" Dawes (Group-Captain) fairly welcomed me with open arms. I was a Squadron Commander of a heavy squadron almost on the spot, and had hardly time to get my breath before I found myself in Yorkshire, cold and miserable, but delighted at last to be taking part in the shooting war.

I reported to Headquarters No. 4 Group, and went into the office of the personnel officer there, a squadron-leader. As I went in I noticed a figure leaning over the fireplace whose badges of rank were obscured by the way he stood. I spoke to the Squadron-Leader Personnel and told him what I had come about, and to my delight Roddy Carr turned round from the fireplace and said, "Hello, Bennett." He had been A.O.C. Northern Ireland during the early stages of the Atlantic Ferry, and as such had been most helpful to me. This meant that although I was only a lowly wing-commander, I at least had met the A.O.C. of the Group.

He gave me 77 Squadron to command, which was nominally a heavy bomber squadron. I was a little disappointed to find that it was equipped with twin-engine Whitleys, aircraft which I had thought were completely obsolete many years before. In due course, however, I learned to respect this very good work-horse, which did a job quite as well as the more famous Wellington. At this time there were still many Whitley squadrons operating and they were carrying approximately half the bomb load delivered to Germany in those days.

I pushed straight on by car to Leeming, a station adjoining the Great North Road about half way between Catterick and York. The conditions of my arrival were typical of those which were to prevail over a large part of my activities at that station—cold, wet and bleak. The heavily-hooded headlights of the car and the total black-out of the countryside accentuated the tedium and discomfort. In some ways, however, Leeming was a very happy station. It had permanent peace-time buildings, a luxury which only applied to one out of three of Bomber Command Stations. The Squadron Commander, from whom I was taking over, was Wing Commander D. O. Young, a very cheery soul who was popular in the Squadron without earning that popularity by any softness or lack of discipline. He was an ex Civil Aviation Instructor and was, in my view, of a considerable higher professional standard than most other Squadron Commanders in Bomber Command. His advice in handing over to me was valuable to me, for the job differed considerably from anything I had previously done in my entire flying career. He painted lurid pictures of the intensity of flak when passing through the Search Light Belt and was fairly impressive in telling me the facts of casualty rates, not to mention flying accidents. Incidentally, the German defence system was modified at about the time I reached 77 Squadron so that the Search Light Belt system was scrapped and each target area was given a tremendous increase both in Search Lights and Guns. This change of German policy made the actual bomb aiming job much more difficult and increased the casualties over the target itself. On the other hand, the route to and from the target became less hectic and until their new fighter system became effective, the casualties en route were not so great.

The Station Commander insisted that I should fly as second pilot on at least two flights before I myself did a trip in command. I therefore chose the two most junior sergeant pilots in the Squadron, and I flew with first one and then the other. It was not particularly educational from the point of view of the job, but it was a really great insight into the nature of young men on bomber operations. On the second trip, which was to Wilhelmshaven, we were just crossing the Dutch islands, where there was a reasonable amount of flak, when the oil pressure on one engine gradually dropped down and then failed. The symptoms were those typical of a failure of the capillary of the particular type of oil gauge in use. I therefore watched it carefully, and did not say anything until I was fairly sure of my facts. I then told the captain that the oil pressure had failed, and that I considered it was due to the gauge. He felt that he knew better, and without the slightest hesitation he immediately feathered the propeller on that engine (stopped the engine and turned the blades of the propeller edge on to airflow so that it did not "windmill"). We were at about 14,000 ft. at the time, and on one engine we slogged along to the target. We were already a bit lower than the rest when we got there, and the flak, of which there was plenty, picked on us unmercifully. We were hit several times, but he was quite unperturbed, and went on with his bombing run. The bomb aimer failed on the first run, and we turned and did a second run. By this time I was getting extremely worried about the situation, as we had hundreds of light flak guns pouring their stuff at us, we were "coned" by the searchlights with absolute solidity, and there was no chance of breaking free. We turned for a third run, and I told the captain that he must drop on that run, or else! The bomb aimer again failed to see the aiming point, which was natural in view of the searchlight illumination on us, which completely blinded him as he attempted to pick up the aiming point. When I was quite convinced that he could not do his job properly, I was eventually forced to take matters into my own hands, as it was quite clear that the captain would have gone on for another run. We were then at 8,000 ft., and it would not have been long before the guns would have brought us down. I therefore jettisoned the bomb load, unfeathered the propeller, and told the sergeant pilot that I was temporarily taking over command—which I did, and flew out of the target area. I then handed over to him and explained to him that I had no wish to interfere with his command, but that I had greater experience in flying than he had and I felt it therefore my duty to do so.

The point was that our bomber operations were largely in the hands of lads like him. He had little experience and little knowledge, but he had the courage of a thousand lions. That was typical of bomber command operations in those days.

Thereafter, I always made it a point of flying with a different crew each night, leaving the captain concerned at home. I was thus able to check up on the efficiency of each crew, and at the same time to give them what I could in the way of instruction in navigation and how best to do their work.

I had taken over 77 Squadron from an ex-civil pilot called Young. The few days in which he handed over to me were most valuable, as he was an experienced pilot and a good one. He gave me the "gen" on the bombing game as thoroughly as he could in that time, and it was a fairly colourful picture which he painted! My first main job in commanding 77 was to tighten up on navigation. Such things as compass swings in the air had never been heard of, and general precision was fairly low. When I arrived, night photography was regarded as a rarity, and there was little proof of what results had been achieved. Bomb aiming was done in those days by the navigator, and was generally of a fairly high order. One fact soon became apparent, however, from interrogation after raids— the angle of bombing considered to be normal by bomb aimers was related to the low level practices which they had done, and not to the height in which they normally operated at night. I had a blitz on this point thereafter, and managed to make people appreciate the fact that the bomb angle was in fact very close to the vertical at anything like operational height.

The results of my navigational efforts soon began to be reflected in our bombing results. We took more and more successful night photos, and all of them proved that we were getting to our target In fact, I used particularly to have any crew "on the mat" who failed to get photos. When I arrived at the Squadron it was a matter of considerable pride if a crew brought home a photo showing the target area at all, but it soon became a matter of considerable disgrace if one failed to obtain a photo of the aiming point itself.

We ranged far and wide during this period of bomber operations. There seemed to be no particular policy so far as one could tell at squadron level. At times we were on the North German ports, sometimes against the ordinary industrial targets inland in Germany, and in due course we were to turn our attention to some very easy targets in

France. The first of these was "money for jam"—it was the Renault works in Paris, and we were told there were very few defences there. I believe that by 3.30 in the afternoon German Intelligence had heard that we were going to attack the Renault works, and that the few available anti-aircraft defences anywhere near Paris were all rushed in in an effort to get there in time.

The raid was laid on very early, and the whole of Bomber Command went in and attacked from relatively low level. My own bombing run was done at under 2,000 ft., and at that height the thump of the bomb bursts below was so severe as to make one almost fear for the structure of the aircraft. It was certainly one of the most thorough and effective raids which I had then seen. It was, in my view, the first decent result achieved by Bomber Command up to that date. On German targets it had always been a source of great sorrow to me to see how ineffective we could be.

Afterwards we did a few more French targets of lesser importance. I remember on one occasion, on the Mat-Ford works on the Seine in Paris, we had a moonlight night and reasonably good conditions. Only two squadrons were put on the job as the works were relatively small. I recall that I spent one and three-quarter hours over the target, mainly because the bomb aimer had poor night vision. I could see the target quite clearly myself and I would begin a bombing run, but as soon as I was level the target disappeared under my nose and I could no longer see it. The bomb aimer, whose job it was to direct me would then fail to see the aiming point because of his poorer night vision, and was unable to drop accurately. During the whole of this period a German night fighter was trying to get on to our tail, and what with doing tight turns round behind him plus the poor bomb aimer, we gave plenty of time to the few gunners down below for their nights' practice. The next day dear old Strang Graham, who by that time was Station Commander at Leeming, gave me a very fatherly talk, as he had counted some fifty-odd holes in my aircraft on return and had even found that one of the control cables had been hit and almost severed.

From the moment I had returned to England from the Atlantic Ferry I had kept in close touch with the Directorate of the Bomber Operations. They had told me on my return that the ideas that I had put forward for leading bomber crews with the target finding force had been turned down, and that there was nothing which I could do at that stage. They therefore suggested that my best line would be to try to get into a bomber squadron, and this is the way things had been going, to their satisfaction, as a preliminary measure. I did, moreover, keep in touch with the more junior members of that department, not only from the point of view of the future, but also to let them know what was going on at squadron levels.

No 77 Squadron taught me much of the deeper sides of humanity amongst young and apparently shallow types of men. I was on one occasion deeply impressed by a tall, dark and extremely handsome boy who told me quite cheerfully that he knew that he would be shot down before long and that I should not try to comfort his relatives with any false hopes that he would be merely a prisoner of war, as he knew quite clearly that he would be killed. He was quite undisturbed about it, without any false gaiety nor any apparent resentment or sorrow. Moreover, he was perfectly content to carry on with his duty as a bomber captain. A few weeks later he was shot down, and I afterwards heard that he had been killed outright.

Affairs of conscience were sometimes difficult. A young Canadian pilot came to me at one stage and asked for an interview. The purport of this talk was simply that on the previous evening he had been asked to bomb an aiming point which was obviously a civilian-type target. He could not, in all conscience, do such a thing, even if they were Germans, and even if they were killing us. He could only make war against the armed forces of the enemy. I tried to explain to him that a modern war is a total war and that the whole population of Germany was in fact fighting against us, whether in making munitions at home or in shooting in a field-grey uniform in the front line. I think I helped him considerably, but there was no doubt about it that for a long period his conscience worried him whenever there was any target which was not glaringly military in character.

The casualty rate at that time was running around 4 to 5 per cent. per raid, and as the normal tour of operations was thirty raids, anybody with a reasonable mathematical training could calculate the risk of survival. Those with more varied mathematical outlooks, however, achieved all sorts of ideas as to what the possibilities might be. Our crews were, in any case, comforted by the knowledge expressed by the Intelligence Officer on each station that at least three out of four crews shot down were made prisoners of war and were not lost completely. The proportions were in reality not quite as favourable as this—but more nearly the reciprocal.

As a slight holiday from bombing I had the pleasure on one occasion of going to Norway on a night on which fog had been forecast for the U.K. and all bomber operations were cancelled. It was a day of national importance in Norway, and it was therefore vital that we should drop pamphlets over Oslo for propaganda purposes. I therefore took my aged Whitley and crew with a big load of pamphlets, and set off. We had a delightful trip across the North Sea, and I gave a navigation demonstration at the landfall, where I took sextant sights off the coast and ran in from these sights to a town called Christiansund. I hit my landfall exactly on the dot, took a photograph of the town exactly in the centre of the lens and then proceeded to Oslo. Unfortunately, low cloud covered the capital itself, but we dropped our pamphlets over the area prescribed and then returned to Leeming. I am told that the Operations Room staff of Bomber Command were most annoyed to be kept awake by one aircraft in the air for ten hours' thirteen minutes that night.

One of the unhappier sides of these operations was the large number of youngsters who crashed on return. Some of these crashes were the result of enemy action which had damaged the aircraft to such an extent that the landing itself became dangerous. At other times, they were simply flying mistakes which caused the accidents. The occasions on which I reached crashes; long, long before the fire brigade did so, gave me a true picture of the value of fire fighting services on aerodromes! I do not think I ever saw any accident occur without my being there three or four times as quickly as the fire tender.

Sometimes the crew might be uninjured, but on other occasions they might all be killed. I remember one particularly hectic crash when a Whitley was coming in and apparently for some unknown reason suddenly dropped in and crashed about half a mile short of the runway. Unfortunately it was just beyond the river Swale. I roared off in my car and drove through a hedge down as close to the river as I could get. The ground was frozen hard, so I did not sink in. I waded through the river and up the far bank, where I managed to get one of the crew out of the already blazing aircraft. He had already his face badly burned and his eyelashes stuck together. This was merciful, because he could not see his hands, which had been burnt off to the bare bone back as far as just short of the thumb, a rather ghastly sight. As I was trying to cope with him up rushed a sergeant air crew member who had not been operating—an American volunteer in the R.A.F. He did his best to fling himself into the flames, which made life a little tricky in view of the presence of the disabled man. Apparently one of his friends was on board, and he was quite frantic. By making him see his responsibility in helping me back with the injured man, I got him also to see the unreasonableness of trying to approach the aircraft, which by that time had burst its tanks and was a sheet of flame 80 ft. high. At first the injured man did not want help, for, as he put it, he "wanted to die" This was because he thought he had lost his sight. I assured him it was merely that his eyelashes were stuck together, and that he would be quite all right. He pulled himself together, and was most magnificent in the circumstances. We held one wrist on each side so that he could not touch his face with the bare bones of his fingers; I explained to him that we had to wade through the river Swale, and he co-operated magnificently. I drove him to Sick Quarters in my car and I thought that all was going well with him. Unfortunately, however, he died of shock two days later, and thus joined the rest of his crew. This was a typical crash.

An episode which really made me angry occurred one day, 12th February 1942, when a couple of German ships, the *Scharnhorst* and the *Gneisenau*, which had been used for many months as an anti-air raid precaution for German cities, decided to leave their harbour in Brest and steam up-Channel to Germany. Coastal Command had spent months and months of effort keeping a watch on these two ships, but by a remarkable coincidence of mishaps the ships steamed out without any information being obtained by Coastal Command. The fact that a press-on type, Group-Captain V. Beamish by name, happened to be sculling round the Channel in a fighter put us wise to their movements, somewhat belatedly but still with plenty of time to take violent action against them. From memory, I seem to recall that Beamish sighted the ships about 10.00 hours that morning, and raised the alarm. They were then steaming in relatively good weather, with a large escort of smaller vessels and a fighter screen overhead. The fighter screen was by that time clearly visible on our radar displays on the south coast, and therefore there was no difficulty whatever in directing British forces on to the target. What followed was rather like a Gilbert and Sullivan exhibition of comic warfare. It seemed to me that somebody was sitting in an office moving chess pieces, one move at a time, directing the attack in a similar tempo. Instead of choosing the moment when the maximum possible effective forces could be formed together and then flung into the attack with every possible speed, the idea of an attack on two warships was to play at it with penny numbers frittered away little by little. There was no cohesion, no co-ordination, and never at any time was there any effective strength deployed against these ships. To give some idea of the mental outlook of our senior officers, I should explain that we, 77 Squadron, had been on operations the night before. As was my custom, I had got up at nine-thirty and in due course had wandered down to the Operations Room. To my surprise I found that 10 Squadron had been called and bombed up ready for an immediate strike against these ships, and everybody was buzzing round trying to find the few armour-piercing bombs available on the station in order to do the job. To my intense annoyance I found that 77 Squadron had not been called. Admittedly we could not carry the same load as 10 Squadron, which had by that time got Halifaxes, but at least we could have bombed the escorting ships whilst other craft both in the air and on the surface went for the two big units. My first request that this omission of 77 Squadron should be rectified, and that we should be bombed up, was immediately turned down either by Group or by Bomber Command. I then pressed the matter further, and insisted that we should be allowed to operate, and received in reply a warm commendation for showing such good spirit and was told that we could therefore prepare to the best of our ability and stand-by. In short, there was absolutely no idea whatever of total effort in the minds of senior officers in those days. Needless to say, I called all crews and bombed up ready to go, then solemnly stood-by the whole day and on into the evening without being called. That a few Swordfish had been put in against such a formidable armada without any top cover whatever, without any diversion, or, for that matter, without any tactics at all, was one of the most suicidal operations I have ever known. My friend, Squadron-Leader Esmond, an ex-Imperial Airways captain, got a posthumous V.C. for it, but that is poor consolation for such a pathetically badly handled affair.

Whether the Admiralty or Coastal Command or Bomber Command or the War Cabinet were to blame for this disgraceful fiasco I was never able to ascertain, nor, I believe, were any members of the British public! Anyway, somebody was to blame. "Salmon and Gluckstein," as these ships were so intimately known by all bomber crews, should never have survived that run up the Channel. My own view is that the attack, involving Coastal, Fighter and Bomber Commands should have been co-ordinated and commanded by the Chief of the Air Staff in close liaison with the Fleet Air Arm and our small ships. So far as the R.A.F. failure is concerned, the head of the Service must surely accept the responsibility.

During this initial period with 77 Squadron my faith in the bomber offensive had been seriously shaken. Like many other Air Force officers, I had looked at this great offensive as the only means of victory. Admittedly, America was now in the war on our side, as indeed was Russia. On the other hand, the operation of getting a foothold back on the Continent of Europe without first weakening the enormous unprecedented military might of Germany seemed to me to be quite insurmountable, particularly when I considered the record of the British Army in the war to date.

The offensive on which I had pinned such faith was clear to me as a relative failure. Admittedly, the total tonnage of bombs was not then very great, but even of this only a tiny proportion was going on any worth-while target. As I continued in Bomber Command I soon learnt that the vast majority of crews were either not finding the target area at all, or, even if they did, were failing to identify the aiming point and in many cases not even bothering to aim. There was a general impression that as we were bombing large German cities it did not matter whether one's bombs hit a particular aiming point or not. The cities were so large that you could not miss. This fallacy persisted right to the end of the war, and must have wasted an enormous proportion of our effort.

I should point out that the bombing of a German target on one single occasion was the equivalent of going through the Battle of Jutland or any other great battle. An ordinary bomber crew in one tour of duty experienced thirty such battles. The battle commenced almost as soon as one had taken off. First of all there was the danger of being mis-identified by some friendly fighter, particularly those manned by our gallant allies, who were so trigger-happy that it was unbelievable. (Humphrey Page, of the Atlantic Ferry, was shot down by some unhappy Pole who mis-identified him as a German.) Then, as we were climbing hard over our own coast, it was almost certain that some odd trawlers or naval units would immediately open up and blaze away at us as we went past. The fact that we might be going west to east just after sunset, quite clearly indicating that we were friendly, plus all the elaborate warning organisations for notifying naval units of our activities, apparently made no difference; they fired away and quite frequently hit us. Then as soon as we reached the enemy coast the heavy flak guns would wait until they were sure of their aim, and would then let fly.

From then on we were tracked by the German defences, and a constant watch had to be kept for fighters. The frequency with which we were picked up by fighters varied. Sometimes we might do two or three trips without being found at all. On other occasions we might get a fighter on our tail, or close to us, on two or three times, and the vigilance of our own gunners plus our own guile in evading the fighter decided whether we were going to get a burst from him or not. Those unhappy crews who were found by the fighter before they found him very often failed to return. The odds were with the fighter. Our own gunners, gallant and conscientious though they were, seemed to me to have fairly poor training in deflection shooting (allowing for the speed of the fighter and their own movement), and I must say their results were not impressive, though occasionally a bomber did manage to shoot down a fighter.

Continuing an operation, we usually had to go close to heavily defended areas where other important targets lay, and often caught quite a pasting in the process. If, as was common in those days, an odd aircraft wandered badly off the prescribed track and went over a major German target, it was possible that anything up to two or three hundred heavy guns might be firing at him at any one time, plus the most impressive array of light flak that always poured forth. Light flak in Germany always contains a very high proportion of "tracer" of various colours, and the result was, to the un-initiated, quite frightening. At first sight it appeared that it would be quite impossible to fly through such a hail of flak. In reality one soon learnt that it was possible, and that the odds were in favour of getting through.

The target itself was always the worst bit, when we solemnly ran up to the aiming point and had to hold straight and level to give the bomb aimer a chance of doing his job properly. The guns knew that we had to do the job, and they were far more accurate on the bombing run than at any other time. Having released our bombs, we then still had to hold straight and level for another twenty seconds in order to have the aircraft steady and with its camera lens directed vertically downwards at the aiming point till the photo flash went off and obtained the vitally important target photo.

The homeward run was very much like the outward bound one. Admittedly, we were flying light and therefore had a somewhat better performance. This was offset by the pre-dominant westerly wind, which slowed down the journey home and gave the enemy fighters a longer chance of getting at us. There was, moreover, a slight tendency for air crews to be less vigilant and less tense on a homeward bound journey, and it seems probable that more aircraft were lost to fighters homeward bound than outward bound. The chances of a reception from the friendly ships in the Channel was always with one, and the risk of the aircraft having been damaged on the operation always made the landing itself somewhat more precarious than normal.

I make no apology for describing this bomber operation in such a way, for I believe that, particularly in the other Services, and indeed amongst the public, it is seldom appreciated that an ordinary bomber pilot was called upon to do about thirty such operations, and that each one of these operations was equivalent to a major battle which in either of the other two Services would be regarded as the experience of a lifetime.

Ninety-nine per cent. of crews did their job conscientiously, and even those of them who lacked precision were quite ignorant of the fact that their shortcomings were of any importance. Most bomber crews did their job extremely well —certainly in their own eyes. I realised, however, that if we were really to destroy the industrial strength of Germany, our bombing had not only to be heavier but also far, far more accurate than it was. The necessity of a target-finding force became more evident than ever, and I hoped for the day when the "powers-that-be" would see the sense of such a force.

In keeping contact with the Directorate of Bomber Operations, quite a lot of good preliminary discussion took place. Those concerned with these early investigations of the idea of a Path Finder Force were originally John Baker, who was the Director, and Aubrey Ellwood, who was his deputy, both of whom have reached very senior rank in the Air Force. One particular friend who was in the Department at the time was Wing-Commander Ralph Cleland, who had been with me in 1930 in No. 29 Squadron at North Weald. He remembered my leanings towards navigation in those early days, and he it was, I believe, who first got the Department to contact me when I was a civilian doing the Atlantic Ferry job in Canada. Then there were Morley, a wing-commander like Cleland, and Sid Bufton, who had commanded a squadron on operations earlier on and therefore knew the job first hand. He had seen the ineffectiveness of some of our bombing. Commanders-in-chief of Bomber Command, I think, always found the Directorate of Bomber Operations somewhat of an irritation. I agree with them that the opinions expressed by the Directorate were not always all they should have been, but nevertheless there was much good thought and many useful suggestions coming from that department, and undoubtedly it was they who finally wielded sufficient influence with the Prime Minister to see that the wasteful and ineffective expenditure of national effort on the bomber offensive must be stopped, and the whole converted into a gigantic striking force better than anything the world had ever known before.

An event which cheered me up considerably was the arrival of Bert Harris (then Air Chief Marshal Sir Arthur T. Harris) as C.-in-C. Bomber Command in place of Sir Richard Pierse. I knew nothing first hand of the latter, but during my period as a squadron commander I had seen little to admire. He refused to believe the evidence of the failure of the bomber effort in those days, and appeared to lack initiative and drive. Bert Harris, on the other hand, I knew and admired. He had been my C.O. at Pembroke Dock when I was in 210 Squadron —and there I had learnt that he was full of fire and dash, was not easily baulked, and was also remarkably intelligent without trying to show it. He was, I knew, a real man, and my hopes for the bomber offensive and its ultimate destruction of Germany were revitalised.

I commanded 77 Squadron from the beginning of December, 1941, until mid-April, 1942, when I was transferred to command 10 Squadron, which was also at Leeming and equipped with Halifax four-engined bombers with considerably greater pay-load than the Whitleys and with a better performance. By this time I had a strange idea that I knew a little about the bombing game, but I was soon to have a small object lesson to bring me back to earth—literally.

Very early in my sojourn in 10 Squadron, we were given a special job up in Norway. It was April, 1942. Hitler's best air-raid precaution, the German Navy, was stationed in and around Trondheim, and in particular the *Tirpitz* was up the Aasfjord, with most of the other major units of the fleet not very far away. The Admiralty worked it out that with the ship lying close in shore, it would be possible to roll some spherical mines down on the shore side of the ship, which was only fifty feet from the steep sloping banks of the Aasfjord, and that these spherical mines would, being fitted with appropriate depth fuses, then get under the comparatively vulnerable bottom of the hull and blow it in. Such an operation would be quite possible with a helicopter, but to do it in a four-engined bomber was, to say the least, a little difficult. Add to this the fact that it had to be done at night and against highly organised and intense enemy defences, and the proposition became quite formidable. Two squadrons were detailed to do this job, with two other Halifax squadrons to bomb from high level in order to cause a diversion.

We moved to advanced base at Lossiemouth, and there we loaded up, carrying five mines each weighing 1,000 lb. The bomb doors would not close properly, but this was of no great importance. We set off before dark for the long journey north, and the weather was clear and beautiful. It was a moonlight night. We hit the coast at an angle, ran up to the chosen island immediately north-west of Trondheim, and then turned towards the target. We had chosen a track which, according to our Intelligence, was free from defences and should give us a good run in across the island. All was peace and quiet before we arrived, but as we crossed the coast everything opened up on us, and we were hit many times. The tail gunner was wounded, and things were far from peaceful. The procedure laid down was nevertheless carried out strictly according to plan, and the tail gunner kept completely quiet in spite of the pain he was in during the whole of the performance.

We ran across our datum point at exactly 2,000 ft. and started our stop watch, descending at the prescribed rate exactly on course and at the right air speed. As we got near the *Tirpitz* herself, all the other units of the fleet to our left picked on us, and by this time the starboard wing was burning fiercely. This attracted more attention, and we certainly had the pleasure of a complete welcoming committee. We were down to the required two hundred feet exactly at the time (as called over the intercom. from the stop watch) at which we should have released. To my horror, the bomb aimer could not see the ship, and with good reason. Below us there was a white haze. I was "mistified"—literally. The mist was not due to Nature, but was a man-made camouflage of which our Intelligence had reported nothing, even although I subsequently discovered that it had been known several months earlier. A split second later the ship's superstructure passed beneath us, but it was too late to let go, and I vaguely hoped that I would be able to hold the aircraft in the air long enough to turn back for a second run. I completed the turn and headed towards the ship, but the flames on the starboard side were now mounting, the starboard undercarriage had come down, and the starboard flap had begun to trail. I pointed towards the ship's position, and released the mines. I often wonder where they went! I then turned east towards neutral Sweden, and tried hard to climb, but things were obviously bad, and I therefore gave the order "prepare to abandon aircraft". I regret to say that one member of the crew became a little melodramatic. He said, "Cheerio, chaps; this is it, we've had it." I told him very peremptorily to shut up and not to be a fool, that we were perfectly all right but that we would have to parachute. Soon it became obvious that I could not possibly clear the mountains which rose steeply to about three thousand feet just beyond the target, and I was therefore forced to turn back west and to give the order "abandon aircraft; jump, jump". I then told the flight engineer to endeavour to assist the tail gunner. The parachute drill went perfectly. I realised, however, after I had given the order and sat there alone, holding the wheel hard over to port with all my strength and with the port outer engine slightly throttled back in order to keep the aircraft on even keel with full port rudder, that I was not wearing my parachute! It was a very nasty thought. Just after this rather uncomfortable fact dawned on me, I was surprised and relieved when the flight engineer, F./Sgt. Colgan, came back to me, found my parachute down in the fuselage, brought it up and clipped it on the hooks on my chest so that I had a chance of escape. He risked his own life in doing this. He then disappeared again, and in due course he went the full length of the fuselage and helped the tail gunner to parachute to safety. For my part, I stayed as long as I could; things were getting fairly hot in the cockpit and the flames were very extensive and fierce in the starboard wing. We were losing height rapidly, and I was heading away from the mountains back towards the east—and towards trouble. The ground was getting very close. Finally, as I was holding the wheel hard over to port, I eased myself out of my seat preparatory to jumping, and just at that moment the starboard wing folded up. I jumped through the hatch below me like a shot, and pulled the rip-cord the moment I was clear. It was only just in time; my parachute opened just as I was striking the snow and all was well. My reaction, I suppose, should have been one of deep gratitude, but instead the only thing I thought of was the shock it would be to my wife; I said out loud a few words addressed to her, and suddenly realised that I should rather be getting on with the job of trying to get back to her. I therefore quickly pulled the white silk of the parachute over the parachute harness which I had discarded, and weighted it down with snow at the edges so that the pure whiteness of the landscape was not blemished by a rather attractive piece of evidence for the Germans to find. The country was sparsely covered with trees, and I immediately headed away from the direction of the crashed aircraft. I particularly speeded up to the best of my ability when I heard voices and thought they were German.

The experience of being hunted is one which I had never

(*Left*) The Lockheed Vega after an argument with Mother Earth at Aleppo, 1934.

Right) GAATZ Calcutta "City of Swanage" at Alexandria. R.A.F. boats in background.

(*Left*) My first Empire Flying Boat, "Cassiopeia".

(*Above*) The Short Mayo Composite taking off, 1938.

(*Below*) Myself with Major Robert Mayo; First Officer Bernard Frost is in the background.

The first direct-flight mail from the United Kingdom to Egypt: loading 1 ton aboard Mercury, December 1938.

Flight refuelling experiment in progress over Southampton Water, with myself as captain of the receiving flying boat.

In front of the railway coach used for accommodation on the siding at Gander, the captains and crews of the first group of seven bombers delivered by air across the Atlantic—including 4 BOAC pilots, 2 BOAC radio operators, 2 Australians (myself on the extreme right) and 13 Americans. This photograph was taken on 10th November 1940.

(*Left*) Air raid damage—Krupps on the right.

(*Right*) Another example of complete destruction of a piece of German industry

Their Majesties with the Pathfinders on a cold day in 1944—at Warboys where G/C Collings (on Her Majesty's right) was the **Station Commander.**

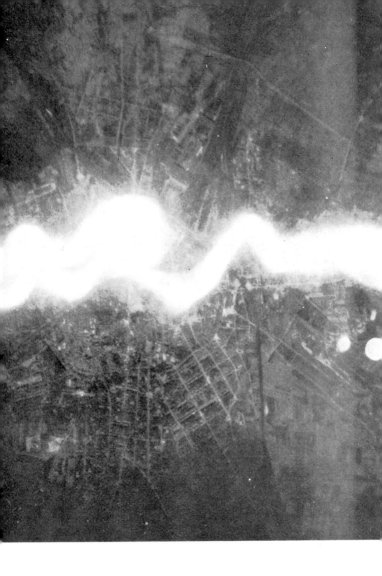

The highest night photograph ever taken: Osnabruck from 36,000 ft., taken by a Mosquito of 105 Squadron.

previously suffered. As a spur to effort it is the most remark-ably effective I have ever encountered. I was not in training, but the running, scampering and floundering in a generally easterly direction, carried out by me in the next few hours, was far more than I had thought humanly possible.

When I had been going thus flat out for about an hour, there came a very dramatic moment. I had entered a belt of trees, and had come upon a mountain torrent sloping steeply down from my right to my left—that is, flowing towards the north. Its banks were steep and coated with ice, and the stream itself was whirling madly—a boiling tumult. I decided that the best way of getting round was to go upwards and try to get round the top of the stream, therefore I set out upwards along its bank. It was almost daylight, but in the depth of the trees it was still quite dark. Quite suddenly I almost ran into a man! In fact, I did not see him until I was within two yards of him, nor did he see me. We both stopped abruptly. I vaguely remembered that I was carrying a small automatic which I always had with me on operations, and in a flash I tried to think whether I had a chance to get to it in time, for I naturally thought he was a German. Before I could decide on this small point, however, the man had raised his hands above his head. Suddenly I realised that he was one of my own crew, and I said, "It's all right. It's your Wing-Co., it's your Wing-Co." It took quite a while to convince him that all was well. It turned out that it was the W/T Operator, Sgt. Forbes, and very glad I was for his company.

We went on together, and as the stream got higher and higher and we feared that we would be overtaken we decided on a procedure which had its elements of risk. I armed myself with a pole which we had found amongst the trees; with this I let myself slip down the ice into the torrent, and fortun-ately found on arrival that the water was neither too deep nor too violent for me to stand satisfactorily. I braced my-self there, and the WOP joined me. We then waded across together, and confronted the problem of getting out the other side. Eventually we did this with a help from overhanging branches, and were on our way. The fact that we went through this stream was, we heard afterwards, one of the reasons that we were able to escape, because the dogs used in the efforts to trace us would not go through this stream.

On we went, higher and higher into the mountains, and eventually came to areas where there were no trees, but simply snow and bare rocks. It was daylight by now, and I was very disturbed in case we should be seen even from a distance and thereby traced and followed. We endeavoured to avoid skylines, and tried to take cover behind rocks and below ridges. By this time my own state was far from satisfactory. My eyes were pulsing in time with my heartbeats so violently that the whole of my vision was throbbing and appeared slightly pink. The effort had been more than I apparently could reasonably stand. Forbes was somewhat better, I think, though at one stage later in the morning when we thought we could see a house, his own vision was apparently the same as mine, because he confirmed that he was quite certain that it was a house and we went to a great deal of trouble to circumnavigate it. Having by this time got the sun on it, the snow was becoming difficult—as the hard crust on top was beginning to soften, and we were literally floundering to our waists for most of the time. The going was extremely slow, and the amount of energy expended was enormous. Having circumnavigated the "house" we discovered that actually there was not the slightest sign of habitation anywhere near us, and that it had been entirely due to our imagination.

Fortunately, both of us had our escape kits in our pockets. An escape kit consisted of a small flat tin in which was a silk handkerchief on which was printed a map of the area in which we were operating. This map was of a tiny scale, but it was invaluable to us in our efforts at navigation. Moreover, there was a tin of Horlicks tablets and a few barley sugars.

This meant about three barley sugars a day and about five Horlicks tablets; not exactly a strengthening diet. In addition, in the escape kit there was a small rubber bag, and we each used this bag to carry water from the streams which we crossed. Later, when there were no streams, we used to fill the bag with snow; we put this in a trouser pocket until it was melted, and then drank it.

By mid-day on the first day we were so exhausted that I weighed up the pros and cons of who was the greater enemy —the Germans or Nature. I came to the conclusion that the Germans were considerably the lesser evil, and therefore decided upon a policy of deliberately trying to find civilisation rather than to shun it and face the rigours of the mountains in that cold and uncharitable region. Forbes had his flying jacket on and might be regarded as fairly warmly clad, but unfortunately I had not, though I was wearing flying boots. These boots were fur lined, and might have been a source of comfort in the normal course of events. As, however, we waded through streams, they were filled with water, and unfortunately when we stopped for occasional rests—as was unavoidable by this time—the water froze in the boots, with shocking results. In fact, I had frostbite down the right-hand side of one foot, though at the time there were so many other diversional pains that I did not even realise it.

According to our maps there was a railway line to the north of us. We therefore, instead of going due east towards Sweden, struck off towards the railway line, and by late afternoon we reached it. There appeared to be no habitation anywhere near, and we therefore went right down on to the line just before dark and walked along it. About half an hour after dark we saw lights ahead, and with great care we moved forward. It was a little town, and we were very careful as we went. Eventually we walked right into the railway station itself, and still nobody had seen us, nor was there any sign of life. We did, however, find a light in one of the offices, and carefully peered through the window to see a man sitting at a desk reading—presumably a Norwegian railway official. Silently we moved through Meräker station in the hope of proceeding along the line, which was such easy going compared to the snow that we were keen to stay with it. Unfortunately we only went fifty yards. There was a railway bridge across a major river, while on the near side was a sentry box, and we imagined we could see a man, We moved closer and closer, and looked at this figure in the moonlight. We retreated and had a whispered conference as to whether it was possible to rush him and try to overpower him, so clearing the way to the bridge crossing. Alternatively we thought we might try to get behind him by climbing underneath and then back up on to the bridge on the other side of him. In either case there was the other side of the bridge to think about. We sneaked up to the sentry box and got within ten yards of it—a long way to rush an armed man, particularly in our state. It seemed from there we should have to come out into the open, and the chances of being seen seemed to be fairly high. We lay there for quite a while, but eventually I decided on retreat. We were, therefore, forced to leave the railway.

We went up a slope to the right of the river, and as we did so we came upon a small house with a light in the doorway. It was now about 11.30 at night, and we were extremely cold and miserable. I decided that we would risk a little investigation. We therefore went to the house and openly knocked on the door. There was no answer. We went into the hallway and called, but there was still no answer. We examined the coats on the hooks in the hall and the various caps. We decided that it did not look like German clothing, and we called again. We still got no answer, and we were at our wits' end as to know what to do. We went outside again and found a shed. In the shed was a heavy fur sleigh rug. We lay down, covered ourselves with this rug, and dog-tired we both fell instantly to sleep, packed close together. The cold was intense, and by about one o'clock we could stand it no longer.

We therefore got up, left the house and took to the mountains once again.

We went up and up. It had been minus 15° Centrigrade by the thermometer on the door of the house, and it seemed to get colder as we went. On and on we went, drinking quite a lot of snow water, and every estimated three or four hours having one tablet and one barley sugar. The barley sugar went down fairly well, but I must say the tablets began to make me feel sick. Therefore I reduced my own ration to half a tablet, and had them somewhat more frequently. By mid-morning we were so exhausted we managed to get a little sleep by lying on a rock in the sun, which was relatively warm by that time.

During the late afternoon we came across a track in the snow, and decided that we would follow it. It tended to go downhill somewhat in a north-easterly direction, but we were once again convinced that the mountains might prove too much for us. Eventually, quite late in the afternoon, we saw a house. We examined it from a distance and from several points of view, and we finally decided it was peaceful and quiet, and that as we were not only hungry but also physic-ally exhausted from a muscular point of view it would be ridiculous to go on without calling. Metabolic reaction (that is, from the cold) is in itself most exhausting. We there-fore chose a place where the woods were closest to the house, and from this vantage point set off across the piece of clear snow directly to the door of the house. We knocked, and a girl aged about ten or twelve years came to the door. She was terrified when she saw us, and ran back into the house. Then her mother came, and in due course her father. They stood there staring at us, and I immediately asked for food. I thought that my requests were not understood as they prob-ably could not speak English, and I repeated them in every way I knew. I pointed to my mouth and opened it; I pointed to my stomach and rubbed it—all to no avail; they simply stared. This was an extremely odd reception, and completely baffled me. What was worse is that they did not appear to be in the slightest bit friendly, and I feared therefore that we were in for trouble. I stopped talking to the Norwegians, therefore, and without taking my eyes off them I said to Forbes, "Get ready to run. I don't like the look of this; when I give you the word to go, run as fast as you can." No sooner had I said this than a grin broke out on the face of the man in front of me, and he said in perfect English, "It's quite all right—come in." I almost collapsed. He explained to me that his unfriendly reception was because he thought that we might be German "provocateurs". Apparently the police were in the district looking for us, and he was frightened that the Germans were trying to trick him, which would have cost him his life or at least a long term of imprisonment.

They took us inside and laid us down in front of the kitchen stove on the floor. I was so tired that I was almost asleep when I hit the floor. Later they woke us up, and I almost went through the ceiling with shock, for I thought that it was the Germans who had come. In fact, it was two young men, one of whom subsequently led us in the direction of safety.

First, however, this good man, whose name was John Dalamo, gave us a very good meal of stew in enormous quantities. I could not help feeling they were depriving themselves of their own very meagre rations for quite a long period in doing so. They had demanded identification right at the beginning of our visit, and I was able to produce a watch which had been given to me by Sperrys, the American gyro makers, on the occasion of the world's long-distance seaplane record in 1938. On the watch was my name. It subsequently transpired that John Dalamo had been working in South Australia at one period, and that is where he had learnt his English.

A young Norwegian, who was to lead us onwards, set out with the two of us at about eleven o'clock at night. Our feet were in a bad way by this time, and we had to go slowly. He walked about a hundred yards ahead of us along a narrow road up into the mountains. He had a cigarette, and it was arranged before we set out that if he ran into trouble he would stop and strike a match to light his cigarette. This signal would mean that we would get off the road and disappear as quickly as we could. He led us on for some miles, which in our unhealthy state seemed an eternity. Eventually we reached a small mountain cottage, and he took us inside. There we found a young man whose name I never learnt, but whose initials were J. G. M., who was living there with his wife and small baby. They put us into their own bunk, and they kept guard while we slept. They let us sleep for two or three hours, and then woke us just before dawn. The young man who had led us went back, and J. G. M. put on his skis. From his own house, leaving unmistakable tracks of a pair of skis and two lots of footprints in the snow, he set off towards the Swedish border. He could speak no English whatsoever, nor could his wife, and my protestations at his actions therefore fell on deaf ears. How he survived such an audacious thing I do not know, but he led us up into the mountains, on to the high plateau, and finally far beyond the tree line. Then he pointed to some distant ridges about five miles further on and said what we took to be the equivalent of "Sweden". He then left us, and skied off back down to his own house. I was terrified that he would be arrested for assisting us. On we went, with hope in sight. The last few miles were—for our nerves—the worst. We did not know where the border was, but it was perfectly clear that it was in a wide open pure white space of snow, and that we were two little dark figures which could be seen from an enormous distance.

Eventually we came to ski tracks running at right angles to the direction in which we were going. At regular intervals along these tracks we would see little hummocks of stone protruding through the snow. We went to one of these hummocks, and discovered that on one side of the stone were two colours, while on the other side were two different colours. This, we felt certain, was the border between Norway and

Sweden. Theoretically we were across the border and in safety. In practice, however, we fully realised that if any patrol came along that track at that time, they could pursue us across the expanse of snow and probably catch us before we could disappear down the slopes, which were miles away. We hurried on as quickly as we could, and kept looking over our shoulders back across the snow up and down the line of the border. Fortune was with us, and in due course we began descending down into Sweden.

By this time it was dark and we went on down and down. The surface of the snow, which in some places had thawed slightly during the day due to the heat of the sun, was frozen like a sheet of ice, and we made good time by the simple process of slipping. The slopes were fairly steep, and very often it was not a question of making oneself slip but how to stop oneself from getting up too much speed. Finally, at about 10.30 at night, we saw a light. Our feelings could hardly be described, for to know that we were across the border, or at least to think so, and then to see a light was the completion of an effort which seemed to have taken a lifetime, but which in fact had taken only three days. On we went towards the light, and I was quite frightened at times that we should lose it. Fortunately the weather was still clear, and I could maintain direction fairly accurately by the stars, even when we lost sight of the light due to intervening ridges and valleys. Finally we reached the building, brilliantly lit, with no curtains. Through the windows we could see that there were couples dancing, and we went closer to get more detail. We had a little discussion, because there were uniforms amongst the men which looked remarkably German. On the other hand we could not ignore the clear indication of what had apparently been the border between the two countries. After a little talk, we finally decided that we would go to the back door and risk it. This we did, and once again the door was opened by a relatively young girl, who on seeing us—and I admit that we must have been a ghastly pair to look at—immediately slammed the door and disappeared. I said to Forbes that once again I did not much like the look of things, and I suggested that we should retreat a little and watch to see who was brought to the door. We turned to go, but there, two yards in front of us, stood two men, and my heart sank. Obviously they were barring our way. To my immediate relief and surprise, however, they once again greeted us—as had the Norwegians—in perfect English, saying, "Welcome to Sweden, and come inside." They opened the kitchen door, took us in and sat us down. Immediately there was great commotion. All the ladies, in their glamorous evening dresses, came pouring into the kitchen, and in spite of the fact that we were haggard and extremely dirty, with three days' growth of beard, many of them kissed us. We were slapped on the back, we were hugged and we were shaken by the hand. In due course we were given a very generous dinner.

Then, and only then, did the official Swedish attitude make itself felt. Captain Skoogh of the Swedish Army formally informed us that we were under arrest and in his custody. He was a quite formal Swedish officer, but performed his obvious duty very courteously and with great consideration. He and his men took us up to a very comfortable bedroom, put us to bed, and then Captain Skoogh locked the door and took the key away.

Next morning we were called early, and were given more food. We felt very much better. We learnt that we were at a Swedish skiing resort called Storvallen, near the small town of Storlien, and to this latter we were duly escorted by Captain Skoogh and his small patrol of ski troops. It was probably only about five miles, but with the night's rest behind me and the resultant thawing-out of my bones, my frost-bitten foot was now giving me a nasty time, and in any case our weakness seemed even greater than whilst we were really on the run. The reaction was almost more devastating than the experience itself. Captain Skoogh was at first somewhat impatient with our slowness, but eventually realised that we could not do any better, and so we went slowly on. From Storlien I managed to get Captain Skoogh to do a kindness for me. By talking about his wife and the separation caused by the war duties on which he was then engaged, I eventually made him realise that my own wife must be most anxious. He therefore sent a cable, not in my name but in his own, in a form which had been common between myself and my wife throughout the whole of my flying career. This form was simply an unsigned cable containing the one word "Love". This cable Captain Skoogh sent, but in view of war-time regulations he was compelled to sign it himself! This he did—for which I shall for ever be grateful.

When my wife received this signal and realised its signifi-cance, she told Strang Graham, the Station Commander at Leeming. He and some of the boys rushed over to the little cottage where she was living near the station, and they found Storlien in an atlas. In due course Strang Graham passed on the information that I was alive and presumably in Sweden. Several days later my wife was officially informed that "from an unreliable source it had been learnt that Wing-Comman-der Bennett was alive and in Sweden". For those who delight in the stupidity of the Air Ministry I should explain that they did this with their tongues in their cheeks, knowing full well that the "unreliable" source was in fact my wife.

From Storlien we were handed over to an Air Force officer who escorted us on the long train journey down to Falun in central Sweden, where we were interned. The Swedish Army, from what we saw of them during the short period in their hands, was quite strongly pro-German and anti-British. On the other hand, the Air Force, according to our escort, was more evenly divided and he claimed that there was a slight pro-British majority, including himself.

The Falun Internment Camp was quite a place. An oldish colonel was horrified to hear that I also was an "Overste". That one so young should hold the same rank as himself was a form of sacrilege which was unbelievable and which obviously did not speak well for the British. He was, however, a kind old man and informed me that he would do everything he could to make life reasonable. The huts were wooden and very, very cold and the fuel supply was insufficient to keep fires going. The food level was also extremely low, but we understood that Sweden was at that time going through very great hardship herself and could do no better. We had ground fir kernels, not closely related to coffee, which were served up as such. We had reasonable bread, but practically no meat. During the first day in camp we were given tickets. I was given a first-class ticket and my WOP was given a second-class ticket and we were sent to the local public baths. I took it upon myself to call at a shop which sold men's wear. I walked in and said in English that I wanted one of everything. Without any apparent surprise one of the assistants said, "Yes, sir, certainly," in good English. I had one suit, one shirt, one collar, one tie, one pair of pyjamas, one pair of shoes and one of everything else. Having laid it all out on the counter I said, "Wrap it up," which they did. I then said, "Charge it to the British Legation in Stockholm." I saw to it that the WOP was similarly equipped, and then we went to the baths. I reflected on the good name of our country when one could purchase a complete outfit of clothes and simply say, "Put it down to my Government." Surely our credit must still be good in Sweden!

At the baths I'll admit I was somewhat shaken at the old Swedish custom whereby the bath attendants are women and they think nothing of providing towels, scrubbing backs or doing anything else that may be required in the way of Turkish baths, etc. In fact, the bath house was a most elaborate concern with a swimming pool, steam rooms, all forms of high- and low-pressure showers, sponge baths and tubs. Apparently the ritual of having a bath in Sweden is a highly organised affair.

In the camp we were delighted to find two of the crew. The

second pilot, Sgt. Walmsley, and the flight engineer who had saved my life by going back to find my parachute, F/Sgt. Colgan, were there, having escaped much more quickly than we did by the very excellent process of putting themselves in the hands of some gallant Norwegian who looked after them to the finish and got them across the border intact. Incidentally, they had already reported that I had been killed as they felt certain that I could not have got out of the aircraft in time. I was very glad that I had got Captain Skoogh to send that cable!

I was the senior officer in the camp, which meant that I was taking over my responsibilities in this connection from a Polish lieutenant-commander who had been nominally in this camp since the invasion of Poland at the beginning of the war. In fact, there were altogether about two-thirds of a submarine crew nominally in this camp, but I understand that in the period before we arrived the idea of staying within the camp had not been taken at all seriously by anybody concerned, including the Swedish authorities. Our arrival apparently altered things—the camp was to be re-established on a formal basis, and we were all supposed to keep within bounds. We were, however, granted leave to go into the local town of Falun, and the Swedish authorities were extremely lax in their requirements. On the other hand, the camp was shocking from the point of view of hygiene, having practically no washing arrangements and very primitive sanitary arrangements. On the first day after our arrival I telephoned to the British Legation, and hoped to contact the Air Attaché. He was not in at the time, but I spoke to his assistant, Squadron-Leader Fleet, and demanded that we should be freed, on the grounds that we were escaped prisoners of war and had therefore lost our belligerent status. Legally, having lost our belligerent status, we should not be interned. He was not encouraging in his reply, and to my demand that he should at least make an attempt in this direction, his answers were far from satisfactory.

The resting in the camp, coupled with the modest amount of food which we were given, soon meant that I was on the road to recovery. I had lost nearly three of my bare eleven stone during the walk from Trondheim, but after I had been in the camp about a week I was relatively strong and well. Not the least of the meals we consumed during that week was one when we had meat. It was a delicious stew, and when I asked what it was I was informed that it was silver fox.

Towards the end of the week we suddenly had a call from the Commandant's office to say that we had visitors. I went with a guard, and to my delight I found a Swede and his wife together with another lady, the two latter being Australian by birth. They had read in the Stockholm newspapers that amongst the air crew who had escaped from Norway into Sweden was an Australian wing-commander, and they had driven from Stockholm to Falun to see me. The Swede, Ake Sundell, was the general manager of the Carbon Gas Company operated by the Government of Sweden during the war for the use of motor-cars.

These kind friends proved extremely useful. I explained that the British Legation in Stockholm did not seem to be pressing for our release very strenuously, and Ake Sundell suggested that I should get parole and come down to Stockholm. This I applied for immediately, and it was granted a few days later.

I obtained a rail warrant to Stockholm, and immediately went to that city. First of all I reported to the British Minister, and met the Air Attaché and the other Service Attaché. All of them were extremely kind and courteous and most helpful, but their approach to the problem of getting us released was far too mild for my liking. I believe if I had left it to them I should have been interned for anything up to a year. By this I do not mean that I hold any hard feeling against them, but merely that I did not wish to depend upon their attitude of apology adopted then in time of war and still adopted by many Englishmen in the world today—an attitude which I believe we can no longer afford to assume.

I met the Sundells again, and he very kindly arranged an interview for me with Count Bernadotte, who was in the Foreign Office (I believe as Under-Secretary of State). I argued my case with him at great length, and quite lightly threatened to take him to law in his own Courts of Law if I was not released. In fact, I believe that I had a fairly good case from a strictly legal point of view, a subject which I had gone to the trouble to study fairly carefully earlier on in my operational career in 77 Squadron. Whether my arguments convinced him, or whether it was simply the line of least resistance, or merely a friendliness to the Sundells, I do not know; but I was allowed to stay in Stockholm for a further short period whilst they discussed the case, and in due course I was released. During this period I was entertained by numerous Swedes, and by the Air Attaché and the Assistant Air Attaché, who both did me extremely well. The Naval Attaché was particularly interesting, as he showed me the reports which he had got through to London concerning defences on the approach to the *Tirpitz*. Had we been in possession of this information it would have made it possible for us to plan a very different form of attack, with better chances of success. As it was, information sent two months earlier had not been transmitted to the squadrons concerned. My investigation into this ridiculous omission on my return elicited the reply from the Admiralty that the information was not considered worth while to pass on to the Royal Air Force, but was purely used for naval purposes. How typical of the Royal Navy and their attitude to the Royal Air Force, even on an occasion where the Royal Air Force was making such a big effort on their behalf!

The return to England was one of the most nerve-racking flights I have ever done. A Lockheed 14 came over from Leuchars, flown by a Norwegian pilot, and the idea was that important diplomatic mail and an unimportant undiplomatic male (myself) were to be taken from Stockholm, preferably just after sunset, and "run the gauntlet" through the Kattegat during the hours of darkness. Whilst we were awaiting departure, the pilot was given a weather forecast that there was thick cloud in the Kattegat, and he therefore decided to leave in the middle of the day. This we did, and to my horror found that the weather was almost perfectly clear with no cloud cover whatever. We therefore ran through the whole of the danger area in broad daylight, without any defence whatever, in an aircraft which was all too slow. That we should get through at all simply proves the magnificent value of surprise. No stupid German could have imagined that any stupid Englishman could be so stupid to do a thing such as that—and so we survived.

On arrival at Leuchars I looked round at the station which I had last seen on 6th October 1938 when I set off in *Mercury* to South Africa. I immediately hitched a ride in an Anson down to Leeming, where I rushed round to greet my wife and children. The Intelligence boys were furious that I had not reported immediately to London to be interrogated. I could not have cared less. From the day I was shot down till the day of my return was just one month.

The crew of my Halifax 2A—B, W1041, was as follows:

Captain	Myself	Escaped
Second Pilot	Sgt. Walmsley	Escaped
Observer/Nav.	Sgt. Eyles	Captured
W./T. Op.	Sgt. C. R. S. Forbes	Escaped
Fl./Engineer	F./Sgt. Colgan	Escaped
Second Op./Mid.-		
Upper Gunner	Sgt. Murray	Captured
Tail Gunner	F./Lt. How	Badly wounded, captured

The interrogations in London by the Intelligence Departments were slightly amusing and slightly irritating. The impression which I gained was that the officers concerned were a little vague about the object of the interrogation. I was able to co-operate by assuring them that I had not killed any Germans during the process of my escape, and that there was therefore no reason why I should not continue operating. This was my main worry, as it had been very customary in the past for the Intelligence Department to recommend that officers who had escaped should not be permitted to operate over enemy territory again. However, all was well, and on arriving back in Yorkshire the following night I was given command of 10 Squadron once again and carried on with my duties.

Unfortunately, this visit to London meant that I missed the first 1,000-bomber raid, but I had the pleasure of seeing the boys off and hearing the interrogation on their return. I was truly annoyed to have missed the party, for the first 1,000-bomber raid was not only an historical event but was also the only really successful of the three 1,000-bomber raids staged by Bert Harris during that period. It was against Cologne, which was a short run in, and which in itself had fairly simple straightforward defences, though they were fairly heavy. The next one, on Essen, was a much tougher proposition, as the target lay in the middle of a vast complex of very heavy defences of all sorts, and the target itself was one of the most difficult to find. The damage done on the first 1,000-bomber raid on Essen was considerably less than that done on a very small raid of a mere handful of aircraft carried out sometime later on the first ever blind bombing raid of this world—of which I will say more a little later.

My command of 10 Squadron was to come to an abrupt end. We were ordered to the Middle East to assist in the bombing of the Italian Fleet, which apparently was considered to be a great strategic danger to our North African campaign. Having seen the Italians quite intimately during my Imperial Airways days, I failed to share this respect for the Italian Navy, and it was therefore a particularly bitter piece of irony that I should be sent out with a perfectly good heavy bomber squadron capable of really hurting Germany and asked to waste its efforts on such a puny force as the Italian Navy. I recalled the memorial to the Italian Navy erected on the shores of Brindisi Harbour; it was a vast massive stone structure meant to resemble the rudder of a ship—as somebody put it so aptly, the only part of the Italian Fleet ever seen by an enemy. I bade my wife and family good-bye, and with the squadron moved down to Hurn ready for the take-off. We refuelled and prepared for the departure. About an hour and a half before we were due to take-off the signal arrived that I was to hand over the command to Seymour-Price, one of my flight-commanders, and to report to Headquarters Bomber Command. To have avoided the somewhat unnecessary journey to the Middle East was gratifying, but behind it all I knew that something far greater had occurred, which in my view was of great importance to the Command.

The next day I reported to the C.-in-C. at Headquarters Bomber Command, and to my great delight this hope was confirmed. The Path Finder Force was to be created.

7

THE PATH TO VICTORY

BERT. HARRIS was blunt, honest and to the point, as always. Roughly, the gist of his conversation with me was that he had opposed the idea of a separate Path Finder Force tooth and nail—that he did not believe it was right to weaken the Command by taking its best crews in order to form a *corps d'élite* as a leading body. He thought it was unfair to the other Groups, and he had, therefore, done everything he could to stop the idea of a Path Finder Force. However, he had been given a direct order from the Prime Minister through the Chief of the Air Staff, and since it was forced upon him he insisted that I should command it, in spite of my relatively junior rank. I was to be promoted to acting group-captain immediately, and as a group-captain could not command such a force, I should do so in his name as a Staff Officer of Headquarters Bomber Command, and I should therefore have a subordinate headquarters to handle the Pathfinders at a station of my choosing convenient to the aerodromes which I also had to choose for the establishment of the Force. He categorically refused to allow it to be called a Target Finding Force, because that was the name which had been put forward by the Directorate of Bomber Operations, and which he, therefore, automatically opposed. He did not put it in quite those words, but that was obviously the implication. He told me that whilst he was opposed to the Path Finder Force and would waste no effort on it, he would support me personally in every way. This assurance was carried

out to the letter and in the spirit from then on to the end of
the war. He never really gave the Pathfinders a fair chance
relative to other special units; but he always supported me
personally to the best of his ability, and did everything he
could to help me. He informed me that he was going to issue
a special badge to signify a qualified Pathfinder Air Crew
member, an idea entirely of his own which I valued greatly
then and all through the war—and now—as one of the best
incentives and one of the best honours which could be granted
to those who led. The tour of operations for a Pathfinder crew
would be sixty operations instead of the usual thirty. He
fully realised that the chances of survival on such a long tour
were small, but agreed that it was unavoidable that if we
were to use the best and most experienced people to lead,
they should go on doing so for an appreciable time.

This was the second time I had appeared before my C.-in-C.
in a month, as I had visited him to be told that I had been
awarded an immediate D.S.O. when I returned from Norway.
From this occasion onwards, to the end of the war, I saw a
great deal of Bert Harris, a man who has been criticised by
many of his jealous colleagues, but who in my view made one
of the greatest contributions to the war of any Royal Air
Force officer.

At that time Bert Harris was getting a little fat, but his
bluff, genial personality kept him young in general impression. His golden hair gave an indication of his character, for
like most "copper knots" he had a fairly short temper, and
was very outspoken and indeed rude when he so chose. On
the other hand, as most people knew, he was very often right,
and his emphatic expression of disapproval for those who
were wrong was generally well justified. Unfortunately, his
outspoken ways, particularly with regard to the Army and
Navy, were so famous that he was fairly unpopular with
both those Services—which I regard as a compliment to him.
Unfortunately he was also a little unpopular with some other
senior Air Force officers on whose toes he had trodden on

various occasions. Nevertheless, as a wartime C.-in-C. of Bomber Command, I do not know of any other Air Force officer anywhere nearly so suitable.

My appointment to command Pathfinders was on 5th July 1942, and I immediately began work on every aspect of the problem. My ideas had already been fairly well formed by my constant discussions with various individuals in contact with the bomber operations, and as the result of my experience as a squadron commander. The divisions of the problems were fairly clear. The human element was undoubtedly the most important, and the selection and training of crews was my most vital consideration. Second was the development and production of the very best navigational equipment available. Third, I had to provide the means of illuminating and/or marking the target in such a way that the main force crews could identify it in spite of all the decoys and dummies and the diversions that the enemy might provide.

Of these problems, the one on which I got moving most quickly related to the equipment. Navigational facilities in R.A.F. bombers in those days consisted roughly of a compass, a sextant, an astro compass and a few other minor instruments. The standard of navigation was elementary in the extreme. Just before I had left 10 Squadron, a new device known as Gee had been introduced. This was very hush-hush at the time, but details of it have since been published. It consisted of a pulse phasing radar system with receiving equipment in the aircraft, displaying signals on a cathode ray tube which could be aligned and measured. The resultant figures gave the position on a hyperbolic grid with reasonable accuracy. It had been hoped that this system would give sufficient accuracy in navigation to make blind bombing of the Ruhr practical. Unfortunately this was not quite so, but its value as a navigational aid was tremendous. In particular its use in coming back directly to home aerodromes was a tremendous help, and saved many stupid flying accidents such as had occurred in the earlier days. Gee was the first radar device used on bombers, and was most valuable. The hope for Pathfinders, however, lay in two other devices. The first of these was an airborne radar ground reflection system known as H2S. The second was subsequently given the code name Oboe.

On the former I went to work immediately, for it seemed to me to be such an excellent device with such tremendous potentialities that it should be top priority. A few days before my appointment to command Pathfinders, the first aircraft fitted with a test rig of this device had crashed and killed all on board. This was a sad loss, and a great setback. I immediately went down to the Telecommunications Research Establishment (TRE) at Great Malvern (in the college), and I worked there and at R.A.F. Defford, its aerodrome, on and off for the next few weeks.

Defford had the vague idea that aeroplanes, even in wartime, had to be wrapped in cotton wool, seldom flown, but in the glorious name of "inspection" repeatedly pulled to pieces and put together again. In short, they had the most old-fashioned pre-war R.A.F. conception of maintenance, and no idea whatever of getting on with the job. The fact that I required them to test-fly at all hours of the day and night shook them to the core. Their own maintenance personnel very soon fell down on the job, so I signalled to Bomber Command to let me have some men from 4 Group who were accustomed to maintaining Halifaxes. A small detachment arrived, and provided the tremendous help that we needed. The scientists ("boffins") rallied round magnificently. The H2S team was headed by Professor Dee, assisted by Dr. (now Professor) Bernard Lovell, with J. P. W. Houchin and B. J. O'Kane at Defford doing the practical side. These boffins used to fly with me, and certainly put in a wonderful effort in getting H2S into being so quickly. In general, such an elaborate device as H2S, with its eight boxes each chock-a-block full of complicated "circuitry", would have taken one to two years to develop, yet so far as the main principles were concerned the whole system was complete within one month. and we had done an enormous amount of flying with fairly good results. Not only could we pick up coast lines and differentiate between land and water, but we could also pick up built-up areas of any appreciable size with complete certainty. The serviceability of the equipment, however, was low, and some skill was required in its operation. I was satisfied that with this equipment we could find all the main German cities with absolute certainty, and mark aiming points within reason in any district in them.

The principle of H2S was simply that it transmitted a directional beam of high energy impulses outwards and downwards towards the ground. This beam rotated with its aerial at the rate of about once per second, and reflections received from the ground of its own impulses were accepted back by the aerial and fed into a receiver, which showed its results on a cathode ray tube which had a radial scanning line from its centre to its circumference rotating in phase with the aerial. As a signal was received, it showed up as a bright spot on the screen, and the retentivity thereof painted a map on the screen similar to the built-up areas and water in the area in range below the aircraft. H2S had various scales, so that the longer range aspects could be appreciated from navigational points of view, whilst the bombing run could be done on the shortest range of all.

How H2S got its name is the subject of so many conflicting stories that I should hate to attempt to confirm or deny which is the most authentic. The one which I believe to be the best is simply that which Lord Cherwell, the scientific adviser to the Prime Minister, gave. When somebody asked him what he thought of it, he said, "It stinks. Call it H2S."

H2S depended largely for its success on a very high power cavity resonance valve known as a magnetron. This was an essential part of its "innards" from the outset; the War Cabinet were well aware that we were proceeding on the lines of using equipment with this valuable invention in it, and they did not in any way oppose the idea. It was only months later, when the Pathfinders were crying out for this equipment and it was being produced in sufficient numbers for a few squadrons to be equipped with it, that they suddenly clamped down and said that we could not use the magnetron over enemy territory. It was a decision against which I had to fight hard, with the support of the C.-in-C. It also seemed to me that Lord Cherwell was most appreciative of the importance of this equipment to the whole of the bomber effort.

Whilst all this high-level activity was going on in connection with H2S, my other radar device, Oboe, was being quietly developed by its inventor, R. H. Reeves, and his brilliant young colleague, Dr. F. E. Jones. Unlike H2S, which was done with full formality and in accordance with the normal procedure, Oboe was developed by the boffins on the job at the Squadron itself, with the test installations being done in the Squadron's own aircraft. Not only did this save time, but it also "achieved the impossible." The difficulty of accommodating the various boxes in so small an aircraft was considerable, and the ingenuity and determination shown by those concerned was outstanding—with subsequent outstanding results.

All of these radar experiments were interspersed with frequent conferences and discussions at all levels, high and low. At the same time, I was in contact with the various pyrotechnic experts made available to me by the Armament Branch, and we got all sorts of fireworks under way. Flares were to be made available in bigger numbers, and development was immediately begun on hooded flares, which had a device in the form of an umbrella above them which helped to prevent the glareback in the eyes of the bomb aimer who was trying to see the ground. The advent of the barometric fuse for opening these and other devices was speeded up, particularly at the request of the Path Finder Force. Some high-powered candles were produced, which we named Target Indicators.

These were my special requirement, and we used them extensively for the rest of the war. They were made in all colours and varieties, plain red, plain green, yellow, white, and each of those colours as a basic colour with ejecting stars of the same or different colours. Many combinations were, therefore, available for us to use as and when we chose, and the enemy could not copy them until he discovered what the colour of the night might be. Dr. Coxon was the "boffin" basically responsible for these Target Indicators, and he certainly made them work to our requirements; they were far better and brighter than anything that the enemy was ever able to produce even up to the last day of the war.

My visit to the Main Force Group Commanders was anything but encouraging. Roddy Carr in 4 Group was friendly, and indeed took a large share of the responsibility for forming the Pathfinders. In fact, at a meeting of Group Commanders before the Path Finder Force was created, he had told the C.-in-C. that in his Group he already had one squadron earmarked for Path Finder duties, and that Wing-Commander Bennett, known to the C.-in-C., was in command of it. This was his idea of the Path Finder technique, and he felt that that was the best way of doing it. I believe that the C.-in-C. felt that this was a good compromise, and even tried to get the C.A.S. to agree to each Group having its own Pathfinder Squadron. He was over-ruled on account of the radar aspects of the problem, and also the lack of general coherence of such independent Pathfinder Squadrons. Anyway, Roddy Carr was friendly and most helpful, and assured me that he would do everything possible to encourage volunteer crews from his Group to man Number 35 Squadron, which he nominated as the squadron to be transferred to me from the Group which I knew and liked so well. No. 5 Group, which was commanded by Alec Coryton, an enthusiastic and most volatile commander, was, on the other hand, openly antagonistic. Coryton did not approve of the idea of a Path Finder Force, and he did not approve of my taking his best crews. However, he was perfectly pleasant about it, and told me that 83 Squadron would be transferred to me on the appointed day. Number 1 Group had been taken over by "Winkel" Rice. I had known him when he was Wing-Commander Training in Calshot, and I was, therefore, on fairly friendly ground. He expressed very little in the way of views either way, but nominated the squadron to represent 1 Group as being Number 156, and assured me that he would give volunteer crews a chance of coming forward. Number 3 Group was commanded by Baldwin, who also had the unhappy task of giving up some of his stations to me. Added to this was the encumbrance of having to administer certain aspects of the stations even although he did not command them operationally.

In selecting the stations, I had started off at the Met. Office and chosen the area in which I wished to operate. This was further encouraged by an examination of the land-line system of the country to see where I should be best placed from a communications point of view. My selection, Wyton, as one of the best weather stations in England was fully justified. I managed to convince the C.-in-C. that I should have that station and also Oakington, both of which were "permanent" built-up stations, and to these I should attach two satellites, Gravely and Warboys. Thus I started with four stations. Number 3 Group's nominated squadron was No. 7, which at that time was equipped with Stirlings. In addition to this, No. 2 Group, which had been on light bombers, was to provide me with 109 Squadron to carry out the Oboe work.

Thus we were to begin life as a Path Finder Force with a total of five squadrons, as follows:

No. 7 Squadron	Stirlings	Affiliated to 3 Group
No. 35 Squadron	Halifaxes	Affiliated to 4 Group
No. 83 Squadron	Lancasters	Affiliated to 5 Group
No. 156 Squadron	Wellingtons	Affiliated to 1 Group
No. 109 Squadron	Wellingtons (pressurised)	Not affiliated to any particular Group

The work on Oboe was carried out not at T.R.E. but at No. 109 Squadron itself. Wing-Commander MacMullen, a fellow Australian, was in command of the squadron, ably assisted by Squadron-Leader Hal Bufton (brother of Sid Bufton). This squadron had been engaged in another little radio job, that of bending the Knickebein beams used by the Germans in their efforts at "pathfinding" during the bombing of this country earlier on. For Oboe the Air Ministry had decided that the pressurised Wellington, with its operational height of about 32,000 feet, would be just the aircraft for the job. The fact that it carried an enormous steel boiler in its fuselage to act as a pressure chamber seriously interfered with its pay-load and its carrying capacity, but as the aircraft would only be required to carry target markers the idea was that it would be satisfactory for such a purpose. This aircraft I was subsequently able to avoid, to the delight of the squadron concerned and to the benefit of our war effort in quite a number of unexpected ways.

On one of my earlier test flights in 109 Squadron I had the misfortune to do myself "a little bit of no good," due to the pressurisation system of this Wellington. I took off by the rather uncomfortable procedure of poking my head up into the astro-dome stuck out of the top of the pressurised chamber. From this position the bulging fuselage obstructed most of the ground view anywhere near the aircraft. It was just possible to take-off provided that one did not run into anything whilst taxiing. The flight in question went to about 30,000 feet, and just after I had completed the Oboe tests which I was carrying out, I noticed that the wireless operator had gone down to the pressurised door in the boiler which we were inhabiting and was fiddling with the catches. Apparently there was an air leak of some fair proportions, and he was trying to fix it. Unhappily he did the wrong thing, and opened the door suddenly, with the result that we changed pressure from the equivalent of about 6,000 or 8,000 feet to 30,000 feet in a split second. Not sufficiently happy with this result, he then closed the door quickly and the pressure built up, equivalent to giving us the reversed process in about twenty or thirty seconds. Unfortunately, I had a very bad cold in the head at the time, and the result was internal infection of both ears. I managed to stay more or less on my feet, but over the next ten days they gave me a very strong course of sulphanilimide which, combined with the ear trouble itself, made it a very unpleasant period for me.

It was not because of this episode, but rather because the squadron was convinced that the Mosquito, which was then available in small numbers, could do the job much better than the Wellington Six, that we changed to the former. We had a few of these bomber Mosquitoes which nobody wanted, but which had been ordered in a small test order by the Ministry of Aircraft Production. They had no armament of any sort, but were indeed very fast little craft. They had a bomb bay big enough to take four of our five-hundred-pound Target Indicators, and it seemed to me that if they could achieve the ceiling we required they would be perfectly suitable. I test-flew the Mosquito by day and by night, and we got on with the "test installation" of the Oboe equipment. At a meeting at the Air Ministry on the subject, Bomber Command and the Air Ministry both very strongly opposed the adoption of the Mosquito. They argued that it was a frail wood machine totally unsuitable for Service conditions, that it would be shot down because of its absence of gun turrets, and that in any case it was far too small to carry the equipment and an adequate Pathfinder crew. I dealt with each one of these points in turn, but finally they played their ace. They declared that the Mosquito had been tested thoroughly by the appropriate establishments and found quite unsuitable, and indeed impossible to fly at night. At this I raised an eyebrow, and said that I was very sorry to hear that it was quite impossible to fly it by night, as I had been doing so regularly during the past week and had found nothing wrong. There was a deathly silence. I got my Mosquitoes.

Thus it was that the greatest little aircraft ever built came into squadron service as a bomber in the Royal Air Force. From that decision grew many other things, not only for the Oboe squadrons but also for the general improvement of our bombing policy.

On the question of pyrotechnics, one might imagine that the situation was simple. I would therefore like to explain to those who had not had the pleasure of bombing Germany, that the enemy went to extreme lengths to divert the fall of bombs from the proper targets on to spots which were more attractive from his point of view. This was done in a number of different ways. Both before and after the advent of the Path Finder Force, one of the most common customs was to create a target area adequately surrounded by defences and searchlights, and to let off dummy incendiaries, like our own, on the ground, so as to look as if there was a town being bombed and being defended. Many a crew would then drop their bombs into the middle of it all, fondly believing that they were giving the real target a real pounding. Unfortunately, all too frequently this was simply a dummy town—in the open fields. The realistic nature of these dummies was quite staggering, and it is no reflection that many crews were caught by them. With the advent of Pathfinders we expected that the Hun would try to copy the markers which we used. Illumination, useful in opening attacks in good weather but useless once the smoke and dust of bombing had started, had certain advantages in the matter of identification of genuine surface landmarks. This, however, only applied to the early Pathfinder crews, and it was quite clear that the main force must aim at pyrotechnics of some sort. The intensity of the target indicators, which we subsequently referred to as T.I.s, was very great, and indeed right to the end of the war the enemy never really produced a very good copy. As we expected trouble, we arranged for all sorts of combinations and variations of colours changing, and colours throwing stars of different colours and the like. We were prepared to use different colours for different purposes, and indeed to change colours if necessary during a raid so as to ensure the correct aiming point even if the enemy were sufficiently alert to watch and copy. In addition, the bursting of the target indicators was carried out by barometric fuses, usually set to burst at relatively low levels between 200 and 500 feet. This meant that there was a slight cascade on to the ground, but that the main burning period was right on the ground itself. Each T.I. consisted of a large number of these pyrotechnic candles, ignited by the initial bursts, which meant that fire-fighters on the ground would take a very considerable time to get around to the job of putting them all out. Moreover, their burning period was relatively short anyway, and so there was no question of their being dealt with in that manner. Continuity of marking was achieved by replenishing from above.

In addition to these target indicators for ground use, we prepared something which was ridiculed and laughed at by a good many people. These were sky markers, and consisted of parachute flares of various colours throwing out stars (or not, as the case might be) so that we could mark a spot in the sky for a limited period, usually three to five minutes. I had done a few calculations on the use of such a method for blind bombing through thick cloud when it was impossible to see the glow of target indicators because of the density and/ or depth of the cloud. These rough calculations seemed to me to indicate that the results to be achieved by such an apparently difficult method would probably prove just as effective as the slap-dash visual bombing that I had so often seen in the past. Roughly speaking, the idea was that the sky markers would be put down by a marker aircraft using Oboe or H2S, in a position so that after it had burned half its time it had drifted, in accordance with the wind found by the navigator, to the correct point through the line-of-sight of a bomber on to the aiming point, assuming that his bomb sight was set to his normal height and that he was approaching the target on the correct heading. This latter point was, of course, the most difficult one to achieve, but as we hoped that the relative accuracy of the fore and aft position would be greater than normal, the error in line was, we felt, acceptable. This proved to be the case in practice, and it was a method which we used frequently for the rest of the war.

It was in August, 1942, that the squadrons of the Path Finder Force assembled. Typical of the attitude of Bert Harris, our C.-in-C., to the Path Finder Force, was the order which he issued to me that the squadrons were to operate the day they arrived, without missing a single night, and that no period would be allowed for preparation or for training. This was quite unreasonable, but the spirit behind it was so thoroughly "press-on" that I made no attempt to argue. In accordance with the general principle of never wasting war effort or of ceasing to strike the enemy, I entirely agreed, and we were therefore prepared to operate the night the squadrons assembled. Actually they did not do so, as all operations were cancelled, but on the next night the Path Finder squadrons went out, using visual methods only, to bomb Flensberg, a submarine base north of Kiel. We had no radar devices working, and the crews were not particularly trained for any special operations. The only thing special about the operation was therefore that we provided the most experienced crews with the means of illuminating the target by parachute flares. Giving them an excellent load of these devices, I sent them off to do their best.

Unhappily, the raid was a complete failure. The weather was quite contrary to the Met. forecast, which had been relatively good. In actual fact there was very poor visibility and considerable low cloud, and the chances of success were nil from the outset. In short, merely creating a Path Finder Force was not magic; if you get no opportunity to train, no special equipment with which to work and an inaccurate weather report, the result must be exactly what one would expect. The Flensberg raid, of course, had the great advantage that it gave the cynics throughout the Command the opportunity to say, "There you are. I told you so; the Path Finder Force won't work!"

That, however, was only the beginning, and soon, with lectures, and training in the air and a general change of direction, the Pathfinder squadrons became effective. Even with the relatively old-fashioned method of ordinary simple navigation, we were able to improve results immediately. This was achieved by the illumination method and with ground marking to concentrate the bombing. Moreover, we were coordinating the efforts of the whole Command, not only from the point of view of concentration of bombing on the target itself, but also by our good tactical routing, which reduced losses.

In the absence of any of the special radar or any other of the pieces of navigational equipment which we were hoping to get, we immediately made progress on the more simple things such as improvement in night vision. Air Commodore Livingstone, the R.A.F. eye specialist, provided "dope" for the eyes in order to give greater dilation of the pupils for bomb aimers, and also provided some useful anti-searchlight glasses. Moreover, Doc McGowan, the Group Medical Officer, who joined us very early in the piece and stayed as a staff officer of Headquarters Path Finder Force for the rest of the war, did much to teach people how best to use their eyes at night. We also did some interesting experiments with high concentrations of vitamin tablets—which I tried myself in vast quantities without any noticeable improvement. Unfortunately, the tests for night vision were such that one could improve at the test by sheer practice, and therefore it was extremely difficult to obtain any exact measurements of improvements in night vision as the result of medicinal or any other trickery.

By the time the Path Finder Force was started, a change of policy in training of air crews had been brought into effect, which not only affected the efficiency of the Path Finder Force itself but in my view seriously impaired the whole strength of Bomber Command. This policy was brought about by the training people at Air Ministry, who insisted that it was impossible to train sufficient pilots to carry two per aircraft in Bomber Command. As flight engineers were in any case said to be sufficient for the large four-engined aircraft which were coming in, the idea, therefore, was that only one pilot would be carried, and in addition one flight engineer. The policy of carrying no second pilot had the result that crews arrived at squadrons with a captain who had never, at any stage of his career, been proved under operational conditions. He had never seen a German target, nor had he been shot at in real anger. This policy was forced on the Air Staff by the Training Staff at Air Ministry, headed by Guy Garrod who, I believe, was principally influenced by Ralph Cochran, who at the time the decision was taken was Director of Training Flying. Personally, I believe that the inexperience of the captains meant that almost all of them were relatively ineffective for a large part of their tour, and in any case the loss rate during the first three trips of any new crew was approximately five times as great as for the rest of the tour. Thus we lost aircraft and we also lost efficiency. Had junior pilots been brought in to act as flight engineers for, say, fifteen trips before they went for their final conversion training to fly in command of heavies, a tremendous improvement in efficiency and a reduction in losses would have resulted. A second such junior pilot could have flown for the second fifteen trips of any captain's normal tour of thirty trips, and all would have been well. As with most of the flying training, this was a typical example of maximum waste for minimum result. Moreover, it was, as with most policy decisions during the war, made by those who had never themselves operated under modern conditions. The fact that this unhappy policy was beginning to have its greatest effect just when Pathfinders started was a coincidence of great misfortune to us at P.F.F., but there was nothing which we could do about it except to try to do our own job properly.

Of the squadrons which reported in August, 1942, No. 7 Squadron went to Oakington, 35 Squadron went to Gravely, 83 Squadron went to Wyton, where the Headquarters of the Path Finder Force was also established, 156 Squadron went to Warboys, and 109 Squadron went to Wyton. During these early Pathfinder raids we did of course learn much in the way of minor tactical detail. For example, the reception given by the few solitary Pathfinders ahead of the Main Force on their arrival at the target area was generally so intense that the difficulty of doing the job was greater than ever. To overcome this we introduced the system of "Supporters", with the opening aircraft, for which purpose we used principally our "under training" relatively junior crews who were not permitted to take part in the marking itself. These Supporters went in with the initial markers, and thus divided the attention of the defences. They could not be used too extensively so long as we were depending upon visual marking, for the effect of their bombing with H.E. was to raise dust and smoke, thus obscuring the visual identification of the aiming point. They could not use incendiaries, as this would have given a glare-back far more serious than the smoke and the dust. Moreover, incendiaries dropped by relatively unreliable crews might mislead the rest of the Force and undo the work of the markers. We also learnt a great deal about the unreliability of the Met. Service during this phase, and the bitterness of these disappointments from that cause was one of the reasons why for a considerable period I gently tried to get the Met. flight under my command. A decision in favour of this was made some months later by the C.-in-C., to my delight and, I believe, subsequently to his entire satisfaction. In criticising the Met. officers, I would point out that they had an extremely difficult job to forecast such a big area without any reports whatever. The whole of Western Europe, from Spain to the top of Norway and right through to the Russian front, was a blank so far as weather reports were concerned, and the Met. officers had to work out for themselves the whole of the weather movement.

Before the end of August was out I had lost Angus Buchan, my Path Finder Force Navigation Staff Officer. I had laid it down as a matter of principle that all staff officers of the Path Finder Force were required to operate moderately frequently, with my approval, in order to ensure that they were thoroughly in touch with the day to day affairs of the Pathfinder Job. Angus Buchan had come with me from Leeming, and it was a sad blow to lose him so early in our existence.

The losses of Pathfinder crews were in fact being carefully watched, not only by myself for my own guidance and action but also by our critics, who declared that we should be hacked down unmercifully and that the result would be catastrophic. In those early days I found that our losses were only very slightly worse than those of the Main Force, and by devising every possible tactical trick we subsequently got them down so that our losses were in fact less per raid. Nevertheless, it was a formidable task ahead of any Pathfinder crew to carry out sixty operations in a leading rôle and to survive until the end. I see from my notes of these early raids that many aircraft still bombed dummy targets, in spite of our efforts at target marking. I raised the question of directing the Force by R.T., but the C.-in-C. turned it down most emphatically. Some eighteen months later, when a certain group commander got busy and introduced the use of R.T. for directing his independent bomber force, the C.-in-C. gave his immediate approval. I often reflect on the bombs we might have saved had we been given permission earlier. On 1st–2nd September we had one example of a mistake which occurred through the still primitive nature of our equipment. On this particular occasion the target was Saarbrucken. The line of approach took the stream of bombers along the valley over Saarlauten. Unfortunately, one of the Pathfinder aircraft dropped his markers on Saarlauten in error. Although the main Marker Force had gone on to the correct target, the diversion was created, and the main weight of the raid fell on

Saarlauten. It was a useful target, full of industrial activities, but not as important as Saarbrucken itself. The C.-in-C. was very kind about the whole thing; he simply said that it was a good German target and at least the Path Finder Force did keep the bombers on *a* target, as opposed to scattering vaguely.

From the beginning of the Path Finder Force I always made it a rule to attend one briefing prior to operations, and one interrogation after operations. I also went out occasionally in person, and saw how things were going actually on the targets themselves. The procedure for laying on an operation was more or less as follows. Each morning I went to the Ops. room of Path Finder Headquarters, together with my Air Staff and Intelligence Officers. We would await the C.-in-C.'s decision as to what the target was to be, and immediately the S.A.S.O. at Bomber Command, Air Vice-Marshal Robert Saundby, would pick up a telephone, and having "scrambled" would tell me what the target was and roughly how many aircraft were to be used on it. In Path Finder Headquarters we would then get our own Met. Officer to give his opinion as to the likely weather, and would lay on our plan of attack. We would decide on the principle marking method, and possibly back it up with a secondary precautionary method. Subsequently, when we got all our equipment, we always laid down the primary method and emergency method as a matter of course, regardless of how good the weather forecast might be. We would then work out the route. All of this was passed to Bomber Command and Main Force Groups, by teleprinter. When we had first started there had been no serious attempt to co-ordinate the tactics of the Command. We evolved our own procedure for informing the Group. Some Main Force Group Commanders decided that they knew so much about air warfare that they themselves should quite seriously interfere with routing proposals and with the direction of approach on the target. This latter point was vitally important, for we soon learnt that the pattern of bombing by the Main Force on to a properly marked target was considerably affected by, amongst other things, the direction of the wind (if appreciable) and the effect of the defences. In taking these two things into account, we hoped to achieve better bombing results. It was extremely difficult to make Main Force Group Commanders understand our reasons, or, at times, to respect them. Daily Planning was not just Aiming Point marking details but more particularly routing tactics to achieve two objectives (i) attract German fighters by Mosquito attacks on other targets. (ii) False route markers with suitable timing in relation to a Main Force route which could remain deceptive until the last moment.

Very few Main Force crews (or even their AOC's) and even some Pathfinder crews ever realised how the PFF and their Light Night Striking Force deliberately stuck their necks out to reduce Main Force casualties—and accepted a higher degree of risk themselves.

For three and a half years I and my Ops. Room Staff planned the routing, marking, spoof raids and fighter diversion as well as the target approach, the aiming point marking and, in order to avoid copying the change of colours of the Markers on most, but not all (Nuremberg!), Bomber Command major targets. The results and the lower than expected casualties speak for themselves.

In December, 1942, we began to use Oboe on operations. To begin with, we had to prove it to ourselves, as there was no doubt that there were many people who were sceptical of these new-fangled devices. In any case, it would have been most unwise for us to rely on an untried method in putting down a big weight of bombs. The alternative in bad weather was no bombs down at all!

Oboe was a responder system worked by two stations in this country which sent out radar pulses. (Radar used to be called R.D.F. before the Americans decided to improve our language.) These pulses were received by the aircraft and sent back to the ground station, which then measured the time element in order to ascertain the distance. The theoretical accuracy of the equipment was very high, and nominally located the aircraft within about 50 feet, in terms of distance from the station concerned. One such station acted as a tracking station, and transmitted a signal with dots on one side and dashes on the other to indicate whether the aircraft was maintaining the constant radius which was required to bring it on to the target. This constant radius was calculated for the height of the aircraft and prevailing wind, and allowed for the tangential throw of the bomb; it was carefully calculated by the "boffins". The other station was ranging on a similar basis, and had set on its equipment warning distances at which it sent out signals that the release was coming near. Finally it sent out a long dash, and at the moment the dash broke the bomb aimer pressed the release and let go the bombs or markers. The boffins (A. H. Reeves, Dr. F. E. Jones and their team) produced the equipment, and it was maintained by 60 Group technically. I was in operational command, and provided the Controllers, headed by one Wing-Commander Finn. The equipment was all virtually hand-made, even including the aircraft equipment, which we then installed ourselves actually on the squadrons.

We had two pairs of stations, with the northern stations in each case up near Trimingham and the southern stations down near Walmer and Worth. Each pair worked on a different channel, so that we could at that stage operate two aircraft at a time. This was one of the limitations of Oboe. Moreover, its range was limited to just a little more than the straight line tangential to the earth's surface. In fact, it was about 1.05 optical range. Thus from these stations on the east of England we could just cover the whole of the Ruhr. Limited though this was, it was of tremendous value in view of its very precise nature and its absolute independence of weather.

The first night on which Oboe was used against the enemy was on 20th December 1942, and the pilots were Bufton, Somerville, Griggs, Campbell, O'Neill and Thelwell. Indeed, this team was the backbone of the Oboe squadrons from then onwards. They dropped 4×500 lb. of H.E. each on a coking plant—as a test target. On 31st December 1942 on a raid against Düsseldorf, we used Oboe to sky mark—the first occasion on which sky-marking had ever been used. We did this with eight Lancasters of Path Finder Force acting as bombers, whilst two Mosquitoes provided the sky-markers. Unfortunately, a gale had blown down one of the masts, and we were therefore working on one channel only. Thus one aircraft acted as marker and one as standby. The Lancasters in the main came in very nicely, with very precise timing, and seven out of eight of them bombed through the sky-markers on the correct headings with good results. The eighth aircraft was a little early, and the flares ignited behind him. He was thus forced to do a circuit, and making it rather wide he unfortunately did not get to the flare before it had burnt out.

It seemed from this, the first test of the method, that we were able to offer the C.-in-C. a means of bombing when there was complete cloud cover below so thick that no ground markers, however intense, could be seen through it. Many Air Force officers would have taken a lot more proof than this before they used the method, but it was typical of Bert Harris that he grasped the opportunity and immediately thereafter used it against Essen itself—one of the most difficult and most important targets in Germany. From 20th December, 1942, onwards, the Oboe boys kept up their operations by dropping sky-markers for targets in the Ruhr, that area which had proved impossible to bomb by visual methods but which contained most of Germany's vital heavy industry. With forces of twenty to seventy Lancasters per raid they attacked Essen six times and Duisburg twice during January, a bad weather month when the whole Command would have been practically paralysed without blind marking. During this period, the end of December, plus January and February, 109 Squadron operated a hundred and six sorties against various targets for marking and for test bombing purposes. The most interesting factor during this trial period was that in spite of the fact that each aircraft had to fly dead straight and level for a distance of about fifty miles into the target, thus helping both the ground gunners and the fighters, and in spite of the fact that the Mosquito was completely unarmed and in the eyes of many senior officers a completely useless aircraft, the loss rate was nil.

The losses on heavies in the early days of the Path Finder Force started off rather badly. In our first month, August, 1942, we averaged 9·1 per cent. lost. This was a rate which we obviously could not maintain if we had any hope of retaining sufficient experienced crews to do the job properly. Fortunately, this unhappy state of affairs did not continue after we began to settle down and become effective in our tactics and our planning. Thus in September the rate dropped to 3·1 per cent. for the heavies, and in October 2·6 per cent. It fluctuated thereafter between $1\frac{1}{2}$ and $4\frac{1}{2}$ per cent., and this was a rate which we could stand without catastrophic results.

Reverting to Oboe, a very historic occasion was a particular sky-marking raid on Essen. This took place on 9th January 1943. The C.-in-C. detailed a moderate little force of Lancasters to bomb on sky-markers, and all went well. There was complete solid cloud cover below, unlike the better conditions which had prevailed on the other sky-marking raids already carried out. Thus it was quite clear to those on the ground that the most valuable target in Germany, Krupps works at Essen, was being hit by a blind bombing method. Hitler immediately called a meeting, at which he himself personally took part, and apparently he was most violent in his denial that such a thing was possible. He insisted that there must have been breaks in the cloud so that the R.A.F. could see the targets. His various experts advised him otherwise, but apparently he was furious at the thought. All this we discovered after the end of the war, when German records of the meeting became available. Oboe had not only shattered the targets of Germany, but had also shattered German morale. It continued the process for the rest of the war, and was probably the most effective single instrument of warfare in our entire armoury. It is interesting to note that the members of the public of Great Britain and the Commonwealth probably have no idea of the existence of Oboe, and have certainly never heard of Reeves, who invented it with the able assistance of Dr. F. E. Jones, and a small team of enthusiastic "boffins". MacMullen, Bufton, Slim Somerville and the rest of the boys in the Oboe squadrons got their D.S.O.s and their D.F.C.s by the sheer weight of their obvious bravery on operations. The inventor of the equipment, however, got precisely nothing. What a grateful and gracious country we live in !

Whilst all this activity with Oboe was going on, we were not stagnant with H2S. The crash programme of production for H2S equipment was carried through magnificently by Sir Robert Renwick, who was Controller of Supply of Signal Equipment and at the same time Controller of Signals at the Air Ministry, a strange dual post which he held as a civilian. By December, 1942, we had a few Stirlings and a few Halifaxes equipped with H2S, largely because the test installations were carried out on these two types by the "boffins" in the first instance, and it was of course in accordance with the C.-in-C.s policy that I should have four squadrons each with a different type of aircraft. The fact that I hoped to get on to only one type of heavy in Pathfinders, in order to simplify equipment installations and crew training and at the same time to help our engineering maintenance, was not appreciated at that time. When these aircraft, fitted with H2S, started to arrive, we were delighted, and started training immediately. To my extreme annoyance, however, a slight obstruction appeared. The War Cabinet suddenly discovered that the much valued magnetron valve in the H2S equipment had never previously been flown over enemy territory, and as it was regarded as a deadly secret, they suddenly decided that we should not be allowed to use our equipment. This was a very serious blow, and an opinion with which I did not agree. The policy so frequently adopted during the war of not using a good thing for fear that the enemy would learn something from it was in my view cowardly and disastrous. I paid a personal visit on Lord Cherwell on this matter, and my own C.-in-C. and his entire staff were using all their influence in any case. Which was the more effective I do not know, but I am pleased to say that after a few weeks the decision was reversed, and we were free to start the use of H2S, with which we could see the ground through the thickest cloud. H2S was far from perfect, and required great skill to operate it and to maintain it. Nothing, however, was so clear to a navigator in the air as the picture painted by H2S when conditions outside were appalling.

Roughly speaking, my policy was to use H2S on all those targets which were outside the range of Oboe, and to use Oboe particularly on the Ruhr, which was too congested for H2S to cover and which was in any case well within the range of Oboe. Thus, from then to the end of the war we Pathfinders had three methods of finding aiming points—first, by visual methods; secondly, by H2S; and thirdly, by the highly accurate Oboe. For those anti-Pathfinder crews, of which we must admit there were a good many, particularly in one rather cussed Main Force group, there was one diffi-culty which was experienced with all three methods—namely, that the target indicators which we dropped some-times had technical faults. These were faults of construction which were outside the control of the Path Finder Force. The result was that the T.I. case was sometimes unstable, and occasionally threw its fins, thus tumbling to earth by a most erratic path. Such faulty markers dropped by one particular aircraft might fall widely apart, causing confusion and lack of confidence in our marking. At the time it gave us consider-able worry, and mystified us completely. It was only very much later that we discovered the cause.

Before H2S came into our heavy markers, we relied entirely on visual methods, and the target finding tactics were roughly as follows: We first put in what we call Finders, with some Supporters at exactly the same time. These Finders were gen-erally at about zero minus five minutes, and they were the best crews available. They had a good load of flares, which they dropped at the point or points where they thought the aiming point was to be found. One or other of these experts would in due course put a bunch of flares over the correct aiming point, and having identified it would then drop further flares on top of it. As soon as this had taken place, the Illuminators would come in, and would put a stick of flares across the aiming point as found by the Finders. After the Illuminators came the Primary Markers, who were accurate bomb aimers, and who dropped target indicators on the aiming point as identified visually in the excellent light of the sticks of flares. Once the aiming point was marked, we then followed up with Backers-Up, who put further target indicators on the mark previously made so that the Main Force had a mark at which to continue to aim throughout the duration of the attack. With the advent of H2S we still carried on with visual marking, as H2S accuracy was not sufficiently good to ensure the results we needed, particularly in some types of built-up area. When conditions were good enough for visual bombing, we therefore used H2S with which to put down the flares, and thus simplified the initial illuminating and found the aiming point far more quickly and with far greater certainty.

So much for the equipment which we could use—the eyes, the H2S and the Oboe. There was, however, the other aspect of the means used to mark; here again the methods fell into three categories. So far as the Main Force bombers were concerned, we detailed the method by three code names. These were "Newhaven" for ground marking by visual methods, when the crews simply aimed at the target indicators on the ground; "Parramatta" was when we ground marked, using H2S only, owing to bad visibility or broken cloud; and finally "Wanganui," which was pure sky-marking, when Main Force crews were required to bomb through these sky-markers on a required course which we detailed. These three code names continued in use for the rest of the war in all the tactical instructions sent out by Path Finder Headquarters each day.

The names for these three methods were chosen very simply. I asked one of my air staff officers, Squadron-Leader Ashworth, "Pedro, where do you come from?" And he replied, "From Wanganui." I then said, "Just to keep the balance with New Zealand, we will call the blind ground marking by the name of Parramatta." Then looking for a third name for visual ground marking, I pressed the bell on my desk and summoned Corporal Ralph, my confidential W.A.A.F. clerk. When she came in, I said, "Sunshine, where do you live?" And she replied, "Newhaven." Thus it was that these famous code names were born.

At this point let me interject a "line shoot". About this time in the affairs of the Path Finder Force I had occasion to go down to Boscombe Down one night to test some pyrotechnics which were being developed for us. On my arrival, the Station Commander gave me dinner, and in due course drove me on a blacked-out aerodrome to an aircraft which was called a B 25, subsequently called the Mitchell. I had never seen a B 25 at that time, and the Station Commander, who knew that I normally required to fly myself, apologised sincerely and said that he felt that it would not be reasonable for me to fly an aircraft which I had never seen, and that he had therefore arranged for a certain squadron-leader to act as pilot for me. To this I agreed, and climbed on board the aircraft. Whilst preparing to start up I gossiped with the pilot, and was not a little disturbed to find that he himself had never previously flown the B 25 at night, but that he regarded it as a considerable handful by day, particularly as he had only flown it for the past two days. I thought that if my neck was to be broken I would prefer to do it myself. I took off and did the test, then came back and landed. I taxied in and drove away. Some months later somebody asked me if I had ever seen a B 25. I replied, "No; I have never seen a B 25, but I have flown one."

In those early days of marking, we did suffer a number of partial failures due to poor timing, and we therefore gave our urgent attention to the problem. As a result of experience with inaccurate wind forecasts, we eventually settled on a method of allowing one additional minute per hour of flying time to the target in order to give marker crews a reasonable chance of being there on time, even when forecasts were wrong. If they were running late, they then kept going to the best of their ability and—quite possibly—with some additional speed, whereas if they were early they lost this extra minute by doing a one minute "dog leg" (one minute sixty degrees off to starboard of the required course, and then one minute sixty degrees to port of the required course before reverting to the course again), thus losing one minute. Any additional earliness was similarly lost. If, on the other hand, they were late in spite of the margin provided, then it was argued that the Main Force bombers would also be late, and would therefore not be embarrassed by any lack of markers on their arrival. In any case, we normally opened at zero minus five or thereabouts in order to ensure that our target indicators or sky-markers were ready for the first bombers on the target.

Thus, by the beginning of 1943 we had the crews, we had Oboe and H2S, we had pyrotechnics and we had a little experience. What was more important was that we had already made a tremendous difference to the effectiveness of the Command, even although it had not as yet grown to the numerical strength which it subsequently achieved. The Prime Minister had regained his faith in the bomber offensive, and Germany had lost faith in her defences. Antagonism within Bomber Command still existed, but the Path Finder Force was doing its job, and it looked as if the future would go on improving.

The Path Finder Force became a separate Group in January, 1943, and the C.-in-C. fought the bureaucrats who wanted some senior and senile stooge to command it. He won the day for me, and I was promoted to Air Commodore to be the first Air Officer Commanding No. 8 (P.F.F.) Group. The staff who had been with me remained when we were upgraded to the status of a Group, and in addition, of course, I had a number of other officers. First a Senior Air Staff Officer had to be appointed, and I was offered C. D. Boyce, who had been a fellow flying officer with me in my younger days on flying boats. He was not a navigator, nor did he profess to any navigational knowledge. He was, however, a solid type, and in spite of an air which was casual at times, he was in general a good average officer. Boyce did not always agree with my ideas or policies, but he served me well enough, and stayed with me to the end of the war. Next, of course, I had to have a Senior Administration Officer, and here I am afraid I had quite a large variety. The Administration of the Air Force is to me something which should serve the operational side and not the reverse. I found it somewhat difficult to find an S.A.O. who was both willing to undertake such a non-warlike duty in the middle of a war and who had at the same time the qualities necessary to serve those who were fighting. I will not go through the full list of those who held that appointment, as I might find it unavoidable in the process to let drop a few unhappy and unkind remarks. I finished up, however, on the best of notes with White, who did a grand job and produced efficiency with the right spirit.

As head "plumber", that is Group Engineering Officer, I had Charles Sarsby, and we introduced planned maintenance in Pathfinders long before it had ever been heard of either in the other groups of Bomber Command or in Coastal Command, where they made such intense propaganda over it. In fact, from the time Sarsby arrived we worked towards standardisation of aircraft—namely, Lancasters and Mosquitoes, and created a maintenance base at Wyton for the former and at Upwood for the latter. Moreover, each Squadron had an obligation to produce sixteen aircraft out of eighteen available each day, and definitely to know that they had the other two available for servicing without fear of interruption. The serviceability of Pathfinder aircraft, in spite of the high damage rate, was as high, I believe, as any ever achieved in the Air Force.

One of the leading characters of Path Finder Force Head-quarters was "Shep"—Squadron-Leader Shepherd—who was the Group Intelligence Officer. He had volunteered to come to me from Leeming, where he had known me, and he re-mained through the whole of the war. Indeed, he rejoined me after the war in civil aviation. He and his staff rounded up the necessary information about targets and the like with the greatest efficiency, and of course it was their duty to col-lect the pilots' reports after every raid. Group Navigation Officer was one of the main appointments in the Path Finder Force, for it was on navigation above all else that our results depended. I lost Angus Buchan, as I have already told, within a few days of the Creation of the Path Finder Force, and the history of Navigation Officers at H.Q. P.F.F. was unhappily on those lines on two more occasions.

One of the most colourful characters of Headquarters Path Finder Force came to us from one of the Pathfinder squadrons in the middle of 1943. This was Hamish Mahaddie, who was the No. 1 Personnel Officer at Group Headquarters and, as such, was primarily responsible for recruiting volunteer air crew from the Main Force Groups. He therefore visited these Groups, and was even permitted to give lectures at times. He became an extremely well-known character, with his strong Scottish accent, and he always started off his lectures by tell-ing of the famous raid in which the Pathfinders went wrong. It was an excellent example, particularly as he was one of the people concerned in the fiasco.

In the Operations Room we made a policy of having young officers who had good operational experience, and of course we changed them over at frequent intervals. This helped con-siderably in our daily tactical planning, as they were able to put forward practical ideas and views based on real know-ledge and not merely on hearsay. Then there was Rathbone, the "Reluctant Dragon", our Armament Officer, who produced our fireworks and bangers; and Howard Lees, responsible for some wonderful photography, particularly at night.

From the outset we had two civilians at Headquarters Path Finder Force. First of these, "Tommy", was the Senior Meteorological Officer for the Group, and his responsibility was tremendous when one realises that the whole of the tactical plans were laid according to his forecasts, including marking methods, the timing and the like. He was one of the best of all forecasters, and I knew it—for, after all, I have some knowedge of the subject myself. There were many difficulties, for in doing his best to satisfy us, little Tommy would often find himself at variance with the forecast given to the C.-in-C., and worse still, the large variety of forecasts which were offered to each Group Commander by their own senior Met. officers. Ultimately, after a lot of trouble in this respect, it was agreed that the Met. officers of the whole Command would have a combined conference on the scrambler telephone to co-ordinate their views before they issued their final forecast. (The scrambler telephone was simply a telephone in which one pressed the button which brought in an interference effect which prevented other people tapping the line, though the message could be deciphered at the other end by means of corresponding equipment.) The other civilian was John Jukes, who, like Tommy, remained with us for the whole of the war. He was the representative of the Operational Research Section. This section was made up of a fine body of scientists whose job it was to investigate the results of bombing and various other aspects of it from an impartial and scientific point of view, and to present their results to the C.-in-C. and to the Air Ministry, and indeed to the Government. Now I have never been very keen on snoopers, so from the outset I made it quite clear to John Jukes that he had complete access to all information, but he was there primarily to help to win the war and not simply to record just how the war went. In fact, I gave him the job of looking after a lot of our mathematical calculations, particularly in connection with Oboe. These duties were of great positive value to our planning, and therefore he fulfilled a useful and not merely an ornamental function. He was a great asset.

Whilst on the subject of O.R.S., I feel that a comment at this stage might be wise. Whilst most of their officers were true scientists and endeavoured to do their jobs impartially, most of us who had anything to do with them found that they did tend to have pre-conceived ideas, and they then set out to prove these ideas regardless whether they were right or wrong. There is no doubt that when a scientist is determined to prove something, it is extremely difficult to prevent him!

There were many others on the staff of Headquarters P.F.F., both officers and other ranks, whom I would like to describe, for they were a grand crowd—and interesting, too. The main point, however, is that I had at Headquarters P.F.F. a band of keen hard-working types determined, in a practical way, to get the war won.

Interrogation of Aircrew after a raid was a ritual on which a lot of false history is based even to this day.

For example a senior crew reported a raid to be a failure with Target Markers very bad. This was reported as a fact by Station to Group, and by Group to Command and then to the Air Ministry. The next morning the Aiming Point photo proved that the "experienced crew" was nowhere near the target and therefore saw nothing relevant. No effort was made to rectify the Raid Report and Summary at Air Ministry or any other level. In particular it is worth noting that one Group Commander particularly asked crews, Squadron Commanders and Station Intelligence Officers to emphasise any Pathfinder errors! There is no reason to question such a direction were it not for the fact that the AOC concerned was openly anti-Pathfinders!

8

INEXORABLY ONWARDS

Aᴛ the beginning of 1943, the mighty sword of Bomber Command was veritably poised for the attack. My own hopes were high, and I believe that the growing effectiveness of the Command was being widely appreciated. My own optimistic estimates of how soon war would end were perhaps coloured by the progress we were making and by the damage which I knew we were doing to the enemy. Unfortunately, I did not fully realise how much our efforts were to be squandered and diverted between then and the end of the war. I saw Bomber Command as a mighty weapon for striking at the heart of the enemy—that is to say, at Germany itself. The frequency with which we were put on to other targets was, however, quite pathetic. I have already mentioned the waste of bombs on the *Scharnhorst* and *Gneisenau* at Brest, and also how we lost a good many crews (including, perchance, myself) with the *Tirpitz* up in Trondheim, but in spite of these obviously ineffective wastages of effort the same policy went on. There were, for example, a few submarine pens in St. Nazaire and Lorient, on the western tip of France, and these enjoyed very special attention from Bomber Command. Bomber Command pointed out the wastefulness but the Admiralty insisted. We could not touch the pens themselves, which were about five metres thick of solid concrete, as we had no bombs capable of penetrating such a cover. The idea was that we should remove brick by brick throughout the entire town of St. Nazaire in one case and

193

Lorient in the other. The simple fact that in any case the submarine crews lived in rest-houses along the coast out of the towns, apparently did not penetrate as far as the Anti-Submarine Committee. Thus it was that we wasted much time on those targets. It is interesting that in order to make absolutely sure of success of a raid on one such target, we were instructed to use Oboe to drop ground markers for the purpose. The target was St. Nazaire, but the dispositions of our stations were such as to suit Germany, and, in particular, the Ruhr. Thus these stations could not turn around and look southwards towards St. Nazaire as was required, and we had to rush around and get a station going at Sennen on the south coast, which worked with Worth, near Dover, to give us the cover we required for this French target. The attack took place on 28th February 1943, and poor old St. Nazaire took a bad beating.

In talking about the diversion of bomber effort from its main task of hitting Germany, I do not wish to give the impression that I in any way minimised the gravity of the submarine campaign and its effect upon our shipping. I should have thought, however, that the then "powers-that-be" would have been sufficiently intelligent to realise that the enormous weight of bombs which we put down on St. Nazaire and Lorient over those few months in the beginning of 1943 were completely and totally ineffective from the point of view of the submarine campaign, and did a great deal to harm our political position with the French people. It was total and wanton destructiveness of cities of an ally, and did no good whatever. After those two towns had been completely destroyed, I believe that a signal was intercepted in which the German Naval Commander-in-Chief passed a message to his Senior Naval Officer in St. Nazaire congratulating him on the effectiveness of his bases as air-raid precautions for Berlin. It was only when this signal was intercepted that we were allowed to go back to our main job of bombing Germany.

Finally we got back to the job, and we ranged far and wide with a variety of targets, including most of the big German cities, particularly those with industrial activities. I will not attempt to catalogue the activities of the Command except to say that the numbers grew, and the weight of bombs grew, and I believe that it is fair to say at the same time that the efficiency of the Path Finder Force also increased. By this time all the twin-engined bombers were dropping out of the Command, and even the Stirling was falling by the wayside in favour of the Lancaster, which was faster, had a better bomb load and a higher ceiling. The Halifax was not as good as the Lancaster, but nevertheless did a sound job of work, in spite of the fact that the C.-in-C. heartily disliked it. We converted 156 Squadron from its Wellingtons to Lancasters, and did the same with 7 Squadron from Stirlings to Lancasters. Thirty-five Squadron stayed on Halifaxes for some time, mainly because 4 Group, its affiliated Group, was also on Halifaxes. Soon, in the interest of maintenance, we converted that squadron also to Lancasters. The effectiveness of Bomber Command against Germany was so great that, naturally, Hitler took quick counter-measures. Priority of production was switched to fighters to meet our attack, and of all fighters produced, greatest priority went to night fighters to contend with Bomber Command itself. This German Night Fighter Force, which had been a matter of a few hundred aircraft before Pathfinder started, was rapidly built up to over 1,500 first-line aircraft and subsequently to over 2,000. This enormous force took a big proportion of manpower, and was assisted by an elaborate defence system of radar, together with an enormous number of guns involving industrial effort and manpower diversion of a very major nature. Nevertheless, by our constantly changing tactics and tricks, we managed to keep our losses relatively low.

In April, 1943, we "hived off" part of 109 Squadron into 105 Squadron, which had been engaged previously as a low-bomber squadron in No. 2 Group. I took over Marham at this time, and ran two Oboe squadrons of two flights each. We increased our equipment accordingly, and generally speaking were able to deal fairly adequately with any required markings within the range of the device.

Concurrently with taking over 105 Squadron for Oboe purposes, thus getting more bomber Mosquitoes, I took over the only other bomber Mosquito squadron of the Royal Air Force, No. 139. This I used as a "supporting squadron" to go in with the early markers, and also to carry out diversion raids to attract fighters away from the main stream at appropriate moments during the attack. This tactic proved very successful, and often diverted the fighters away from the main target to a likely one within visual distance of it just before the main raid started. Thus the fighters might be fifty or eighty miles away before they suddenly realised their mistake. I also used this squadron for nuisance raiding—an idea entirely of my own, which I quietly insinuated into the operations of the Group, without its being particularly noticed for some time. When the C.-in-C. did notice it, he thoroughly approved of it, and the idea grew.

Mosquito bombers were being produced in goodly numbers. They were coming out of the factories faster than had been anticipated, largely due to the nature of their wooden construction. Moreover, the losses were relatively small—in fact, almost negligible. I, therefore, adopted a policy of an expansion of Mosquitoes which had very far-reaching results. I had my own Mosquito Training Unit for converting crews to Mosquitoes, and ran my own Group Maintenance Unit for Mosquitoes, as by that time I had started to do also for Lancasters under the able guidance of the Group Engineer Officer, Group-Capt. Sarsby. The resultant position with regard to both aircraft and crews was highly satisfactory, and with the low loss rate I found that I was able to go to Bomber Command quite frequently and say that I wished to form a new squadron, as I had surplus crews and surplus aircraft. The A.O.A. would grudgingly give me a squadron number and get it approved by Air Ministry, and I would then build that squadron up to full strength. I kept on doing this until ultimately I had nine squadrons of Mosquitoes (twenty aircraft each) in addition to the Oboe Mosquitoes and the Met. Mosquitoes. When one realises that these Mosquitoes carried a 4,000 lb. bomb, commonly known in those days as "blockbuster", it is clear that the real damage done by such a force was appreciable. In ordinary nuisance raiding on Berlin or similar cities these aircraft, each carrying a 4,000-pounder, would go out in bunches of up to 120 a time, or more frequently in small batches of 10 to 20, at intervals throughout the night, and thus cause chaos amongst the German civilians, lowering their morale and reducing their productive output. All this took time, but it began in April, 1943.

I also increased the Mosquito Oboe squadrons from two flights to three flights each, which gave me the strength I needed to do all the marking necessary for Bomber Command.

During this main flogging match against Germany, our losses in Pathfinders varied between 3½ and 5½ per cent. on monthly average, mostly heavies. Unhappily, amongst these losses were often people whom I regarded as good friends. We worked so closely with the squadrons in the Path Finder Force that I got to know most of the senior pilots fairly well, and therefore when they went missing it was a personal blow. This naturally had its effect on one's nerves and spirits, and occasionally driving home from interrogation in the early hours of the morning it was hard to avoid breaking down and shedding a few tears—which was probably a good safety valve in any case. To have this constant strain over such a long period, night after night, and month after month, had its wearing effect, however tough one tried to make oneself superficially.

One particular loss was subject to a fairly happy ending. Squadron-Leader Price, the Group Headquarters Navigation Staff Officer, went flying one night in a Mosquito, and failed to return. Next morning the administrative wheels started turning, and his next-of-kin were informed. The following morning I went into my office, and as I passed through the outer office, there was Price; I stopped in amazement. I suddenly realised that instead of wearing a squadron-leader's uniform he was wearing a flying officer's badges of rank. My amazement apparently showed on my face, and he immediately spoke and said, "It's O.K., sir. It's not Price, it's his twin brother. I am Flying Officer Price from Iceland." I invited him into my office, and he explained what had taken place. Apparently, twenty-four hours earlier he had gone to his Commanding Officer in Iceland, where I believe he was in a Coastal Command unit, and simply told him that by telepathy he knew that his twin brother had gone missing, and that he wished to have leave in order to go back to England to comfort his parents. His Commanding Officer apparently had the good sense to believe him and give him the leave which he requested, and the means of transport to England. He immediately went to his parents, and assured them that his twin brother was alive and well. He then came on to Headquarters Path Finder Force, and told me the same good news. It transpired later that he was perfectly right. His brother had lived through the crash, and had been made a prisoner of war. This was truly a wonderful example of the power of telepathy at times of great human stress.

During the early summer of 1943, we kept flogging away at the Ruhr, using Oboe in this difficult and important task. We also went to such places as Hamburg, Berlin and all the other main German cities, using H2S. The Ruhr itself was at last being dealt with effectively, and a reflection of the success of our raids was shown on the Russian front, where the German lack of heavy equipment saved Stalingrad. Indeed, the Russians recognised this by awarding me one of their decorations, the Order of Alexander Nevsky. This vast and important industrial complex, the heart of German industry, fortunately fell into British hands when victory came, and it is good to know that the British Army saw the results of the might of Bomber Command and what R.A.F. bombing really means.

Towards the end of July, 1943, we achieved what I regard as the greatest victory of the war, land, sea or air. This victory was in the Battle of Hamburg. The first raid was on 24th July, when a fairly big force of about 700 and 800 aircraft attacked, using Parramatta ground marking, and everything went according to plan. All of these aircraft were four-engined heavies, and with the relatively reasonable range to Hamburg, they were all carrying a big load of bombs. The result was absolutely staggering. The fire-fighting services failed completely, and enormous infernoes raged on the ground. So great were these fires that the smoke reached 20,000 feet, and it was subsequently discovered from German reports that the wind speed, due to this violent convection, reached about 100 miles per hour on the ground, blowing bicycles along the streets and, it is said, even blowing over pedestrians who were attempting to run for better cover. One report claimed that the pedestrians were blown into the flames by the force of the convection winds. However true these stories may be, the result was certainly devastating. On the following night we reverted to Essen, in order to fool the German defences, but I sent a few Mosquitoes along to Hamburg just to ring the alarms and make the frightened people of Hamburg frightened once again. On the 26th I did the same with another handful of Mosquitoes, just to keep their nerves on edge. Then on the 27th the C.-in-C. laid on another big one, and once again it was wonderfully successful. A few Mosquitoes kept the pot boiling on the 28th, and then on the 29th we went there in force again. The final raid was on 2nd August, four days later, when we finished off the job. On each of these raids, three of them with the full force behind us, and one with half the normal maximum behind us, together with a few nuisance raids, we virtually destroyed 75 per cent. of Hamburg. We had moved the aiming point suitably in order to cover the area adequately, and Bomber Command had really done their stuff in a big way.

I endeavoured to convey to the C.-in-C. what I felt about the staggering success of this raid, and what it must be doing to the German people and to the German High Command. I myself held views that if some appropriate political action were taken at that time, peace feelers might very well have started to emanate from Germany, which would have been the beginning of the rot which would bring about her end. Unhappily, nobody seemed to realise that a great victory had been won, and certainly nobody realised its effect on the German people at that time. This became evident many weeks later, when it was clear that the Gestapo had lost their grip on the population and that the whole of North Germany had panicked. It was an opportunity which we missed. Whatever the chances of success might have been, it would certainly have been worth while to try to have weakened German morale by some appropriate political action.

In the nine days of the Battle of Hamburg the Path Finder Force and its attendant "Light Night Striking Force" of Mosquitoes flew a total of 472 sorties, with a loss of thirteen aircraft. Cloud varied from 4/10ths to 9/10ths over the target throughout the period.

A satisfying aspect of the Battle of Hamburg was the fact that it was here that the Path Finder Force once made its classic bloomer, and managed to bomb a small town on the western side of the city instead of the main aiming point in the docks themselves. This failure was the subject of one of our lectures to newcomers to Path Finder Force, and therefore was a very famous affair. Fate put matters right—or was it, perhaps, some element of skill?

Incidentally, at this time a counter-measure for use against the German radar was introduced. This was given the code name "window", and it consisted of throwing out bundles of metallised strips of paper. These metal strips gave excellent radar reflections at the ground stations, and thereby filled their screens with responses, making it impossible to differentiate between the "window" and the aircraft. This code name "window" was no doubt given to this device by the Air Ministry, but it suited Pathfinders down to the ground, for it fitted in with our description of the early aircraft which we called "openers". Thus thereafter we detailed "window openers" to begin every attack, going in with the early markers to spread plenty of "window" and drop their high explosive, thus confusing the issue for the gunners as well as discouraging them with their bombs. "Window" was also used by the Mosquitoes detailed for spoof attacks, when they increased their rate of throwing out "window" in order to give the impression of a big bomber force going to that particular target. I often wonder whether the Main Force crews appreciated the fact that the Mosquito crews were completely unarmed, and yet were deliberately enticing the fighters on to themselves in order to protect the main stream.

Whilst on the subject of counter-measures, there was one episode at this time which was quite amusing. My wife, who lived in a married quarter on Wyton Station near to my Headquarters at Huntingdon, often had official visitors. On one occasion we had a number of such visitors, and at dinner she announced that I had presented her with a new Alsatian puppy. She insisted that it should be called "Tinsel", and she could not understand why I very peremptorily insisted that she should not use that name, but any other she chose. My embarrassment at this name was simply due to the fact that it had recently been allotted as a code name for a radio counter-measure which we used on our aircraft. This counter-measure was simple straightforward radio jamming, and was carried in Pathfinders, as they were the leading aircraft. I could not, of course, explain to my wife that this was a code name for anything, because that in itself would have been a breach of secrecy. Without giving a reason, it was quite awkward to try to convince her that she must not use that name.

The Path Finder Force continued to grow. Marham was taken out of service for the building of runways, and instead I was given Downham Market. I extended to the south to Bourne, and finally to Little Staughton. No. 5 Group gave me an additional squadron, Number 97, and No. 4 Group gave me 635. In addition to this I gained another squadron, No. 405, when 6 Group was formed. This raised an awkward matter of principle, as I had insisted from the outset that I would not have any segregation or differentiation in the Path Finder Force. Thus, when the Australians came to me at one stage and asked whether I would have an Australian squadron, I refused point-blank, much to their surprise. The question of the 405 Squadron was different, because it was affiliated to a complete Main Force Group. Nevertheless, I insisted that the crews of this so-called Canadian squadron must not be more than 50 per cent. Canadian. I maintained this principle right to the end. I did agree that the C.O. would always be a Canadian, and it started off under the command of Wing-Commander Fouquier, a thoroughly "press-on type" if ever there was one.

Whilst talking of "press-on types", I feel I should tell of the case of a wing-commander of the Light Night Striking Force—a name incidentally which I used for that Force, much to the dislike of my C.-in-C. This wing-commander commanded one of the squadrons with such enthusiasm that it was positively dangerous. His name was Guy Lockhart, and I never, throughout the entire war, met anybody so fanatically courageous and "press-on" at all times and in all circumstances. Virtually nothing would stop him. For example, on one occasion he took-off in a Mosquito carrying a four-thousand-pound bomb, and after take-off had a complete engine failure. The Mosquito is twin-engined. Nevertheless, he went all the way to Berlin and back on one engine, and dropped his bomb on the target. Needless to say, he was nearly an hour and a half late on his return, and we were all extremely worried. His determination passed all bounds, and the inevitable result was that eventually he lost his life. Before he had joined me, he had done a tour on fighters, and his advent to bombing was with the utmost modesty.

Amongst the many visitors to Path Finder Headquarters we had on one occasion an American lady of some distinction, Mrs. Ogden Reid of the *New York Herald Tribune*. She was brought to Pathfinders by one of the members of the Government, who felt that she would be of considerable influence in presenting a true picture of the British war effort. It so happened that bad weather brought about the cancellation of the heavy bomber attacks for that night, but, of course, my Mosquitoes still functioned. I therefore took her to see a Mosquito squadron take off. We stood at the end of the runway, and the Mosquitoes roared off in quick succession close behind each other, one on each side of the runway, so as to give moderate spacing without interfering unduly with the rapidity of take-offs. As the last aircraft left she said, "I won't ask what their destination is, but I can guess that it is the usual milk-run to Berlin. Tell me, what is their bomb load?" I said, "The Mosquito bombers carry a 4,000 lb. blockbuster to Berlin." She thought a little, and then she asked, "And what do the B 17 Flying Fortresses carry to Berlin?" I replied, "At present, with the routing which they use and with the larger load of ammunition necessary for daylight operations, they are carrying 3,500 lb. In any case, they cannot carry a blockbuster, as it is too large for their bomb bays." Mrs. Ogden Reid looked very solemn. "I only hope," she said, "that the American public never realises those facts." I should explain that later on the Americans were able to exceed the 4,000 lb. load on their attacks on Berlin by more direct routing and somewhat less ammunition, coupled, I believe, with an increase in take-off weight. In any case, the comparison is still obvious—the little Mosquito was a master aircraft.

It was about this time, or perhaps a little earlier, that we lost Alec Coryton from the Command. Alec Coryton was a very great leader, and his Group, Number 5, was certainly the strongest in the Command at the time he left it. The story has it that the C.-in-C. one day ordered Coryton and the A.O.C. of No. 3 Group, Ralph Cochran, to detail twelve Lancasters each to attack Berlin. This was at a time when the Main Force was not able to give their attention to that city. The C.-in-C.'s idea was that, being a small force, they might slip through, and the chances were that they would not suffer appreciably, whilst the political result would be good. Cochran, being new to the Command and being Cochran, immediately replied, "Yes." Coryton, on the other hand, declared the great risk for the crews concerned was unjustifiable, and said he would not order aircraft on such a raid. Knowing Coryton, I should imagine he expressed himself violently. Knowing the C.-in-C., I'm equally certain that his rejoinder was equally prompt and violent. In fact, for other reasons as well, Alec Coryton was relieved of his Command, and Cochran was given 5 Group instead of 3 Group. This was most unfortunate for the Path Finder Force, because, although Coryton had never been very friendly towards us, he was fair and reasonable. Cochran, on the other hand, was in my view neither fair nor reasonable. In saying this I do not mean that I have anything personally against Cochran as a man, but as an Air Force officer I found him most unfortunate—of which I shall say more hereafter. Coryton had been a thoroughly good group-commander, and I for one was very sorry to see him go, though he was extremely difficult at times.

We continued our pressure on the Ruhr, and some good raids took place. We introduced a new set for Oboe at about that time, and increased our channels to three and subsequently four—a tremendous help in achieving continuity of marking.

In addition to the Operational Command of Pathfinders and the tactical planning of the marking method and of the diversions, etc., I had to administer a Group which grew to a fairly considerable size. This resulted in all sorts and varieties of work, some of which was irksome, but sometimes was indeed of the utmost interest. In this latter category fell the interviews of N.C.O.s recommended for commissions. When interviewing anybody for a commission it is generally customary in the Air Force for the A.O.C. to ask some such questions as what public school they went to and similar facts of their existence. My method apparently was somewhat unconventional in that I regarded the first essential of a good officer to be efficiency, and that automatically meant a knowledge of his own job. I therefore tested each N.C.O. who came before me in his knowledge of his work, whatever it might be. This apparently shook them to the core, but it also shook me to find that some who put up for a commission were utterly incompetent in so far as their own jobs were concerned. This was more usually so in the case of gunners, many of whom had not the vaguest idea of deflection shooting and who had very, very little mathematical background at all. One amusing aspect of it was that although pilots and navigators expected me to know something of their jobs, the others were taken completely unawares. Apparently they expected a senior officer to have no idea of the details.

Another aspect of administration was the purely disciplinary side, including the legal aspects which unfortunately did occasionally arise. I think I am right in saying that there were fewer courts-martial in the Path Finder Force than in any other body of similar size. This was natural, in view of the fact that we had selected volunteers in all our air crews and the general spirit was therefore of a high order. On petty offences, however, I was constantly having trouble, particularly with the R.A.F. Provost Corps. These excellent chaps seemed to think it was their duty to make life irksome for those who were fighting for their country. They constantly put people on charges for most ridiculous petty offences, until finally I had to get extremely tough with the Provost Marshal from Cambridge and make it quite clear that I would not tolerate any more petty victimisation of air crew members. On my own stations I also sometimes ran into stupid peace-time mentalities so far as Standing Orders and red tape were concerned. On one occasion, I was paying one of my un-announced calls on a Station Commander, and as I went into his office I found that he was just about to take a charge and that the airman concerned was already in front of him. He immediately suggested that he should postpone the case, but I insisted that he carried on and that I would listen to the pro-ceedings. Strictly speaking, I should have left the Station Com-mander to give his judgment without any interference. As I listened to the case, however, it transpired that the airman was charged with walking from the Photographic Section directly across the grass to the Squadron Office in the hangar, and that walking across the grass was contrary to Station Standing Orders. As soon as the facts had sunk into my thick skull, I took one deep breath and said, "Station Commander, tell me, what is the straightest line from the Photographic Section to the Squadron Offices?" The Station Commander looked anxiously at the Station Warrant Officer, who, without any hesitation, said, "Across the grass." Without taking any more deep breaths I let it be known emphatically that if any-body on any station of mine walked along any other than the straightest possible line between the places in which he had to work, he would be on a charge for sabotaging our war effort. The case was dismissed.

The mentality which was so often displayed in admini-strative matters was absolutely unbelievable. For example, shortly after I took over full command, I gave orders that the rifle range on the aerodrome at Wyton should be removed. This miniature range consisted of a brick structure about twenty-five feet high, filled with earth so as to permit small arms training for the officers on the camp. It was so sited that it was only about ninety yards from the edge of the main runway. As a matter of policy, I laid it down that all aero-dromes were to be kept completely clear of obstructions, so that if an aircraft swung or ran off the runway on return from operations, either through its own unserviceability or that of its crew, then it had the sure knowledge at all times

that it would hit nothing. The rifle range at Wyton was obviously a major danger, and I therefore insisted that it be
removed. In doing so I made it quite clear that we had no
intention of replacing it with any other range, as we could
quite easily carry out the small-arms training on the aircraft
butts, or indeed elsewhere. This rather remarkable requirement of mine was promptly refused by Works and
Buildings, and when I insisted that it was an order they
then referred it to Headquarters Bomber Command. Bomber
Command sent down a team of administrative people to investigate; and having investigated, they came to tell me
that they had decided that it could not be removed. I made
it quite plain that if they insisted that it would remain there,
the first fatal accident which it caused would be attributed
to them, and I personally would see that they were
credited with the deaths concerned. This shook them somewhat, and apparently they passed the matter on to the Air
Ministry. The Air Ministry similarly sent a party, with similar
results. On each occasion I became more and more emphatic.
My final words were that if they would not remove it, then
I myself would promptly do so. Needless to say, they
went off and did precisely nothing. An old 250-lb. bomb did
all that was necessary as far as I was concerned. When the
rubble was removed and the site was levelled and rolled, we
had a good aerodrome again, and from my own personal
knowledge I twice saw aircraft in trouble which passed
exactly over the spot where that massive structure had stood.
In both the cases which I witnessed it would have meant the
loss of all of those on board the aircraft concerned, one a
Lancaster and one a Mosquito.

As the summer wore on we continued our attacks against
Germany herself. One raid of considerable interest was a very
precise raid by Heavy Force against Peenemünde, the site on
the Baltic coast where the German scientists were concentrating on rockets and buzz-bombs. The conversation I had
with Lord Cherwell before this raid indicated that the British

Government was extremely worried about these secret weapons of the Germans, and proposed to divert quite a lot of effort to stopping them. I myself was fanatically single-minded on the more hopeful line of sticking to the offensive rather than responding to Hitler's threats of action against us. Cherwell, on the other hand, was quite clearly worried about the potentialities of these secret weapons of Hitler. The Peenemünde attack was a full-scale Bomber Command show, and we were allowed to use a Master Bomber to assist in directing the attack, largely because 5 Group had started their intense line of independence and had been allowed to use a Master Bomber on an easy undefended target at Friedrichs-haven in a little show which they did on their own. Our results on Peenemünde, with Group-Captain John Searby as Master Bomber, were excellent, and the whole of the plant was very severely damaged and a number of scientists killed. The C.-in-C. and the A.O.C. of No. 5 Group had much excitement and amusement by laying on some of the Main Force bombers from 5 Group to check the reliability and accuracy of the Path Finder Force, by doing a timed run from a landmark outside the target area. This had long been a procedure adopted by the Path Finder Force for cross-checking their own results, and it was quite quaint that there should be such a "to do" over what was a perfectly normal navigational procedure. In fact, at the time, it was the "be-all and end-all" of the war so far as the A.O.C. of No. 5 Group was concerned, and he carried the C.-in-C. with him, as he always did. He had also persuaded the C.-in-C. that H2S was useless at that time. Whilst I freely admit that Mk. II H2S, which was the first equipment we got, was often unserviceable and never available in sufficient quantity, we did in fact achieve remarkably good results in the circumstances. In any case, the failures or partial failures which occurred were nearly always attributable very largely to factors other than H2S. For example, it was not uncommon for the Main Force to arrive so late, as the result of poor forecasting, that they failed to arrive with the limits set down for the laying of markers. However, we were busily engaged on the production of Mk. III H2S on 3 cm.; this gave better definition. and, because it was designed and engineered at greater leisure, it gave greater reliability. H2S was used on most of the mid-German cities such as Kassel, Mannheim, Nürnburg and Stuttgart.

Then on 18th November we started the main battle of Berlin. The German capital had been visited on various occasions before Pathfinders had been formed, and also on three or four occasions after the beginning of Pathfinders. These attacks had been made mainly with fairly small forces, but had been useful in that we had had the opportunity of seeing this comparatively large built-up area swamp the screens of our H2S equipment. This early experience was therefore most valuable in the tactics which we adopted for this the great battle. Unlike London, Berlin was placed more or less at the far side of enemy territory, which involved a long crossing of fighter-infested sky with a consequent high risk of interception. Berlin itself had very heavy defences in the way of flak and searchlights. Moreover, the Germans had largely overcome the effect of "window" by using different radar equipment and reorganising their methods both on the ground and in the air. Also, Berlin was attacked in the middle of winter, and the weather was bad for most of the time.

This battle was indeed the bitterest part of the war for me, for not only was it gravely important that we should succeed and thereby confirm the effects of Hamburg, but also it was bitter because of the great losses which we suffered. So far as the Path Finder Force was concerned, these losses were particularly serious because they included a large proportion of very experienced and good Pathfinder crews. I lost a number of squadron commanders and senior flight commanders, and at one stage I thought that the backbone of the Path Finder Force was really broken. I lost two Wing-Commander Hiltons, one of whom was the C.O. of 83 Squadron, well liked and an old Pathfinder who had been with us a long time. Unhappily he did not survive. The other was a friend of mine who had only just joined the Path Finder Force. He spent the rest of the war in a prison camp. (He is now a Commandant of the civil airport at Bovingdon.)

Between 18th November and 24th March 1944, Bomber Command carried out 16 heavy major raids on the German capital. This was done with no element of surprise except for very occasional diversions to other German cities when the weather was too bad for us to go to Berlin. We knew Berlin on the H2S screen, from the earlier raids, and our methods were largely influenced by the weather forecast given to us by the Met. Service. By this time 1409 flight, that magnificent band of weather pilots, was under my command, and flew daily all over Germany in their unarmed Mosquitoes, obtaining weather observations for us. Unfortunately, they could not change the weather.

Thus it was on almost every raid we laid on "Wanganui" blind H2S sky-marking as a primary method, and backed it up with blind Parramatta ground markers just in case these might be seen, with a few aircraft detailed for visual methods in case the impossible occurred and we got clear visibility. In fact, in the event, all the raids were carried out blind, and we were never able to obtain any bombing photos to prove our results, though we did take photos of the H2S tube at the moment of the bomb release, in order to estimate results. Thus we slogged on and on with bitter losses and tough conditions—on a directive from the Prime Minister to do so, without ever knowing for certain what had been achieved. The P.R.U. aircraft which went out each day could get absolutely no photographic evidence, and so I had to estimate my results entirely from H2S photos and reports from my Pathfinder crews, particularly the H2S operators. I moved the aiming point methodically around the city, and managed to achieve directions of approach suitable to give the required pattern on the ground. This was not always easy, as the Main

Force group commanders were inclined to object to my ideas of the best line of approach, particularly if this meant going all around the target in order to approach it.

When we ultimately did get photos, the results on Berlin were said by the C.-in-C. to be disappointing. What he did not seem to realise was that what I had been saying throughout the whole series of the attacks was perfectly true, however unpalatable it might be. This was to the effect that the crews had been particularly worried by the defences of Berlin, and had been doing everything they could to be as defensive as possible. In particular, they had been encouraged to believe that height was their salvation, and height they tried to get at all costs. Unhappily, someone had decided (I am not quite sure who was responsible) to add 3,000 lb. to the all-up weight of the Lancaster in order to increase the bomb load on Berlin, which was of course a considerable range from England. In fact, the range effect alone knocked about 1,500 lb. off the pay-load of a Lancaster and about 2,000 lb. off the pay-load of a Halifax compared to the short target such as Hamburg or the Ruhr. This was a fairly substantial reduction, and there was a tendency to put on more fuel and fewer bombs in view of the bad weather, etc. The idea of offsetting this by putting up the all-up weight of the Lancaster by a further 3,000 lb. was in my view quite wrong, as the rate of climb with a normally loaded Lancaster was already sufficiently slow to be extremely worrying to a captain approaching hostile defences. The result was inevitable, and I reported it raid after raid, only to be told that we were imagining things! What I reported was that senior Pathfinder crews at interrogation were constantly saying that they had seen scores of bombs being jettisoned in the North Sea on their outward bound flights. Experienced Pathfinder crews do not mis-identify bomb bursts. More particularly they do not mis-identify "cookies" (4,000 lb.) with their light cases. These cookies could not be dropped "safe", because they always exploded in any case. Thus the aircraft which were jettisoning these bombs gave away the fact that they were doing so, and, incidentally, letting go of the most valuable bomb in the whole of their load. The net result was that of the bombs which left England, a very large proportion did not reach Berlin. The captains concerned felt justified in acting in this way as they were quite unable to climb, and indeed, in many cases, were apprehensive of icing in the clouds ahead. In their view it was thus a question of necessity. Had they been lighter at the outset, they would have been of higher morale, as well as had a good performance from the outset. By being too ambitious, we in fact dropped less. Another thing which seriously reduced the effect on Berlin, and which was also reported by Pathfinders was that the bombing was more scattered than on other targets. Whether this was due to the weight of the defences, or the psychological effect of believing that a vast area of targets lay beneath, it is hard to say. In any case, the results were not as good as they should have been. Nevertheless, Bomber Command achieved a very great victory, and achieved it by sheer hard fighting in bad weather, and against the strongest defences which the enemy could muster. His skies were teaming with fighters, and the target itself was plastered with flak. It is surprising that our loss rate was not higher. Bomber Command itself averaged something over 6 per cent., and Pathfinders, which started badly and at times reached as much as the 13½ per cent. lost on one raid (1st January 1944), averaged about just over 5 per cent. The total area destroyed in the main battle of Berlin was about 5,500 acres. Hardly disappointing!

The Mosquitoes had joined in the party, and I kept up the alarms with these Mosquitoes every night that I possibly could. During this main battle, the Mosquitoes went to Berlin on 16 nights other than the 16 Main Force attacks, and it is interesting to note that with the same weather and with the same system of defence determined to prevent us getting through to the capital, the Mosquitoes lost about 1 per cent.

With the battle of Berlin completed, we were able to return to more general bombing, which meant that we could exercise more surprise and thus reduce our losses. We paid a few visits to the Ruhr, including one on Essen, and also gave Nürnburg quite a heavy load. We also did occasional bombing of German fighter aerodromes with Oboe aircraft and the like, partly nuisance and partly training and testing.

Towards the end of the Battle of Berlin the C.-in-C. rang me up one day and said that Cochran had been talking to him at great length, and had convinced him that the way to mark the target at Berlin was to put in low-level Mosquitoes at 50 feet above the roof tops to find the exact aiming point and to mark it with T.I.s. I pointed out to him that the T.I.s could not be seen through the clouds with the prevailing weather. What was more important was that I had myself had some considerable experience of flying over densely built-up areas at low level, when I had been in the 29 Squadron at North Weald and on many other occasions during my flying career. I was quite convinced that at high speed it was virtually impossible to map-read over a densely built-up area at low level. The field of view was limited to a few hundred yards, which at 200 knots meant split second identification of any landmark, if indeed one even managed to recognise landmarks as such at all. I entirely agreed that the method was excellent for other than densely built-up areas, but not for Berlin. The C.-in-C. was obviously peeved, but I hardly admired then or now the action which resulted. Within half an hour I had a message to report personally to the C.-in-C. Bomber Command. I flew down in an old Hurricane which I was then using as a hack, and landed—with a little undercarriage difficulty, just to make life more interesting—at Halton. I drove over to Bomber Command, to be received with a frigid and formal notification that I was immediately to send 83 and 97 Squadrons (Lancasters) back to their parent group, 5 Group, together with one Mosquito squadron, and that in future 5 Group would adopt the method which I had refused to accept

—namely, the low-level marking method—and would then mark a large number of their own targets themselves. This was, in itself, a tremendous slap in the face to a Force which had turned Bert Harris' Bomber Command from a wasteful and ineffective force into a mighty and successful one. It meant in the eyes of the rest of the Command that in the opinion of their C.-in-C. the Pathfinders had apparently failed. What was worse was that it left us with very seriously reduced heavy marking strength to carry on and do the same job as we had been doing in the past. This was still necessary because 5 Group would often still be in the Main Force, and the nature of targets and duration of attacks was not going to be any less on most occasions. What was worse was that we had to provide these squadrons with equipment, and we had to give their crews initial training before they reported to 5 Group for operational control. Most members of these Pathfinder squadrons, even after they went to 5 Group, still remained intensely loyal to the Path Finder Group itself.

It is perhaps wise from the point of view of students of air strength and its history, to pay Ralph Cochran the compliment of expanding a little on his methods and on his results. I would emphasise that I have never fallen out with Ralph Cochran, and those who used to gossip during the war, saying that there was a feud between us, overlooked the fact that we were personal friends and I believe we still are.

Ralph Cochran is an energetic and conscientious man. Seldom have I known any Air Force officer who had more ardour and more zeal than he. In my opinion, however, Cochran's decisions were most unfortunate. He was mentally restless, and had to be doing something all the time. I believe that if Ralph Cochran had been given the opportunity to operate as a captain of a heavy bomber for fifteen or twenty raids before being given a Group, he would have been a wonderful Group Commander. When he first came to the Command, he was given No. 3 Group in place of Baldwin. Having had no experience of bomber operations in the current war, he immediately complimented his predecessor by grounding practically all squadrons for intensive training, thus weakening the Group's operational strength very considerably for a period. Whether the quality was better after the training period or not, is something which was hard to discern. On arrival at 5 Group, he decided that the Command was not sufficiently "aggressive". He stressed that gunnery should be brought to the forefront, and that bombers should seek out fighters rather than being frightened of them. The unintended result was that there was some wild shooting from 5 Group aircraft on to "friendlies", and in fact it was only when a 5 Group gunner, being interviewed on the B.B.C., admitted that he had shot down an aircraft without identifying it, that 5 Group was restrained at all in this particular activity. Next Cochran, having heard about timed runs into a bomb release point, which was a cross check which Pathfinders used, decided that this was the "be-all and end-all" of bombing technique, and tried to have it enforced as a primary method rather than the tactics laid down by the Path Finder Force.

However, he had now done great damage to the Path Finder Force, to the benefit of his own independence. We were interested to see what the result might be. In dealing with Cochran on this occasion and others, I despaired of ever influencing the C.-in-C. in any way. When I referred the matter to Saundby, he simply shrugged his shoulders and said that he and Cochran had once been flight commanders together, under Bert Harris, in the Middle East, and that the same situation had then prevailed. Cochran could do anything, and the C.-in-C. would always support him; any attempts to convince the C.-in-C. that Cochran could ever be wrong were inevitably doomed to failure. Saundby recommended that I should not try to do anything about Cochran, since it was quite hopeless. With the loss of these squadrons to 5 Group, I did a little analysis of the results achieved by that Group for the rest of the year. It must be remembered that they were taken from me by the C.-in-C. ostensibly so that Cochran could adopt a method of low-level marking with a Mosquito squadron, backed up by the two heavy squadrons, on built-up important German targets. Of course, the one target for which the method was particularly proposed was Berlin, but fortunately for Cochran that battle had come to an end before he was in a position to try his method on it. It must, however, still be remembered that this was the basis of the transfer of these squadrons.

In the rest of 1944, according to the Operational Research Section at Headquarters Bomber Command, 5 Group sometimes joined in with the rest of the Command on proper P.F.F. marking, but otherwise attacked on their own a large variety of small targets, most of them comparatively undefended, such as Wesseling, Scholeen, Dammstadt, Königsberg, München Gladback (with the help of Oboe markers provided by us), Dortmund-Ems Canal, Kaiserlautern, Harburg, Mitteland Canal, Heilbroun, etc. In addition to these targets. 5 Group did go to a few German cities alone. They went to Munich on three occasions, Brunswick twice, plus Wilhelmsleven and Nürnburg, with very mediocre results. Their first big raid on Munich was carried out by the method which they proposed. Their Master Bomber went in low level in a Mosquito, with three others to back him up in doing the job at very low level. He tried gallantly for nearly twenty minutes to get his markers on the correct aiming point, but in view of the difficulties of very fast flight very low over a built-up area he was unsuccessful. By this time his reserves had had to leave for home owing to shortage of fuel, and he was, therefore, forced in due course to call upon the P.F.F. high-level Master to take over and mark the aiming point in accordance with the usual Newhaven procedure, which was done satisfactorily. From then on the raid was controlled by our Master Bomber with fairly good success. Incidentally, quite a number of aircraft were lost due to fighters whilst the P.F.F. Master Bomber held them circling the target waiting for the low level marker to do his stuff. In apparently criticising this failure I make no reflection whatever on the very gallant attempt he made to do his job properly. The difficulties, however, were greater than he had expected, and the ultimate success of the raid finally depended upon normal Pathfinder methods.

I feel at this point that I should explain more fully the work of the Met. flight. No. 1409 Flight was stationed at Wyton, and was equipped with Mosquitoes. Its Commanders—Braithwaite, Nigel Bicknell and Michael Birkin were amongst them—had a small handful of crews, and the navigators were particularly trained in weather recognition so as to be able to make their reports reliable when they returned. When a flight was called for, the code name "Pampa" was used, and normally came from the C.-in-C. Bomber Command, although we often flew Pampas specially for other commands when they required it, and for the other Services occasionally. No. 1409 Flight flew by day or by night as and when required. Sometimes there might be one aircraft out, sometimes there might be three or four. Their total time in the air very often covered most of the twenty-four hours of a day. Their penetrations into Germany were quite deep even in broad daylight in clear weather. Naturally they flew high and fast, but the danger was extreme, and it was a most nerve-racking job for the crews concerned. Admittedly in the final analysis their losses were extremely low, although not quite so low as the rest of the Path Finder Force Mosquitoes and the Light Night Strikers. Generally they would be required to report either at a particular spot or down a particular line in Germany. They would plan their route with suitable changes of course to throw off possible enemy fighters, and would pass through the area required, taking a full record of the weather at the appropriate positions. They had no guns of any sort, and nothing offensive. I often wonder whether it was appreciated at Headquarters Bomber Command, or for that matter by any other senior officers who called for a Pampa, that in doing so they were asking an unarmed aircraft to proceed deep into the heart of enemy territory, often in broad daylight, without any cloud cover. The ease with which they called for Pampas was sometimes quite frightening. No. 1409 Flight, on the other hand, never hesitated for one moment, and never failed to do their job with absolute reliability and consistency. In fact, even when aircraft unserviceability interrupted the flight, it was only a matter of minutes before an alternative aircraft was in the air on the same job, or alternatively, if the unserviceability occurred when the flight was well in hand, it would be completed in spite of the unserviceability. There were some harrowing experiences for the crews of 1409 Flight when they were intercepted, particularly by the German jets just towards the end of the war, which could out-pace them but not out-manœuvre them. The anxiety to run for home had to be overcome whenever the enemy closed, so as to take advantage of the Mosquitoes' ability to out-turn the enemy.

Mark III H2S was coming along nicely on three centimetres, but at about this stage we had quite a battle with Coastal Command over the use of this equipment. I had no intention of being "dog in the manger" over my valuable boxes, but Mk. III H2S had, in fact, been largely developed at my request and with the full co-operation of Path Finder Force. The fact that it was discovered that this equipment could be used in A.S.V. (Aircraft/Surface Vessel) with such success that it could actually pick up a Schnorkel did, of course, make it extremely valuable for Coastal Command. My contention, however, was that the main job of defeating the enemy was more vital at that stage of the war than merely sinking a few more U-boats, and that the priority, therefore, should be largely on Pathfinder's requirements and not Coastal Command's. I recall a meeting at which the C.-in-C. Coastal, who was then Jack Slesser, crossed swords with me at the Air Ministry for some hours on this sore subject. His technique was something which I shall always remember, for it was a combination of charm and stubbornness which I have seldom seen equalled. Needless to say the outcome was that there was a compromise, and Coastal Command got a substantial proportion of the equipment which had been intended to be used by the Path Finder Force.

The Mosquito force kept on keeping on, and thanks to the advent of FIDO its consistent attacks against Germany had an even greater effect upon German morale than in the past. Their consistent visits to Berlin from the time of the Battle of Berlin to the end of the war received considerable publicity at the time, and therefore most people know of this, the "Milk Run". FIDO helped very largely in this consistency.

I think it was about Christmas Eve, 1943, that a moustached Wing-Commander called Wooldridge knocked at the front door of my quarters at Wyton and asked to see me. It was just about dinner-time, so I invited him in. He came diffidently inside the door and said he had some friends outside. Before inviting the friends in, however, he waved a letter in my face and asked me to read it. I glanced at it, and saw that the signature was that of Winston Churchill. Briefly it said that the scientists had promised that fog could be cleared, and that he wished all of those concerned to grant the best possible co-operation in bringing this about. I more than welcomed Wooldridge, and asked him to bring in his companions. These proved to be Geoffrey Lloyd, who was Minister of Petroleum Warfare, together with two of his advisers, Colonel Medlicott and Mr. Hartley, whom I had met in one of the petroleum companies in the Middle East. Needless to say, the idea of clearing fog was something which I more than welcomed. In fact, I was simply staggered at the idea of the possibilities of such a device, and I said so in no uncertain terms. The four visitors looked at each other, and almost burst into laughter. They explained that the contrast of finding somebody who was keen to have fog cleared compared to the discouragement and disappointment which had faced them for the entire previous ten hours in the Northern groups was almost too much for them. The C.-in-C. Bomber Command, who was enthusiastic about the idea, had sent them to the Main Force Groups first, as he did not wish me to be diverted by a development not peculiar to our needs.

They stayed for dinner, and during the meal we discussed the possibilities. I listened to their proposals and hopes, and to the requirements they laid down for the aerodrome on which an experiment was to take place. They had been unable to find any aerodrome from the Northern groups, all of whom made various excuses as to why it could not be arranged. I immediately nominated Gravely as the most suitable aerodrome, and they enquired when they could inspect it. I replied "immediately". We got into a car, drove over to Gravely and inspected it forthwith. I give those people full credit for the magnificent way they then went about the installation of this comparatively new equipment. They had 1,000 yards of approach and 1,000 yards of runway equipped with FIDO burners within about six weeks of my giving the O.K. to go ahead. The burners consisted of long lengths of pipe, with the feed along a pipe over the burners so that the flame from each jet impinged slightly on this top feed tube, thereby vapourising the petrol that it fed along it, and ensuring that no neat petrol came out of the jets, but only pure vapour. It was not until the pure vapour came out that the smokiness of the flame disappeared and a clean burning was achieved. This was obviously essential if it were to improve visibility and not to do the opposite. These burner pipes were laid parallel with the runway and about 50 yards from it; thus the burners were a total of 150 yards apart. They extended along each side of the runway and out into the approach area, so that the intense heat which they generated cut a chasm through the fog which could be seen from above and the aircraft could fly down into this chasm and land on the runway.

The element of doubt was not only whether sufficient heat

could be generated to disperse the fog as planned, but whether in view of the intense heat and glare of the flames it would be practical for an aircraft to land down the centre line of this inferno. To test this out I took a Lancaster myself from Oakington over to Gravely one night, and did the first landing with FIDO burning. I had vague thoughts of seeing lions jump through a hoop of flame at the circus. The glare was certainly considerable, and there was some turbulence, but it was nothing to worry about, and I expressed the view that FIDO was a usable project and should be developed with the utmost speed. I am pleased to say that we got it extended at Gravely, and later on had it installed at Downham Market. Thus I was equipped with two aerodromes at which we could land in practically all weather with reasonable safety. I made it a rule that whenever I wished to fly I did so regardless of the weather, on the basis that FIDO was always there to save my miserable neck should the need arise. Indeed, I was on some occasions caught out by fog and had to use FIDO—sometimes with quite amusing results.

One night I had been visiting some other aerodrome, and came back to my own Group to find that things were completely fogged in and that most of England was closing down rapidly. At Gravely they announced that although FIDO was going full bore, a substantial cross-wind was blowing the fog across the runway so rapidly that it was quite impossible to land. I was in the Beaufighter which I used as a hack in those days—not the most pleasant aircraft for blind approaches, but one which I had very fully equipped with SBA and with pilot-operated Gee. When I got to Gravely I called up and told them I was coming in to land. I did my approach on SBA, and having had a full description of the direction of the wind, I deliberately swung out to starboard, since the wind was from port to starboard of the runway. As expected, I found the chasm cut in the fog exactly as planned, but instead of being vertical it was sloping very sharply over to the right and was inclined at about 50 degrees from the vertical. When, however, I entered the chasm, I could see the flames of the FIDO on my port bow quite clearly, and I simply did a slanting approach on to the runway and landed quite normally. I had informed Flying Control of my movements, over the R.T., and as I ran out of the FIDO cleared area on my landing run into the thick fog beyond, I stopped as soon as possible and called up and asked them to provide assistance. This apparently left them completely speechless, and they asked me, Would I please report my position? To which I replied that if I was able to do that I would have been able to taxi in on my own. Would they kindly send a vehicle to guide me from the runway to the taxi track?—as I was unable to see more than 10 yards ahead of me. Once again, they repeated their request for my position. Finally I realised that they were under the impression that I was still in the air, and I made it quite clear that I was firmly on the ground, after which I got the assistance I needed. In discussing it with the Flying Control Officer afterwards, he explained that he had been in constant touch with the A.C.P. (Aerodrome Control Post) at the end of the runway, who assured him that I had not landed. What in fact had happened was that because of the roar of the flames the A.C.P. had not heard the throttled-back approach of the Beaufighter, and as I had had come in from starboard to port he had failed to see me, since he was attempting to look straight along the line of normal approach which was thick fog. In short, this little episode proved once again what a magnificent blessing FIDO was, and what wonderful potentialities it had—and still has. The fact that all our civil aerodromes are not equipped with this simple and *economical* device is to me one of the most blatant examples of the grievous "malade" which besets our aviation today. Thereafter I always operated Mosquitoes even when fog was forecast, but simply cut down the numbers to what I thought was reasonable for landing back, by using FIDO. One of the factors which I at first failed to appreciate in calculating the number which I could put out in such circumstances, was that whenever FIDO was lit it attracted other aircraft in difficulties like flies to a honey-pot.

Early in 1944 Bomber Command formed a new group called 100 Group, which took over some of the sundry duties which the Pathfinders had been carrying out before that date. They were the counter-measure group, and they carried all sorts of very powerful jamming equipment and radar homing equipment. Their job was to confuse the enemy and to make his defences ineffective. Addison was the first A.O.C., and continued to the end of the war, doing an excellent job.

During 1944 Bomber Command Headquarters took more and more interest in the day-to-day tactics, and the C.-in-C. himself was keenly studying all the possible ways of avoiding losses by varying our tactics and our diversions. One of these methods of variety was to divide the bomber force on to two different targets, or to divide any attack on a particular target into two quite separate phases. This was excellent from a defensive point of view, but it meant that the Path Finder Force was called upon to mark twice as many targets, which, with our reduced strength due to the absence of our squadrons up in 5 Group, meant that at times we were sorely pressed to spread our aircraft over the many duties which came our way. When one remembers that we were, as a matter of principle, endeavouring to lay on three different methods for each target, and that the C.-in-C. sometimes called on three or four different targets for one night, it can be appreciated that it was not easy to find the aircraft and the skilled crews. This was particularly so if the targets were all outside Oboe range, meaning that we had to use heavies only for the job of marking. With six squadrons each turning out about sixteen aircraft per night, of which only about ten or twelve were qualified markers and the remainder supporters, it can be seen that anything more than two targets was a very severe strain. Even with two main targets, only about thirty qualified markers would be available, and these had to be divided, depending upon the methods used, into at least three categories. Thus if the weather was expected to be fairly clear we would lay on H2S Illuminators followed by Visual Markers, and possibly a Master Bomber, with continuity ensured by Backers-Up at the rate of about three aircraft every two minutes of the duration of the attack. From this it can be seen that unless the attack were kept to a very, very short period, our thirty aircraft could hardly be expected to do the job, particularly when it was remembered that as a precautionary measure we had to lay on blind marking by H2S aircraft using Parrammatta ground marking as the secondary method, with the final reserve of Wanganui sky markers carried in their bomb bays should that be required. This in itself meant markers every minute, so that there were flares in the sky ready for Main Force bombers to aim at should the weather be bad enough to necessitate it.

The Mosquitoes of the Light Night Striking Force sometimes did duties other than their routine bombing raids. One amusing example of this is worth quoting, as it shows the spirit and intensity of their operations, particularly in comparison with some others of Bomber Command, who always had to go in for intense training for a considerable period before they undertook any special duty, and, without being unduly rude, had to ensure that the Public Relations Department was well informed. The little incident which I now quote was laid on at 9.30 one morning, with the C.-in-C.'s approval which I obtained over the telephone. I simply detailed one squadron to go and practice during that morning, doing low-level flights across the Great Ouse at shallow angles. They would descend from a considerable height from a point about five miles back, and should cross the canal at not more than 50 feet and at an angle of approximately 20 degrees to it. They did not, at that stage, know what they were training for, beyond the fact that it would be to drop something in the canal. After their morning's training they got particulars of the raid which was to be carried out that night. The job was simple "gardening". For those who are not aware of it, "gardening" was mine-laying from aircraft. The target was the Kiel Canal, which is, after all, the most important canal in Germany, connecting the Baltic with all the North Sea ports, and which was used very extensively by the Germans during the war. It was of particular importance for the movement of heavy submarine parts and the like from the Baltic areas to Wilhelmshaven, Bremen, Hamburg, etc. It was also considerably used by the submarines themselves.

With but a few hours' training, this squadron of the Light Night Striking Force went out that night and successfully laid mines in the Kiel Canal, keeping it virtually out of action for two and a half weeks. One aircraft struck the ground in the process, but all the remainder returned. Unlike some other pieces of water in which things were dropped, Kiel Canal did of course have defences at various points along its length, and was particularly heavily defended at each end. (Total defences were 97 guns and 25 searchlights.) Moreover, instead of being a fairly vast sheet of water, it was narrow, and the precision with which the mines had to be dropped was therefore only to be achieved by great care and at a low level. It is an interesting reflection on the appreciation of the efforts of various people during the war that this little episode was not even mentioned to the British public, and no honours or awards were given in relation to it.

During all this long period of bombing of Germany by the Light Night Strikers, No. 139 Squadron, fitted with H2S, acted as their marker squadron. Nominally, No. 139 Squadron was not a Pathfinder Squadron, but it did in fact carry out all Pathfinder duties for the benefit of the rest of the Mosquitoes. It did a wonderful job, and made that Force a really damaging factor and not merely a set of nuisance raiders—which was the general opinion of it held by many people in the Air Force at the time. Perhaps Londoners might be interested to know that on an ordinary "milk run" to Berlin the Mosquitoes of the Light Night Striker Force were properly guided and given aiming point markers by No. 139 Squadron, and, as they often reached as many as one hundred aircraft, they dropped a total of about 400,000 lb. of bombs in any one raid on Berlin. Talking to Berliners a few years ago, when I was carrying out civil flying into that city, I discovered that in general the inhabitants of Berlin did not regard the Mosquitoes as nuisance raiders, but as genuine heavy raids in their own right. Admittedly, they fully recognised the difference from the main heavy raids of the Battle of Berlin itself, which were far, far worse, but they never regarded the Mosquitoes lightly. To them the Mosquito raids were heavy attacks, and when one works out the tonnage of bombs dropped one realises that their views have considerable justification.

The experts on the Air Staff who turned down the Mosquito as a type in the early days might be interested in the argument which subsequently became current to the effect that one Mosquito was worth seven Lancasters. For those mathematically minded, here is the exercise: A Mosquito carried a little over half the bomb load of a Lancaster to Berlin. Its casualty rate was about 1/10th of that of the Lancaster. Its cost was 1/3rd of the Lancaster, and it carried two people in its crew instead of seven. Personally, I think it is a little hard to get an exact mathematical result from that set of figures, but it is quite clear that value for war effort was certainly well on the side of the Mosquito compared with any other aircraft ever produced in the history of flying.

9

SLEDGEHAMMER

THE battle of Germany had gone on for not quite a year when we were diverted to other things. During that year the Command was by no means at anything like the strength that had been intended. In fact, we started with only about 550 heavies and a few mediums in the battle against Germany, and by the time we were diverted from it we had reached about 1,000 heavies, with no mediums.

The first diversion which took considerable strength from Bomber Command was the bombing of the "buzz-bomb" sites in the Pas-de-Calais area and a few in the Cherbourg area. From these permanent sites Hitler had intended to launch about 6,000 buzz-bombs a day, aimed mainly at London, but also at the other south coast targets such as Portsmouth, Southampton and the coastal towns. It will be appreciated that 6,000 of these things would have taken an awful lot of shooting down, and the results might have been extremely serious. Naturally, the organisation required to launch 6,000 of these missiles was considerable, and involved the laying of railway tracks, stores, etc., so that the launching would be rapid from each particular site. Thus, 64 permanent sites were set up, and it was these which we attacked. They were in open country, and were to a certain extent camouflaged. We attacked them in daylight, and started the raid with a few Oboe markers to ensure that no difficulty was encountered in map-reading on to the sites themselves. This involved an enormous amount of day to day calculations, for these targets were not in our original work on Oboe aiming points, and had to be calculated almost on the spot when required. Generally, fairly small forces of bombers were used on each site, and we used Master Bombers to assist in keeping the Main Force exactly on to the aiming point. At this stage we started using coloured smokes, which were quite effective in daylight, in preference to the T.I.s. Particularly T.I.s lying on the ground, would be obscured by the smoke from the high explosives, whereas the coloured smokes rose with the H.E. smoke and could still be seen. These smokes were emitted from candles and we were able to use yellows, mauves, greens, etc.

The Command dealt effectively with these permanent launching sites, so much so that when the great day came that Hitler had chosen to go ahead there had to be a deferment, while even when the raids did start they were on a very much reduced scale. In fact, Hitler was forced to improvise sites of a temporary nature and to move their positions in order to be able to operate at all. This meant that he had no railway tracks on which to bring up the V-bombs, and no concrete foundations, etc. Moreover, the personnel were disorganised domestically, and the net result was a very much reduced effort. The effort was indeed but a very tiny percentage of that originally intended, and practically all buzz-bombs launched were from the temporary sites. These sites were dealt with as soon as we discovered their whereabouts. A further and very effective means of dealing with the menace was to attack the dumps of V-bombs which were reported to us through French Intelligence. These dumps were underground warrens. We put in some very heavy attacks on these supply dumps, and they were really churned up. Flying over France to this day, one can still see the results of these raids.

Our next great duty was in preparation for the invasion. In this connection Bomber Command had two duties. The first of these was in connection with the transport system of western Europe. In their choice of landing places, the planners had studied the vast and efficient network of railways, and realised that, wherever we set foot on the Continent, Germany could bring her troops quickly and efficiently by rail. Railways, in the main, had always been considered to be difficult and unproductive targets, and many were of the opinion that we should not attempt to attack them. It was, however, realised that if we attacked marshalling yards, with their complex networks of points and difficult mechanisms, and containing as they did the workshops and repair centres of the rolling stock as well as the tracks, we could and should prove effective.

Bomber Command played the major part in dealing with the marshalling yards. All main marshalling yards, including all those with repair facilities west of the Rhine, right through to the Atlantic coast of France, were included in the scheme, and originally about 55 per cent. of these were allotted as Bomber Command targets. We proceeded to get on with the job. Most of the targets were but lightly defended, and even when the Hun discovered that it was our plan to destroy these marshalling yards he was not able to spread his defences over all of them with sufficient weight to make the targets really difficult. The net result was that our crews had a relative holiday from the intense receptions to which they were accustomed in Germany.

Our technique was generally to use fairly low-level methods, and when cloud was bad we even went down to 1,000 or 2,000 feet to do the job. We used Oboe considerably, and on all occasions used Master Bombers. No. 5 Group operated successfully on their own on this type of target, and did good work. The Command as a whole soon achieved excellent results—to the great satisfaction of Eisenhower and Tedder. All the target areas were really ploughed up, and their workshops, breakdown facilities, etc., were destroyed. Early efforts at repair soon gave way to a policy of despair, and the enemy no longer made any effort to repair the damage which we did. By a strange irony of fate, Squadron-Leader Cranswick, the boy to whom this book is dedicated, was shot down on one of these relatively easy targets. He came below cloud and went down to about 1,500 feet in order to control the attack (he was Master Bomber), and was shot down by the light flak guns defending the area. He was, I believe, on his 143rd raid. When one appreciates that each such raid was generally as dangerous as a major battle on land or sea, one gets something of the idea of the sacrifice made by some bomber crews. I believe that Pathfinder Cranswick had carried out more operations than any other Bomber Command pilot; yet the public have never heard of him.

Intermixed with these raids on the marshalling yards we also attacked coastal defences. The idea was that we were gradually to wear down the radar sites and the heavy batteries defending the coast, but that we had to spread our efforts from North Holland right round to Ushant, so as to give the enemy no idea of the area in which we intended the invasion should land. We had a rule that we had to do three targets away from the landing area for every one which we did in that place. Thus, three-quarters of our effort was virtually wasted. This wastage was, however, necessary in the interests of security. On 13th March 1944 we did one big raid which should be quoted as an object lesson. It was on Nürnberg, when the unhappy record of 94 aircraft lost was sustained. This loss of 94 out of 795 aircraft was considered by many at the time to be a catastrophic accident which just happened to occur. Without being in any way bitter about it, or trying to make any accusations, I simply believe that it would be best from an historical point of view and as a lesson for the future to realise that it was caused, and not simply accidental. As I recall the occasion, it was one of those very common events where the Main Force Group Commanders objected to the routing planned by Path Finder Headquarters. On this particular occasion I believe the idea originated from 5 Group, as was quite common, but was supported by "Winkel" Rice in 1 Group and, I think, also by 3 Group.

Moreover, the new Canadian Group, No. 6, apparently concurred. As far as I was concerned, Saundby simply rang me up and told me that my routing had been over-ruled by the C.-in-C., who had decided to give the Main Force Group Commanders a chance to see whether their theories were correct. In the circumstances we did a long straight run into the target without any jinking or tactical trickery. Why the Main Force Group Commanders should be so critical and intolerant of the methods which had saved so many lives I could never quite make out, beyond the fact that it seemed merely human weakness that they should revolt against the loss of their power to a youngster in another Group. This is putting it at its lowest level, but I feel that this was basically the trouble. Added to this, one must remember that practically no senior officers of the R.A.F. had any appreciable first-hand operational experience in the current war, and they were therefore at a grave disadvantage in any tactical planning. This, I would emphasise, was not generally their own fault, and should not in any way be held against them. It should, however, be held against the Prime Minister, the Cabinet and the Air Council that it was their policy to prohibit operational flying by senior officers over enemy territory. It cost us thousands of lives and many failures, and was, in my view, the most deplorable of all mistakes which we made during the war. On this particular occasion it was, of course, a simple straightforward matter for the German defences, which by this time were recovering from the effects of "window", and were therefore able to deal with us fairly effectively, to plot the track and to put their fighters on to us. The results speak for themselves. Pathfinder's own losses were about in proportion to the rest of the Command, being eleven out of 119 aircraft which set out.

During one of the pre-invasion conferences held by the Army, Navy and Air Force, I recall that I was there with "Oxo" (Air Vice-Marshal Oxland) and we were asked by the naval representative to give an absolute guarantee that there would be no heavy guns firing on the area of the beaches during the landings. There were no less than ten heavy batteries covering the landing beaches, and these were well protected in concrete gun emplacements which would take quite a lot of destroying. At this meeting I recall that the naval representative explained that each of these guns could sink a landing craft with a single round if it scored a direct hit, and that in the relatively easy conditions prevailing they would be extremely accurate. He asked Bomber Command to give a definite 100 per cent. guarantee that none of these guns would be firing. Poor old "Oxo" looked at me, and said that it was up to the A.O.C. Pathfinders. What was asked was indeed a tall order. It was not a question of whether we could destroy the targets; but to be able to give the guarantee regardless of the weather, was quite a different matter. We were not going to be allowed to attack the target at all until six hours before the landing, and then all ten batteries had to be dealt with. I did some quick thinking, and my reply was that provided I had the whole weight of Bomber Command behind me I could give a 95 per cent. certain guarantee that we would destroy the guns. I explained that we would do it even if there was a layer of low cloud or fog over them; and that we could do it quite simply if the weather was clear. I also then went on to explain that if there were solid fog merging into thick cloud continuously up to very high level, so that no marking methods whatever could be used, then it would be impossible to destroy the guns. I also explained that such weather was not likely to be prevailing if the Supreme Commander had given the word to go, as he would have had to consider the marine craft themselves and would not have sent them forward in such circumstances. This seemed to satisfy the Navy, but I often wonder whether they realised that they were asking me to accept a gigantic responsibility. The casualties would have been enormous if the guns had been firing and might, indeed, even have been catastrophic. By this time, however, people had become quite accustomed to asking the Path Finder Force to do something of which they themselves had no idea whatever of the method or the means of doing it.

As the Railway Plan made progress, it was soon apparent that the targets allotted to the Tactical Air Force were not being dealt with, and the larger number given to the Americans were also well behind schedule. Thus it was that eventually the Bomber Command had to take on considerably more than their original allotment, and they did so effectively. This was interspersed with raids on coastal radar and guns, and also frequent visits to the V-Bomb sites. Very occasionally, if the weather was bad over the western areas, we were allowed to go and do the odd raid on German targets. These were, in the main, on German cities associated with the aircraft industy, as the Hun was putting an enormous effort into building up fighter strength. It is a measure of the success of Bomber Command that the greater portion of these fighters were night fighters, and of the Americans that the rest were day fighters. Practically no effort was put into production of bombers with which to hit England or to deal with an invasion. The lack of these bombers was of tremendous importance when eventually the great day came when the armies of America and Britain and the British Dominions set foot on continental soil once again. They had virtually no air attack directed against them, and this was a result of the diversion of the German aircraft industry to the production of fighters with which to try to stop Bomber Command and the American Air Force.

By this time our targets were being attacked by day and by night, and the number of targets involved was considerably more than when we were concentrating on the big cities of Germany. This naturally entailed a great deal of Operations Room work and tactical planning. Added to this, I was having a fairly busy time with the invasion planning, for although much of the detail work was nothing whatever to do with me and I was not in any way Bomber Command's representative, I found that I was often called on to attend at the Joint Planning meetings with "Oxo," who was Bomber Command's official representative. By this time, Saundby had been made Deputy C.-in-C. instead of S.A.S.O., and his place in the latter post had been taken by Hugh Walmsley. Saundby continued to be a tremendous help to me at all times, not only by being able to understand the Pathfinder problem and my own point of view, but by having a very patient nature and an ability to express himself to the C.-in-C. even when the latter was in a non-receptive mood, which did occur at times!

One afternoon at about this stage of the war, I had the pleasure of attending a meeting in the C.-in-C.'s office at the request of A.O.C. No. 5 Group. Cochran, eternally agitating for something to keep himself out of the rut, had decided that he would attack some lock gates, the name of which I have forgotten, lying between Hanover and Berlin. These gates were particularly deep, with an enormous lift of water, and their foundations were vital to their functioning. It was thought that if heavy bombers could drop some special 8,000 or 12,000 lb. bombs close beside the foundations, with a fair penetration before exploding, then the lock would be out of action for many months. It was an excellent idea, and the purpose of my being present was that Cochran wished the Path Finder Force proper to lay flares over the targets, so that his visual markers could themselves then mark the aiming point and control the raid, which would be carried out entirely by his own aircraft. I need not comment on the remarkable nerve of the A.O.C. of 5 Group in asking us to co-operate in view of the way he had treated us, and weakened us both in strength and in name. The point of the story is that during the discussion he called upon Cheshire, who was present at the meeting and was the Squadron Commander of the special squadron concerned, to explain that they had thrown out the Mark XIV bombsight, which had been sponsored by the C.-in-C. himself and adopted after considerable

tests by the Path Finder Force, and that they had fitted the
Mark IX. This bombsight had no gyro-stabilisation, so that
any roll or pitch of the aircraft was not corrected, and this
resulted in very erratic movements of the target through the
sight. On the other hand, it did have an automatic ground-
speed measuring mechanism in it, which could result in a
very accurate interpretation of ground-speed being fed into
the mechanism so that the sight was very accurate for distance. In practice, we in the Path Finder Force had long
before come to the conclusion that under operational conditions, with flak bursting close by, it was quite impractical to
have any bombsight which was not "gyro-erected". In the
process of convincing me when I expressed surprise at their
decision, Cochran called on Cheshire to tell the meeting how
wonderful their bombing results had been with this sight.
Cheshire then claimed that from 20,000 feet they had been
dropping 11½ lb. practice bombs, and that the error in
distance had never been more than 20 feet, and in line had
never been more than 2 to 3 feet. This latter, of course, was
quite fantastic, as the ballistic error of an 11½ lb. practice
bomb from that height is in itself at least 30-40 feet. I therefore expressed some surprise, only to have it thrust down my
throat once again that these were, in fact, practical figures
obtained without any doubt and that of course they were
correct. I first asked Cochran whether he meant that that was
the bombsight error alone, after an analysis had been made
to remove other possible random errors. He insisted that this
was the overall or total error of all the very many bombs
which they had dropped with this sight, and not merely a
"centre" of them—and that the figures were accurate. I
looked at the C.-in-C. and I looked at Saundby, and I said,
"Do you accept those figures as being total errors?" And they
both quite solemnly and happily agreed that they accepted
them. I inwardly shrugged my shoulders, and realised that
the C.-in-C. of Bomber Command and the Deputy C.-in-C.
seemed to have failed completely to take in what had been

said. In short, Cochran had mesmerised them once again, and it was no good my arguing. It is perhaps possible that the figures quoted had been achieved by some remarkable chance. My point is, however, that neither the C.-in-C., his Deputy, the A.O.C. 5 Gp., or Cheshire seemed to remember the ballistic error of the practice bombs used.

Incidentally, we never did the raid!

As the day for the invasion grew nearer and nearer there was more and more intensity of planning, and we were watching the weather carefully. None of us knew, of course, the exact date when the invasion would take place, and I, for my part, tried to take the line that I did not want to know until I had to.

We plugged away at the pre-invasion targets, and as the great day drew near we were put on to radio and radar stations near the coast. One Signals air commodore at the Air Ministry called me into his office one day with great glee and told me that he was going to show me the latest secret radio-counter measure. Radio counter-measures were at that time being produced in all sorts and sizes, and were of tremendous importance to us. I thought he was going to tell me one of the latest secrets. Instead, he produced a photo of a radio station on the coast of France, heavily bombed, obviously by Bomber Command. I said, "Well, it has simply been bombed." To this he replied, "Yes, and it is the best counter measure for radio I know."

It is not my job to tell in this book of the details of the Army and the Navy and their affairs in the greatest invasion in history. It was apparent to all of us that big things were happening: the assembly of vast numbers of varied surface craft, the creation of such things as the Mulberry harbour and the PLUTO pipeline, the latter being produced by my friends who had developed FIDO for us. In short, the air was charged with excitement and activity. Many of us—in fact, most of us—had anxieties, for there were many strange tricks that the weather could play, and none of us knew the real strength of the German Army on European soil, where the Germans were theoretically fighting on their own ground and with the backing of their own industries not very far behind them. The operation "Overlord" was building up to its climax, the landing itself.

What with tides for the Navy and their landing craft, and weather for the Air Force, it was indeed a tricky situation. As the world now knows, General Eisenhower and his senior commanders, both British and American, met on 3rd June to make the decision as to whether everybody should embark on 4th June ready for the first chosen D-Day, which was dawn on 5th June. The forecasters were pessimistic, and the situation certainly looked fairly hopeless. These men on whom such a grave decision rested met again on 4th June, in the early morning. The Navy were against the operation in the light of the latest forecasts, and Lee Mallory for the Tactical Air Force also said "No". The Army were entirely in the hands of these two Services, and in due course Eisenhower made the decision that a twenty-four-hour postponement should apply. Some troops were already on board their ships, but the order went out, and everything came to a standstill until further orders were received. I was in the know, and I must say I felt the burden of the secrecy quite considerably. I was, however, greatly relieved—for the guarantee which I had given months earlier at that joint meeting weighed heavily on me when I thought of the prevailing weather and the difficulties of being certain that we should put out of action those heavily defended guns on the vital beach head.

On the evening of 4th June, the Met. boys gave the Supreme Commander a somewhat more favourable forecast, and the operation was laid on once again. This time it went forward, and that night we planned the bombing of the beach with the full weight of Bomber Command except for a few Lancasters and some 100 Group aircraft who did diversions trying to give the impression of movement of ships further down the Channel. It always struck me as being rather strange, in view of the fact that actual light marine craft could easily have done this operation quite effectively without going to the somewhat ponderous and relatively risky procedure of using valuable aircraft which could have been doing more important work elsewhere. Being clever for cleverness' sake has never had much appeal to me! That night we attacked two targets before midnight, and then the remainder between midnight and dawn. The main attacks were started only four hours before the invasion. Of the ten aiming points which were so vital, all were marked with Oboe markings, and eight of them were then controlled and marked by the Path Finder Force proper; the two remaining targets were controlled and marked after our initial Oboe marking by 83 and 97 Squadrons, and 5 Group bombed them. The weather was not entirely satisfactory, as there was broken cloud at various low levels and it was hard to be certain what was going to prevail at the moment of any particular raid. In the event, however, our markers were always seen, and the results were excellent. It was another triumph for Oboe, for this provided the basic method of marking for all targets. The Master Bombers also did a wonderful job, and the spirit of Bomber Command that night was at its peak. From all the eight targets marked and controlled by the Path Finder Force I believe there was not a single gun firing. Of the remaining two batteries, 5 Group did a really good job on them, and with the exception, I believe, of one gun which was firing on manual control, these batteries, too, were out of action. I believe that I am right in saying that this made a vital difference to the Navy and the Army in their difficult task, for in those few critical hours when the die was first cast it would have been possible to inflict enormous casualties on our troops, and mere gunfire from our ships could have done nothing against the solid concrete emplacements of those coastal batteries.

The intensity of the excitement of D-Day and the strain of the night itself came to a strange and very unusual anti-climax for me. The next day at lunch time I had a long-standing engagement to address the Royal Institute of International Affairs at Chatham House on the subject of World Peace and the formation of an International Police Force to enforce it. This had been arranged by Lord Hinchingbrooke and one or two other members of Parliament, who knew my views on warfare and its suppression in the future, and they wished to encourage me. I must admit that I was hardly in a fit state to do justice to the subject, but I could not cancel without a breach of security. Therefore, although I had known that it was highly likely to clash with this operation, it so happened that as it came immediately after the critical period I was still able to attend without at any time giving away the fact that I was deeply involved in something important and secret. As it was, by that time the world already knew that we were ashore in Europe; even Hitler knew!

I do not think that the audience at Chatham House was in exactly the right receptive mood to listen to a dull lecture, even though it was from one who was involved in the present conflict. I hope, however, that I sowed some thoughts that day which may yet reap some reward in the future and help to establish the world peace which I am convinced could, and would, come if we had but a tiny grain of courage in the heart of any honest, leading British politician. I am convinced that Britain could still lead the world, and I am certain that if we could overhaul our political machine we should again get great men at the head of our affairs.

The days which followed were critical and tense. The build-up was taking place, and things were going fairly well, with a few exceptions of a tactical nature. Some of the airborne stuff had not been at all accurate in their positioning, and some of the results achieved by them had been disappointing. Moreover, the enemy fought us hard and viciously in many places, and took a great deal of moving. We in Bomber Command were theoretically not intended to be used for short-term tactical purposes. It soon became evident, however, that the vast weight of bombs which Bomber Command alone could put down was a weapon so potent that the temptation to use it could not be resisted, least of all by Montgomery. On the night after the invasion we marked no less than eight tactical targets, whilst the Light Night Striking Force went, as always, to Germany. On the following night, that is to say, the night of 7th June, we marked six more tactical targets by the same method, Oboe Mosquitoes backed up by heavy Lancasters. We had, of course, arranged our Oboe stations to suit the invasion area.

We had four channels working on Mark II Oboe. Moreover, both 105 and 109 Squadrons were now at three Flight strength, that is to say, making the equivalent of three squadrons. We needed all of them, as the amount of work increased day by day. On the night of the 8th to 9th we reverted to marshalling yards, and marked two which were of direct importance to the movement of troops up to the beachhead. We also did a tactical choke-point at Rennes. Just to show the Germans that the invasion itself would not relieve them of their worries at home, I sent three dozen Mosquitoes to Berlin. We carried on on these lines, and gave local airfields which had fighters on them a good pounding every now and again just to help keep any possible air force animosity at bay, or at least suitably discouraged. Most of the airfields west of the Rhine had received a fairly good plastering both from Bomber Command and from the American Air Force, in order to ensure that their fighter activity was restrained as much as possible. Thus we carried on with our tactical targets, using practically the whole of Bomber Command's strength for the purpose. Only the Mosquitoes of the Light Night Striking Force kept on with their visits to Berlin, Cologne and similar main German cities, to let the population know that Bomber Command would not forget them. Politically, I believe this was of tremendous importance, and I am glad that we had those Mosquitoes available to do it—in spite of the bureaucrats.

As the days passed, the Army suddenly discovered our value, and brought us nearer and nearer to the actual front-line fighting, so that by the 12th we were attacking Caen itself right in front of our own troops. These Caen attacks soon produced the famous remark from Bert Harris that for the British Army it appeared that Bomber Command should invent some "suction bombs". We were called upon to blast the enemy in front of the troops with such vast tonnages of bombs that it seemed quite out of all proportion. The Army would then move forward to the extent of our bombing through the dazed and stupefied German troops, and when they had thus advanced they would stop again and wait for us to lay down another heavy load of bombs. The irony of it was that they then complained that we made the ground impossible to pass through with their vehicles. Bomber Command was available by day and by night, and that meant that the Path Finder Force was similarly involved. Moreover, the work of the Met. Flight 1409 in all directions was more intense than ever. We ranged over airfields and ports as well as purely tactical pinpoints.

Heavy bombers in close tactical support of troops had never really been used on any great scale. The problem, therefore, was considerable. The fear of hitting our own troops was indeed great, and I believe there was some justification. When we first started these tactical targets, I myself was extremely worried about this danger, particularly as I knew the frequency with which odd aircraft would undershoot the target quite substantially through either the mistakes of the crew, or sometimes electrical faults of the bomb release circuits. On the early tactical raids in support of our troops I was generally able to arrange the line of approach to take this into account. On one of the earlier close support raids I went along myself to see how things went, and I was very relieved to find that the bombing was extremely compact, and that there were no "strays" whatever on that occasion. On another occasion, however, a little later, I believe early in August, things went quite seriously wrong for a short period. I myself was at the Air Ministry that afternoon, at a meeting which I could not avoid. Whilst I was there, reports came in that Bomber Command aircraft had been bombing our own troops, and I was certainly put in a most difficult position by some of my seniors present. Naturally, I do not blame them, because the accident was a serious one. I feel, however, that they might at least have investigated the cause of the trouble before giving me quite such a hot time. Eventually, after much investigation, it turned out that one aircraft had accidentally dropped its load of bombs short of the target, and as the route—contrary to Pathfinder's wishes —had been due south from the coast over the heads of our own troops, these bombs fell in a most dangerous position. Immediately the local Army officers let off smoke candles of a colour which apparently was the identification colour for the day. This was a code system used between the Army and the Tactical Air Forces, but unfortunately our magnificent liaison had failed to convey this information to Bomber Command. In fact, we did not even know that such a system existed. Unfortunately, the colour used that day was the colour which was also our aiming point mark dropped by Pathfinders themselves. The net result was that the unwary or thoughtless among the Main Force bombers saw the colour and bombed it. The majority, however, realised that it was a mistake, and flew on to the correct target and the correctly marked aiming point. The casualties among our own troops were quite serious, including many Canadians. There were many hard feelings at the time, but I feel sure that the Army realised in due course that it was not entirely Bomber Command's fault, and certainly no fault of the Path Finder Force. In fact, I believe that our C.-in-C. had made a definite arrangement that the Army would not use coloured smokes when Bomber Command were operating.

Material was building up satisfactorily behind the American and British forces, and the Americans were making some progress forward. The British Army was, however, very heavily contained by the Germans, and it was indeed a compliment to our troops and to Montgomery himself that the vast weight of armour was concentrated against the British. In fact, the Panzer Divisions gave practically no attention to the Americans. We in the Air Force were of course guilty, as were most people in England, of considerable impatience regarding the proceedings on the Continent. They seemed all too slow to us, and we were "champing at the chocks" in real earnest. Things were, however, going more or less to plan so far as Montgomery was concerned. On one occasion during those days I had a fit of impatience with what I regarded as poor liaison, and went to lunch with De Guingand, Montgomery's brilliant Chief of Staff. I hoped that my visit helped him to understand what the Pathfinders could do and, therefore, what Bomber Command could do for them. Although Bomber Command and the C.-in-C. in particular were terribly keen to help the Army, and constantly told them so, I must say I thought that the machinery for liaison between the two was totally unsuitable and too unwieldy to be able to handle the quick-changing situations which occurred. In fact, it seemed that no heavy scale support could be given to the Army with less than two days' notice and very laborious joint planning. I, on the other hand, took the view that Bomber Command should be able to put on a hundred heavies at a half-hour's notice at any time. Needless to say, I made it quite clear that these were purely personal views, but that I was sure that in a real emergency Bomber Command would always come to the help of the Army, even at quite short notice, and that my C.-in-C. was keen to help in every way.

One example of this occurred very shortly afterwards. The Americans had broken through in the west, and were coming round in a left-hand encircling movement whilst the main bulk of the German armour and their main troop concentration still opposed the front of the British beyond Caen. Canadians were brought in on the British left and advanced in a slightly right-handed movement towards Falaise. Close support was laid on to assist in the decisive battle of the campaign. We marked numerous aiming points, and gave heavy support which I believe was extremely valuable to the Army. Late one afternoon, however, while this was going on, I had a call from Saundby to say that he was very sorry, but that the Army had suddenly discovered that the Germans were retreating down what was called the Falaise Gap towards Argentan and Gace. This west to east road had to be blocked, but it was quite impossible to take Bomber Command off the targets already detailed for the night. He was not pressing the matter, but he wondered whether I could mark and put a few supporters on with some other stragglers of Bomber Command to do the job. I naturally said yes, and about 120 heavies were, I believe, raised for the occasion. We did completely blind marking on the vital road in a place where the surrounding country made it almost impossible for vehicles to move once off the road. We ploughed up the whole area over a considerable distance, and, I believe, brought the traffic completely to a standstill, as well as causing considerable casualties among those German vehicles already in that position. It stopped the "rat-run" and thus bottled up the Germans in what became their slaughter ground—slaughter far greater than the people of England ever realised. The defeat which the Germans sustained in that bottled-up area, with the road closed behind them, with the Canadians to the north of them, the British to the north-west and the Americans to the south, was probably the most serious of the whole war. The enormous casualties in dead and captured would, one have thought, have made even a Hitler have serious thoughts about surrender—particularly when he realised that his Fatherland had already been laid in waste by the heavy bombers and that now his Army was being destroyed unmercifully.

I rather feel that this effort, which closed the Falaise Gap at a time which was vital, was not appreciated even by the

Army at the time. Their operational research into the great success of that battle apparently overlooked this little raid entirely. It was again so when we interfered seriously with the enemy during the later Ardennes offensive by Rundstedt.

And now the armies of Britain, American and Canada "swanned" along towards the Seine after the receding Germans. Some of the Canadian armour caught a bad beating on one occasion, driving on in high spirits and apparently with some carelessness. They were badly ambushed, and lost a great many of their tanks and men, from which it can be seen that even after the shocking defeat at Falaise the Hun was still fighting back.

As our armies rolled eastward, they left various pockets of resistance, outflanked them and carried on. These pockets were, of course, a source of considerable danger to our troops, and had to be dealt with. This gave us some copybook practice seldom equalled.

The first of these was Le Havre, which was outflanked when our troops crossed the Seine and carried on to the north-east. I always recall this raid as an example of the staunch loyalty of the British Press to the Senior Service whenever possible. At the request of the Army, we had been bombing various gun emplacements and the like around Le Havre; then one day a really big show was put on in which we in Bomber Command delivered a very great weight of bombs. From memory, I believe that almost all heavies turned out, which by that time must have made something over 1,000 heavies each carrying about six tons of bombs. This would mean that over 6,000 tons of high explosives were put down on to the target area by Bomber Command. Even the unimaginative can realise that this is a very great weight of high explosives, and bombs are, of course, a very efficient form of high explosive. Fifty aircraft were, however, diverted to attack some gun emplacements on the coast to the north of the town, facing towards England. These fifty aircraft dropped some 300 tons of high explosive in order to silence these guns. The sole purpose of the guns was to shoot out to sea, and they were not in any way an embarrassment to the Army, nor to its attack on the town. These three hundred tons therefore were dropped purely to silence anti-naval guns. The reason was a good ship called, I believe, *Erebus*, a gun-boat of very ancient vintage which had gallently decided to join the party. I had known the *Erebus* in the old days when I had been a "coastal" pilot, and I remember the quaint ship with its bulging bilges and its ponderous, very slow cruising speed. I am told that the *Erebus* actually fired for many hours as a result of our silencing these guns, thus making it possible for her to come within range of Le Havre. In all the hours of shelling which she did, however, I believe she delivered something less than 50 tons of high explosives, a somewhat adverse balance compared with the 300 tons wasted in order to make this action possible. I am not belittling what the *Erebus* did, but what I am saying is that the great British Press the next morning need not have carried banner headlines to say that the British Navy had shelled Le Havre and that gun-fire from Le Havre was heard in London when, in fact, this action on the part of the Royal Navy was indeed a very minor one in relation to the might of Bomber Command. Incidentally, it was a raid which I watched myself throughout its entire duration; I had the pleasure of seeing the *Erebus*' gun flashes, but never, I am afraid, the fall of her shells.

During all these activities we did not neglect Germany. Bomber Command's main weight often went back to the German cities, particularly those connected with the aircraft industry, whenever the tactical situation allowed us, and, of course, when weather made it more profitable. Mosquitoes also kept up their attacks against Berlin, and occasionally other cities such as Munich. Incidentally, one of the best "line-shooting" pieces of the war occurred on a raid to Munich. I always shoot this line to demonstrate the gentle art of navigation! One Mosquito from Gravely took off with its fellow squadron mates on its way to Munich, and similarly amongst a squadron that was taking off from, I believe, Wyton, another Mosquito joined the party. These two distinguished Mosquitoes each came back and reported a strange bump. They each said that in black darkness about fifty miles short of the target they felt "a bump in the night". After they landed at their respective stations on return, examination of the aircraft showed a strange cut vertically in the nose of one aircraft and a strange round dent in the rudder of the other. The cut in the nose of the one aircraft was exactly in the centre—need I say more?

As soon as the armies rushed forward, I followed them up with my Oboe stations, which had been produced for me by the boffins in a mobile form so as to be ready for such an occasion. I had to increase the number of Oboe controllers; 60 Group increased the technical personnel available and produced the vehicles, etc., to do the job. I give the Signals people full marks for the wonderful way in which they met the occasion and produced the goods in time. The results of this were that by moving the ground stations forward, Oboe became effective deep into enemy territory in a manner never previously possible. We followed fairly closely behind the Army, and usually had our stations functioning within a matter of days of the Army passing. Thus we were able to give the accuracy and reliability under all conditions which Oboe alone could guarantee. This was particularly valuable for open country tactical targets, where H2S was at a disadvantage as there were no built-up areas to differentiate on its screen.

In February, 1945, I had occasion to call on an American Air Force Commander who was operating in the Italian campaign. These American forces had been equipped with the equivalent of what we called GEE-H. This was a radar equipment in which the responses were the reverse of Oboe. Instead of emanating from the ground and being re-transmitted back to the ground from the aircraft, the procedure was the opposite; that is to say, the aircraft sent out a pulse which was received at the ground station and re-transmitted back to the aircraft, so that the whole of the control of the equipment was in the hands of the crew. Basically, it should, of course, have been possible to make that equipment as accurate as Oboe, but owing to the frequency used and other factors this was not so. It was, however, possible to achieve accuracies of a matter of a few hundred yards at ranges equivalent to those used in Oboe. These American aircraft in the North Italian campaign were using this equipment, and it was important that I should know all about it.

As an indication that the Mosquito was years ahead of its time, I think the itinerary of that visit is worth quoting. I rose from my bed at Wyton in the usual way, and had a cup of tea. I took one of my staff navigators from Headquarters Path Finder Force, and we climbed on board a Mosquito. We flew to an aerodrome near Florence in north Italy, and had breakfast. While there we learned that the American Commander I wished to see had moved his headquarters to Corsica, and therefore we took off again and flew over there. Incidentally, it was a strange contrast to leave the depths of an English winter and land in Italy where all our chaps, including a number of South Africans, were in khaki shorts. We flew over to Ghisenaicca, south-west of Bastia. There the Americans showed us their equipment, and generally looked after us most generously. We had lunch with them, and afterwards we heard all about the excellent fishing and the wonderful life which they led at their headquarters there. Again, it was a strange contrast to the life we were leading in England in those days. We boarded the Mosquito, flew back to Wyton, and sat down to a cup of tea at ten past four in my quarters. Even today, with fast modern aircraft, it is hard to equal the itinerary of that day eleven years ago.

At this time I was carrying out considerable experimental

work with automatic control of the aircraft, using Oboe as the means of holding it on track. We did, in fact, make considerable progress with some new automatic pilots, and I believe that we would in due course have perfected automatic flying fed through electronic circuits from the Oboe set. In fact, the war was progressing so rapidly and there was so much preoccupation with day to day events that we never actually got this system going in Operations. I did, however, have the pleasure of doing some completely automatic landings at Defford on a rig which they had arranged with a radar beam which they devised, and a Eureka beacon for range. (The Eureka beacon is a ground responder beacon which can be used in conjunction with REBECCA, which is an aircraft radar transmitter-receiver.)

After the capture of Paris and the crossing of the Seine, it was an unfortunate fact that the Army generals were all fighting among themselves. The American generals, Patton in particular, were openly abusive of the British generals, and appeared to be completely undisciplined as a matter of principle. Without being unduly rude, it seemed that Eisenhower was loath to give any direct orders to his generals, particularly to the Americans. Montgomery wanted to concentrate on a relatively narrow drive into northern Germany. Patton and Co. wished to spread as opportunity allowed. It is not for me, a mere Air Force officer, to express views on which policy was correct, but it does seem that the arguments in favour of Montgomery's single thrust plan in a north-easterly direction were far more sound than the wild spreading which ultimately took place either as the "Eisenhower plan" or in spite of Eisenhower—I never could quite tell which. The Americans, on the other hand, certainly had all the guts in the world, and enough drive to get anywhere; certainly they moved. However, I believe that it would have produced a quicker victory if we had grabbed the Belgian ports as quickly as possible and cut up into the north of the Ruhr as planned by Montgomery, who, despite his acknowledged carefulness, was a soldier of far more brilliance than any of the Americans, even including the Supreme Commander. As one who received the daily intelligence reports and saw a good deal of the area concerned, I must say that I—often a critic of Montgomery—heartily side with him in this matter of the main thrust at this critical period. In my view, it would probably have saved a very long period of the war, and thereby saved many lives.

Once we were across the Seine the whole of the Army pushed onwards, and the British were on the left gaining the important ports so vital to our supplies. They pressed on, captured Brussels and Antwerp, and headed for Holland. Many of us thought that the drive would go straight on into Germany, and that the end was near. But the enemy still fought doggedly. As ever, however, the Army was delayed not by its spearhead but by its supply lines. It is a strange thing that even in a relatively modern war the whole of the forward troops depends on the roads, and the roads alone, for supplies. It is easy to see how inadequate these are, even with thousands and thousands of lorries at the disposal of the Army, when one realises the narrow strips which roads present on the surface of the earth. The vast spaces of the air were virtually unused. This, I believe, is also one of the greatest lessons of the war—the inability of either side to use the air for the transport of its ground services requirements.

In order to speed up this north-north-easterly advance, a plan was laid on to use airborne troops and to take some of the canal bridges. The places particularly vital were at Arnhem, where a big bridge could easily be destroyed by the enemy before we reached it by normal means, and where a similar situation occurred at Nijmegen. The troops were dropped first on 17th September and for several days thereafter. Reading the reports of these affairs, I must say it made me somewhat sick that the Air Force should solemnly put its parachute-dropping aircraft straight down a line of defences which were quite clearly shown in our own Intelligence

Records, and apparently were found in fact to be there. Moreover, the aircraft flew, I believe, at about 2,000 feet and were, therefore, absolutely sitting targets for the light flak. The casualties were heavy. What was more important, however, was that the "drops" in the days which followed apparently made no attempts to use any greatly improved routing or tactics, and the casualties remained high. The idea was that these airborne troops should hold the vital bridges and areas essential to our subsequent advance, whilst the ground troops further south should come on up behind them as rapidly as possible. At first things went well on the ground, but the heavy losses involved by the troops going in by air had its effect, and the enemy's reaction to them around the bridges themselves was intense and included some Panzers. Owing to poor weather, moreover, practically no air supplies were reaching the airborne troops, and their situation was very dangerous indeed. I rang up Headquarters Bomber Command and suggested that we should drop supplies blind, as it was inevitable that the ordinary visual methods used by the Army's own tactical units and supply droppers were quite inadequate in the bad weather which prevailed. On the third day, the 19th, the weather was worse, and we began to get reports of a most serious nature, indicating that the operation was likely to be a complete failure and that a large number of troops were holding out in almost hopeless circumstances. I talked to Saundby again, and pleaded that I should be allowed to put down at least some supplies by Oboe aircraft. Still my suggestion reaped no reward. I don't know whether Bomber Command ever offered our services to the Army; but whether they did or not, it was a deplorable thing that we were not allowed to help. It is, of course, impossible to say whether such help would have made any real difference to the result, but it seems likely with the high calibre of parachute troops that reasonable supplies might have made all the difference to them. Had they been dropped supplies of anti-tank weapons and ammunition, I feel sure that they might have destroyed the German tanks which, after all, were relatively few in number. The gallantry of our troops was magnificent—their support from behind was dismal. Moreover, I believe that the tactical planning of the initial drop was pathetic. Finally, on 25th September, Montgomery ordered the withdrawal from Arnhem, and an unhappy chapter was ended.

The failure to hold this vital bridge was, I believe, of tremendous importance in the termination of the war, which in my view would have come to an end in a very short time had we been successful. As it was the spearhead was blunted and we lost momentum, so that the enemy was able to recover, to reform and, indeed, even to retaliate.

As the winter approached, the Army appeared to be building up their supplies and to be getting ready for something big, but of course we in the Air Force were not fully informed of those parts of the overall strategy which obviously had nothing to do with us. For ourselves, we continued hammering away at the German cities, with occasional diversions for tactical purposes of all sorts, and on the occasional V-Bomb sites more or less at any time. After Le Havre we had cleaned up Calais and Boulogne in quite short order by similar types of raid, and the Canadian forces moved in. Enemy airfields also received a fair pounding at odd intervals, particularly when it was important that no fighter activity should bother our land operations.

On 16th December 1944 I had a telephone call from across the water from the senior Oboe controller at one of my units sited just beyond the Meuse up on one of the hills in the western portion of the Ardennes, which we then held. He reported that the Germans had suddenly launched a counter-attack, and that he had been forced to retire at high speed and was therefore off the air. He insisted that the offensive was a major one, and that the Americans, mostly green troops who had just taken up position, were collapsing like cheese. It was the beginning of the Runstedt offensive through the Ardennes. Apparently nobody at Bomber Command knew anything about it when I telephoned; nor did they appear to take it very seriously. The weather in England was very bad, and I believe it was bad right from the beginning of the attack on the other side. This, no doubt, was intentional on the part of the Germans, as they had relatively no air support for their Army and they obviously did not wish to have the full force of the 2nd Tactical Air Force against them—nor, for that matter, any British planes if it could be avoided. The fog was their best friend. To me the attack certainly seemed serious, and I tried to convey my impression to Bomber Command, though with little effect. It was obvious that the Germans were endeavouring to drive westward to capture Liège and Brussels and our supply port at Antwerp, thereby cutting off the whole of the British troops to the north, and the 1st U.S. Army as well. This would have been extremely serious, because neither of these two armies would then have been able to maintain their supplies at anything like an adequate level and the results might have been catastrophic. I have heard some British senior officers say that the Ardennes offensive was doomed to failure from the outset, but I would not for one moment agree with this. The situation at the time was extremely serious, and if Montgomery had not reacted very quickly, as indeed he did, to bring troops southwards in order to hold the spearhead of the German offensive, then Rundstedt might quickly have driven through and disorganised the whole of our affairs.

I would, however, also like to emphasise that even in spite of Montgomery's coming south so rapidly it would have been relatively difficult to hold the Germans' offensive, fierce-fighting troops as they were, had they not been short of supplies brought about first in a general sense by the effect of Bomber Command's bombing of Germany, particularly at that time of their synthetic fuel supplies, and secondly by the direct result of our own attacks against them.

The fog over England, Belgium and most of the battle area was generally fairly thick. We in Pathfinders had our fair share of it, and things were extremely difficult. Nevertheless, during the Ardennes offensive, Bomber Command laid on eight major raids, and on all of these Pathfinders operated and marked, regardless of the weather at our own bases. In all cases blind marking was necessary, for even on the daylight raids one could not see the ground, and therefore it was essential to use T.I. ground marking for the heavies to aim at. Of these raids, the transportation targets against the marshalling yards and railways behind the German offensive were fairly straightforward, as were the attacks on the big troop concentrations at Houffalize. The raid which I believe, however, was the most vitally important in stopping the German advance, was that which we carried out by day against the St. Vith crossroads. This was in the heart of the Ardennes mountains, and the roads converged to it from all directions. It was, in fact, impossible to go from east to west at all except by passing through the St. Vith, and this choke-point was therefore of vital importance to the supplies to the German spearhead. It was thick fog; we marked the target by T.I.s in daylight, and the bombing was excellent. The net result was that the German tanks had to dig themselves in at the tip of the spearhead and try to fight without any fuel and with little ammunition. I had these reports first-hand from my own Oboe controllers, who were still in the neighbourhood awaiting the opportunity to return to their site.

Incidentally, during the Ardennes offensive the Pathfinders often had to take-off to mark for the northern groups—that is to say, 6 Group and 4 Group, when they were in relatively clear weather, even though the area in the Path Finder Force stations was itself still completely fogged in. The take-offs were done down the edges of the run-way, and we had FIDO at Gravely and at Downham Market on which to land our aircraft back, which was indeed very necessary!

This heavy support for the Army, in what was really quite

a critical situation, was one of the things which I believe was seldom appreciated, particularly the vital effect of the St. Vith raid.

The Light Night Striking Force was still active during all this period, keeping up its general nuisance value in Germany. In addition to its very substantial raids against Berlin and the other great cities, at this stage of the war it undertook what were called Siren Tours, which consisted of laying on a party of Mosquitoes to visit a number of German targets in turn. This meant that there were odd aircraft flying in all directions, and the air-raid alarms were being sounded in many German cities, which in due course each received a few bombs. We usually managed to include about four or five big cities in each such Siren Tour, and they must have been an awful nuisance to the German population. This did of course mean that any one city only received a small number of bombs, and the total damage was therefore relatively ineffective, but the effect on German morale must have been enormous.

On 1st January 1945 some of the Mosquitoes did a job which was quite a matter of skill and of considerable importance to the supplies to the Army in the vicinity. It must be remembered that both British and American Armies were fighting back to recover the ground lost during the Ardennes offensive, and this little operation did, I believe, assist materially.

At Path Finder Headquarters we selected a large number of railway tunnels in the relatively hilly district immediately behind the German front, and we arranged for the Mosquitoes to do skip bombing by approaching the tunnels at low level and dropping their bombs with delayed fuses into the mouths of the tunnels concerned. We attacked fifteen tunnels in this manner; most of the attacks were successful and caused some paralysis to the rail services in the district. Moreover, it took valuable effort for the Germans to rebuild and to clear the lines. The total effort on our part was one squadron for one day, which, compared to some better known operations, was remarkably economical.

Our efforts against Germany and her war effort never flagged for one moment, though we could see that success was in sight. On the contrary, we piled on the pressure with every aircraft available, and the numbers were steadily increasing. The strength of Bomber Command was at its peak, and we really could hit hard when necessary. Our duties, however, were varied, and early in 1945 we became involved in the problem of feeding the Dutch. Unfortunately, we were not allowed to do much until quite late, when I believe the situation was becoming extremely serious in that country. We then had the pleasure of dropping food supplies from the air—a mission which was thoroughly enjoyed by all the crews of Bomber Command, and filled them all with a very great appreciation of the difficulties and privations which had been suffered by our Allies in the occupied countries.

Our attacks on the German cities with the Mosquitoes were now being spread into a number of raids per night. Thus we usually sent about three dozen Mosquitoes to Berlin on one attack, and then several hours later another three dozen. And so the gallant little Mosquitoes kept on contributing toward the final victory. Incidentally, it is not always appreciated that the number of flights carried out by Pathfinders was very considerable. Take February, 1945, as an example: the Oboe Mosquitoes carried out 427 main operations, whilst the Lancaster heavies carried out 866. The little Light Night Striking Force, however, carried out 1,809 operations against the enemy in that month. Thus the total for my little Group was 3,102 operations for the month, with a loss of only 17 aircraft. The work of the Met. Flight was additional to these raids. In these days of peace, however, it might be more interesting to realise that we never worked more than seven days in any week, and never more than twenty-four hours per day.

The following month we did 604 Mosquito Oboe operations and 1,355 Lancaster Pathfinder operations, while the Light Night Strikers did 2,242, making 4,201 for the Group with a loss of 22 aircraft. Our targets ranged from the V-sites and tactical targets in support of the Army; right through to the far side of Germany on such places as Berlin, Lübeck, etc.; we also went to Czechoslovakia and other distant targets. Oil, incidentally, had suddenly become a top priority target, and the C.-in-C., who had previously always opposed attacks on oil targets in view of their difficult nature, suddenly became fanatically in favour of the job. I could not understand this, but eventually he put me in the picture by telling me of the German oil situation, and it certainly was a well worth-while objective at that stage of the war. The synthetic plants in the Ruhr were given a good pounding every now and again, and I believe we virtually brought Germany to her knees more by this particular "panacea" than by anything else in the closing stages of the war.

In the spring our great last offensive started. The armies of America and of the British countries crossed the Rhine and attacked the enemy with the utmost vigour, with the support of the Air Forces as and when necessary. The use of heavies, however, in these last stages was not so vital as it had been when the enemy was tough and still fighting with plenty of strength. Indeed, the Tactical Air Forces looked after most of the Armies' requirements, and we were only called upon to do our stuff when really heavy loads of bombs were required. I personally did a good deal of visiting on the Continent during this period, moving up the Oboe stations and being prepared for anything the Army might require or, for that matter, for any other form of bombing when necessary. They were exciting days—to be moving into Germany, and to see for the first time the people whom we were conquering was an experience long awaited. For most fighting men there was a supreme satisfaction that the German, our No. 1 enemy, was defeated or almost so, and most thoughts were beginning to turn towards Japan.

As the end drew near, Bomber Command did the work it had done at the beginning—took to leaflet raiding! It was a strange full turn of the clock that Bomber Command, which started its offensive with leaflet raids over the enemy-occupied territory and over Germany before bombing proper started, should start dropping leaflets once again as bombing proper finished. This time, however, it was very different, for these leaflets were dropped over prisoner of war camps, trying to get pamphlets into the hands of our own men. These leaflets were dropped in order to try to convey to the prisoner of war camps the true situation as it existed, and instructions as to behaviour and the procedure which would be followed to safeguard our men as quickly as possible. Incidentally, long before the end came I had carried out experiments with the Lancaster to see how many people I could carry in one such bomber aircraft. They were hardly suitable as passenger-carrying machines, but we managed to get in about twenty-two quite comfortably. Finally, when the end came the R.A.F. pushed the idea that we should bring the prisoners of war back by air, and I personally did my best to get the idea adopted. The Army and the Navy had laid on their ponderous method of bringing them home by surface transport, and had plans involving a period of four months for the process. I personally could imagine the thoughts and feelings of men who had been imprisoned for years, waiting another four months before they got home to their loved ones. I fought hard for that, and the C.-in-C., who had always wanted to do this job, gave me permission to carry prisoners of war home from a camp up near the Baltic coast and to use the Path Finder Force for this purpose for one day as a test period. We ran a shuttle which was just about as rapid as could be. I was in the first aircraft to land, and we had machines coming and going every few minutes, taxiing off one end of the runway, around the perimeter track to load, then on to the runway again to take-off. We each carried a full load, and all the Lancasters of Path Finder Force which were available functioned for the purpose. The troops were cramped, but delighted to be taken home so quickly. The effect was magical. The next day, the whole of Bomber Command was put on the job of ferrying prisoners of war back to England, and they functioned on this purpose most magnificently. I was pleased that I managed to foil the sluggardly plan which had been laid on to bring these men home so slowly.

The final collapse of Germany ultimately came, and, as the world knows, by pre-arrangement between our political leaders, Russia moved forward to prescribed lines and we were thus curtailed in our advance. Indeed, it was a great political calamity that America, thanks to her depraved outlook on Britain, which she regarded as a colonial power, should be friendly with Russia rather than with us. The calamity of the division between Russia and the rest of the world which occurred after the war was, in my view, created entirely by Roosevelt, due to his policy of sabotaging England in order to appease Russia. In any case, we took up our positions, and the war with Germany came to an end.

Between 18th August 1942 and 8th May 1945 the Path Finder Force and the Light Night Striking Force flew 50,490 bombing sorties and dealt with 3,440 targets. Casualties were 3,618 dead.

The contribution of an aircrew member of Bomber Command who completed an operational tour or died in the process—measured in terms of danger of death, both in intensity and duration—was, in my view, far greater than that of any other fighting man, R.A.F., Navy or Army. The contribution of a Pathfinder, in the same terms of intensity and duration of danger—and indeed of responsibility—was at least twice that of other Bomber Command crews. Particularly the ice-cold courage of an air gunner was phenomenal and deserves the highest possible praise. Great Britain and the Empire have, in the goodly time of ten years since the end of the war, strangely failed to erect any Nelson's column in memory of Bomber Command, the most powerful striking force in all British history. There is not even a Bomber Command Campaign Medal (with or without a Pathfinder Star)! We are not bitter, for we know in our own hearts just what we did—and that is our reward—the truest reward of all.

10

PRATTLE

To the victors, turmoil; and to the vanquished, peace.
I have finished this book so far as the practical things matter, but there are, perhaps, equally important matters, not physical and not practical, which decide the destinies of man even more bitterly than war itself.

I saw a good deal of the Russians towards the end of the war, because they made frequent efforts to visit my headquarters, obviously with the intention of obtaining some of our secrets. Finally the Air Ministry gave in and granted them permission, and two generals and six colonels arrived at my headquarters just before victory in Europe was achieved. Indeed, their four-day visit lasted over the victory celebrations—much to our dismay. They were all smiles and courtesy and were most charming and likeable persons. Their distrust of us and their obviously disguised views of us as an enemy were, however, quite apparent. One of the occasions of their visit was to show them a demonstration of the latest Pathfinder markers of all sorts and sizes—which we laid on one night. When we told them that this was to take place and that they would fly with me in a Lancaster, there was immediate confusion. Our interpreter finally explained to me that they were not permitted to fly in Royal Air Force aircraft owing to the dangers involved. The interpreter had apparently overheard the conversation in which it had been made quite clear that they did not trust us to fly them, as it was obviously a trick in order to kill them all. The interpreter explained this to me, so I told him to point out that I myself was flying with them and I hardly intended to risk my own life in any way and that therefore they were quite safe. This apparently helped, but they still had to ring up their Embassy in London to ask permission. In due course this permission was given, provided I was pilot of one aircraft and only one general was with me, whilst the other general and some of the colonels flew in another Lancaster. This was arranged, and the demonstration took place. I was amused to find the relief when in fact we landed back safely without killing any of them!

Another little incident which clearly showed the nature of the Russians occurred one afternoon when we were inspecting one of the Pathfinder stations. We had been in the Operations Room, and later went on to the Officers' Mess for tea. Whilst the Russians were washing their hands, they had left their overcoats hanging on the hooks in the hall. The Station Intelligence Officer beckoned me whilst they were washing and quietly told me that he had seen one of the Russian colonels pick up a signal off the Operations Room table. The S.I.O. wanted to know what he should do about it. I thought a moment, and then said that I suggested that he should simply go to the great-coat hanging on the hook and take the signal from the pocket. The S.I.O. grinned from ear to ear, and said, "Good—that is what I have done, sir." I approved of his methods, and told him to keep the signal. In fact, it was a weather report, and so I am afraid the colonel would have been extremely disappointed even if he had managed to keep it. His reaction on finding it missing must have been quite amusing!

Which reminds me, of course, of the little matter of the radar station which was overrun during the Russian advance on the Eastern Front. When we heard of this, in accordance with the agreement of sharing all secret information, we sent out scientists up through Persia up into Russia to inspect the station. When they got there, everything of any importance had been taken away. The Russians simply said that there was nothing other than what was then remaining, which our scientists knew to be quite wrong. Our boffins were admittedly a little peeved, and they therefore decided that if that was the co-operation of the Russians, they would reciprocate. They therefore smuggled certain remaining parts into their suitcases to bring back to England without telling the Russians that they had done it. All went well, and they returned to Teheran, where they opened their suitcases to find that all the things which they had put in had been removed. Thus there was trust amongst allies!

All through the war, from the first night when I had heard the first distress signals of the first ship torpedoed in the Atlantic, right through to the end, I had always maintained that this war was not being fought for mere survival. I had always opposed the Prime Minister's theme that we are fighting to win and that we had "no war aim." I openly expressed my thorough disapproval of what appeared to be a fight for mere survival without any worthy aim. "Give us the tools and we will finish the job" did not mean to me to be finishing the war. I held then as I hold now, that the job was to establish peace, and that this could be done simply by applying the ordinary rules of law and order to nations, as indeed applied already to citizens within each nation. The evolution of the principle of law and order had gone a long way, and only the last final step was needed. My views on this subject gained attention from a good many senior members of all political parties in this country, and I was encouraged to press on with my ideas. All three political parties invited me to join them, and promised me a seat in Parliament at a by-election if I would accept. Geoffrey Mander, the P.P.S. to Sir Archibald Sinclair, the Secretary of State for Air, particularly encouraged me and arranged for a publisher to take a book which I would write on the subject—and this I did. I submitted the manuscript to the Air Ministry, and obtained ap-

proval in writing for its publication. To my surprise, just as
the actual book was about to come out I had a message from
Bert Harris one day that the Chief of Air Staff wished to see
me. I went up and was "on the mat" for nearly an hour and a
half before the man who should have been the most busy man
in the whole of the Royal Air Force. The sole purpose of this
was to try to stop me publishing this book. With all his
wonderful charm, he tried to dissuade me; he tried every
method at his disposal. I pointed out that we had not fought
the war in vain, that I was virtually a civilian, and that the
Air Ministry had particularly made me so; that in any case I
was leaving the service very shortly in accordance with the
Swinton plan for civil aviation, in which I was nominated
as the head of an air line to South America; and finally that
I already had written permission, and the publishers were
proceeding and had finished the printing. All this had no
effect on him, for in spite of his charm Portal was, above all
else, stubborn. Finally, he gave me a direct order that I was
not to publish the book, and I replied simply that without
breaking any Air Force law I would publish the book. He
said, "Don't be a fool, Bennett," and I left him. I particularly
recalled this unhappy episode when Portal graced the platform of a great Albert Hall meeting which I held a couple of
years later, when I was Chairman of the United Nations
Association in the cause of Peace. His opposition to my book
was solely based on the fact that he did not approve of the
principles which I was putting forward. His appearance at
that Albert Hall meeting must have meant quite a mental
somersault!

I went straight along the corridor to Sir Archibald Sinclair's office, the Secretary of State, and told him that I was
willing to accept the by-election which the Liberal party had
offered me that morning. Three weeks later I was Member
of Parliament for Middlesborough West. During the period of
the by-election I resigned from the Air Force, in accordance
with an A.M.O. on the subject, and returned to the Air Force

immediately thereafter. Thus I published the book whilst I was out of the Air Force, and, therefore, of course, I did not break any order from the C.A.S., even though the order given had been, in my opinion, improper. There was nothing in the book which in any way referred to any service matter, nor gave away any secret or other information concerning the Services. This episode shook me. It seemed that the Chief of the Air Staff, the head of the service which had sacrificed so much, was himself, at least at that time, apparently without any ideals or any ambitions concerning future generations and the danger that they ran of being exterminated in another great war.

At that stage this disillusionment and frustration was just beginning for me, and Lord Portal was but a tiny example of it. In the House of Commons I found that a Member was impotent in all worth-while matters, with practically no voting power and no speaking power. His sole purpose seemed to be that of a slightly exalted social welfare officer. The Whip system had completely strangled all democracy; the Party system had made a farce of our administrative arrangements, and our voting system was outdated. No sooner was victory in Europe assured than the parties divided and started fighting, sabotaging the country in the process. Moreover, the United Nations Association, of which I had become Chairman, soon proved to me the true nature of human beings. The determination and the effort and the sacrifice to which I had become accustomed during the war was replaced by misgivings and distrust and doubt. In fact, of the fifty members on the Executive Committee of the United Nations Association, all of them were so expert that they knew that everything was impossible.

I personally can see nothing wrong with a national sovereignty and being proud of one's own country. I recognised, however, at the end of the second German conflict that if we were to prevent another world war some organisation to prevent international murder was necessary. When the

United Nations was formed, I was therefore extremely disappointed to find that it contained practically no useful measures to ensure that the peace would be kept. An impartial examination of the Charter of the United Nations showed an organisation which, in almost every aspect, it would be hard to equal in absurdity. Take, for example, the voting arrangements in the Assembly of the United Nations. The Yemen had the same voting power as the United States of America, Great Britain or Russia. The Security Council, with its right of veto, was obviously designed to be unable to function if any one of the great powers were involved in a dispute—which, to say the least, is an absurd situation in view of the fact that it should be world war which we are trying to prevent, and not merely tribal friction. And similarly, the siting of U.N. in the United States of America instead of one of the smaller, less conspicuous countries was in itself bound to cause suspicion and jealousy which must inevitably weaken the organisation. Moreover, it was clear that it was going to bring the United Nations under the influence of America, and this has happened. We have seen many cases where the United Nations has made no attempt to express any views until the United States Government has itself made up its mind—a deplorable reflection of the true state of affairs. This particular weakness is somewhat offset by the voting system on which I have already commented. This system ensures that the Asian/ African group can control the affairs of the world without any trouble. But of all the shortcomings of the United Nations, undoubtedly the one which, in my view, is the most serious was that it had no armed police force with which to maintain the peace. This to me made the whole thing a farce, because I am not interested in a lot of pious platitudes when no practical action is possible and everybody knows it. Very soon, moreover, it became clear that the Military Staffs Committee was not going to function, and it also became clear to me that the British Government, amongst others, was not doing very much to try to make it function!

And as the victory receded into the past, I began to appreciate that in England the only thing which we had achieved was the right to be lazy, the right to preserve and protect every little dictatorship which set itself up, and to conserve and cultivate every bureaucratic encumbrance that was possible. I looked across the Channel and saw Germany working hard, really hard, long hours and continuously, and staging a come-back which made us look childish. At one stage I watched the housing programme of Hamburg, one single city of Germany, exceed all the houses built in England in a period of twelve months. I saw German trade expand and grow. It is not my intention to carry on this book beyond the end of the war, but it is appropriate to point out that we, the victors, have gained nothing, whilst our enemies, the Germans and the Italians, have both been sponsored and supported by us, helped and befriended. This, combined with their own industry, has made their prosperity many, many fold greater than ours. Moreover, neither of them suffer from any sense of guilt for the war, or for the many disgusting crimes which took place during it. Many of those in both Italy and Germany who were associated with atrocities of the most repulsive nature are again in positions of power. Moreover, I am convinced that they have no intention whatever of remaining the vanquished, and that their plans for the next world war have already been drawn up.

I am the first to want a truly United Nations functioning in this world. I am sure, however, that with its present ineffective organisation the U.N. can do nothing for us. We therefore can only prevent war against ourselves by being sufficiently strong to deter it. We have the spirit and the courage, but have we the political leaders and the men of wisdom and knowledge to find the path?

Recently our present Prime Minister stood up against blatant cold blooded aggression. This aggression was one of the most dishonourable in human history. It was for greed—for the Falklands have never been Argentine. "No robaras",

"Thou shalt not steal", is a commandment conveniently forgotten by these allegedly Christian Argentinians. They stole. Great Britain, thanks to one honourable leader, stood firm against this crime. New Zealand and Australia gave their moral and political support immediately. Our EEC partners sat on the fence for a week (rapidly signing contracts with the aggressor) and then supported us, for a "limited period" and not, of course, related to any existing contracts. The Exocet missiles fired at our ships were not, of course, armed by the French experts who were there for that purpose. When the "limited period" was up only two of our "partners" actually sided openly with our enemy and went on supplying him!

The British troops put matters right and the vast majority of our people were proud and thankful—in the Mother Country but also in goodly measure in the British Crown Commonwealth.

We had the courage to fight for right.

This example of honour backed by strength is an isolated case. We grovel to all sorts of tyranny internally—the Party System and the Trade Unions; the former with its Whip System and farcical elections destroys any vestige of democracy, and the latter destroy the value of our money and our competitiveness in the world. We asked thousands of our best young men to die for freedom and independence—and then turn around and surrender our sovereignty and right of self-government to our late enemies with disastrous practical and political results. We grovel. With over 3 million unemployed we continue our EEC membership when arithmetically it is certain that our adverse balance of trade in manufactured goods represents about a million jobs lost.

The EEC is harmful to the world, to Europe and to us. I will not rest until we are free again. The British Anti Common Market Campaign, of which I am Vice Chairman, works towards that noble aim.

Strikes will never prove the right or wrong of any claim

or argument—and they cost the nation dearly. That is the reason for the Inflation Prevention Association—of which I am Chairman.

Similarly I am Chairman of the Political Freedom Movement which aims to replace the present Party dictatorship with Free Democracy in which voters would have a real vote (by the Points System of Positive Voting), and where Parliament would revert to the Constitution with a Free Vote on every issue. We have virtually no democracy at present; it is time we tried it.

We in Great Britain must rise again to honour our greatness, by work and by loyalty to ourselves and to our own.

To ourselves let us be true.

Victory Message

To: The Path Finder Force.
From: Air Vice-Marshal D. C. T. Bennett, C.B., C.B.E., D.S.O.

Great Britain and the Commonwealth have made a contribution to the civilised world so magnificent that history alone will be able to appreciate it fully. Through disaster and triumph, sometimes supported and sometimes alone, the British races have steadfastly and energetically over many long years flung their forces against the international criminals. They have fought the war from end to end without a moment's respite, in all theatres, and with all arms—land, sea and air.

Bomber Command's share in this great effort has been a major one. You, each one of you, have made that possible. The Path Finder Force has shouldered a grave responsibility. It has led Bomber Command, the greatest striking force ever known. That we have been successful can be seen in the far-reaching results which the Bomber offensive has achieved. That is the greatest reward the Path Finder Force ever hopes to receive, for those results have benefited all law-abiding peoples.

Whilst you have been hard at work through these vital years, I have not interrupted you, as I would like to have done, with messages of praise and congratulation. You were too busy; but now that your great contribution to the world has been made, I want to thank you each man and woman of you personally and to congratulate you on your unrelenting spirit and energy and on the results you have achieved.

Happiness to you all—always. Keep Pressing On along the Path of Peace.

DON BENNETT.

Headquarters, Path Finder Force,
European V-Day, 1945.

Appendix A

APPOINTMENTS ASSOCIATED WITH THE BOMBER OFFENSIVE

Secretaries of State for Air, 1938-45

	Appointed.
The Rt. Hon. Sir Kingsley Wood, M.P.	16. 5.1938
The Rt. Hon. Sir Samuel J. G. Hoare, Bart., G.C.S.E., G.B.E., C.M.G., M.P.	5. 4.1940
The Rt. Hon. Sir Archibald Sinclair, Bart., K.T. C.M.G., M.P.	11. 5.1940

Parliamentary Under-Secretaries of State for Air, 1938-45

Captain The Rt. Hon. H. H. Balfour, M.C., M.P.	16. 5.1938
Lord Sherwood (Under-Secretary of State, House of Lords)	22. 7.1941
Commander R. A. Brabner, D.S.O., D.S.C., M.P.	22.11.1944
Earl Beatty, D.S.C. (Under-Secretary of State, House of Lords)	5.1945

Chiefs of the Air Staff, 1938-45

Marshal of the Royal Air Force Sir Cyril L. N. Newall, G.C.B., C.M.G., C.B.E., A.M.	1. 9.1937
Air Chief Marshal Sir Charles F. A. Portal, K.C.B., D.S.O., M.C. (later Marshal of the Royal Air Force, G.C.B., D.S.O., M.C.)	5.10.1940

Commanders-in-Chief, Bomber Command, 1938-45

Air Chief Marshal Sir Edgar R. Ludlow-Hewitt, K.C.B., C.M.G., D.S.O., M.C.	12. 9.1937

	Appointed.
Air Chief Marshal Sir Charles F. A. Portal, K.C.B., D.S.O., M.C.	3. 4.1940
Air Marshal Sir Richard E. C. Peirse, K.C.B., D.S.O., A.F.C.	5.10.1940
Air Chief Marshal Sir Arthur T. Harris, K.C.B., ·O.B.E., A.F.C. (later G.C.B., O.B.E., A.F.C.)	22. 2.1942

BOMBER COMMAND GROUPS

Air Officers Commanding No. 1 Group, Bomber Command, 1939-45

Air Vice-Marshal A. C. Wright, A.F.C.	3. 9.1939–22.12.1939
Air Commodore J. J. Breen, O.B.E.	27. 6.1940
Air Vice-Marshal R. D. Oxland, C.B.E.	27.11.1940
Air Vice-Marshal E. A. B. Rice, C.B., C.B.E., M.C.	24. 2.1943
Air Vice-Marshal R. S. Blucke, C.B.E., D.S.O., A.F.C.	12. 2.1945

Air Officers Commanding No. 2 Group, Bomber Command, 1939-43

Air Vice-Marshal C. T. Maclean, C.B., D.S.O., M.B.	25. 5.1938
Air Vice-Marshal N. M. Robb, C.B., D.S.O., D.F.C., A.F.C.	20. 4.1940
Air Vice-Marshal D. F. Stevenson, D.S.O., O.B.E., M.C.	17. 2.1941
Air Vice-Marshal A. Lees, C.B.E., D.S.O., A.F.C.	17.12.1941
Air Vice-Marshal J. H. D'Albiac, C.B., D.S.O.	29.12.1942

(Group passed to Fighter Command on 1.6.43)

Air Officers Commanding No. 3 Group, Bomber Command, 1939-45

Air Vice-Marshal J. E. A. Baldwin, C.B., O.B.E.	22. 8.1939
Air Vice-Marshal The Hon. R. A. Cochran, C.B., C.B.E., A.F.C.	14. 9.1942
Air Vice-Marshal R. Harrison, C.B., C.B.E., D.F.C., A.F.C.	27. 2.1943

Air Officers Commanding No. 4 Group, Bomber Command, 1939-45

	Appointed.
Air Commodore C. H. B. Blount	25. 5.1938
Air Commodore A. Coningham, D.S.O., M.C., D.F.C., A.F.C.	3. 7.1939
Air Vice-Marshal C. R. Carr, C.B.E., D.F.C., A.F.C., (later C.B., D.F.C., A.F.C.)	28. 7.1941

Air Officers Commanding No. 5 Group, Bomber Command, 1939-45

Air Vice-Marshal A. T. Harris, O.B.E., A.F.C.	14. 9.1939
Air Vice-Marshal N. H. Bottomley, C.I.E., D.S.O., A.F.C.	22.11.1940
Air Vice-Marshal J. C. Slessor, D.S.O., M.C.	12. 5.1941
Air Vice-Marshal W. A. Coryton, C.B., M.V.O.	25. 4.1942
Air Vice-Marshal The Hon. Sir Ralph A. Cochran, K.B.E., C.B., A.F.C.	28. 2.1943
Air Vice-Marshal H. A. Constantine, C.B., D.S.O.	16. 1.1945

Air Officers Commanding No. 6 Group, Bomber Command, 1939-45

Air Commodore W. F. McN. Foster, C.B., C.B.E., D.S.O., D.F.C.	2. 9.1939
Gp.-Capt. H. S. P. Walmsley, O.B.E., M.C., D.F.C.	16. 3.1942

No. 6 (B) Group became No. 91 (O.T.U.) Group on 11.5.42 and No. 6 (R.C.A.F.) Group formed 25.10.42.

Air Vice-Marshal G. E. Brookes, O.B.E.	25.10.1942
Air Vice-Marshal C. M. McEwen, M.C., D.F.C., (later C.B., M.C., D.F.C.)	29. 2.1944

Air Officers Commanding No. 8 Group, Bomber Command, 1939-45

H.Q. Path Finder Force formed 15.8.42 and became No. 8 (P.F.F.) Group, 13.1.43.

Air Commodore D. C. T. Bennett, D.S.O. (later Air Vice-Marshal, C.B., C.B.E., D.S.O.)	13. 1.1943

Air Officers Commanding No. 91 (O.T.U.)
Group, Bomber Command, 1942-45

Appointed.

Gp.-Capt. H. S. P. Walmsley, O.B.E., M.C., D.F.C.
(later Air Vice-Marshal, C.B.E.,M.C., D.F.C.   16. 3.1942
Air Vice-Marshal J. A. Gray, C.B.E., D.F.C., G.M.   8. 2.1944

Air Officers Commanding No. 92 (O.T.U.)
Group, Bomber Command, 1942-45

Gp.-Capt. H. A. Haines, O.B.E., D.F.C.   14. 5.1942
Air Vice-Marshal H. K. Thorold, C.B.E., D.S.O.,
D.F.C., A.F.C.   17. 3.1943
Air Vice-Marshal G. S. Hodson, C.B.E., A.F.C.   23. 2.1945

Air Officers Commanding No. 93 (O.T.U.)
Group, Bomber Command, 1942-45

Gp.-Capt. C. E. Maitland   15. 6.1942
Air Commodore A. P. Ritchie, A.F.C.   25. 2.1943
Air Vice-Marshal O. T. Boyd, C.B., O.B.E., M.C.,
A.F.C.   24. 2.1944
Air Vice-Marshal G. S. Hodson, C.B.E., A.F.C.   9. 8.1944

Air Officers Commanding No. 100 (Special
Duties) Group, Bomber Command,
1943-45

Air Commodore E. B. Addison, C.B.E. (later Air Vice-
Marshal, C.B., C.B.E.)   8.11.1943.

Main Appointments in No. 8 (P.F.F.) Group,
Bomber Command, 1943-45

A.O.C.   *Appointed.*

Air Commodore D. C. T. Bennett, D.S.O. (later
Vice-Marshal, C.B., C.B.E., D.S.O.)   13. 1.43
(H.Q.B.C Staff Officer commanding the Path
Finder Force   15. 7.42)

S.A.S.O.

Gp.-Capt. C. D. C. Boyce (later Air Commodore,
C.B.E.)   18. 2.43

Air Staff

Wg.-Cdr. R. Hilton, D.F.C. (Ops. Rm.)	28. 1.43
Wg.-Cdr. J. A. Slater, D.F.C.	25. 1.43
Wg.-Cdr. T. G. Mahaddie, D.S.O., D.F.C., A.F.C.	20. 3.43
Wg.-Cdr. G. H. Womersley, D.S.O., D.F.C.	27. 4.43
Sqn.-Ldr. R. O. Altmann, D.F.C.	25. 1.43
Sqn.-Ldr. D. T. Witt, D.F.C. (Trg.)	25. 1.43
Sqn.-Ldr. Ashworth	
Sqn.-Ldr. E. W. Anderson (Flyg. S.N.)	25. 1.43
Sqn.-Ldr. G. F. Georgeson, D.F.C. (Nav.)	25. 1.43
Sqn.-Ldr. J. Collier, D.F.C. (Flyg. Con.)	9. 2.43
Sqn.-Ldr. A. F. Chisholm, D.F.C. (Air Bomb.)	10. 3.43
Sqn.-Ldr. J. E. Partridge, D.S.O., D.F.C. (Instr.)	14. 3.43
Sqn.-Ldr. D. F. Allen, G.M., B.E.M. (Instr.)	20. 2.44
Wg.-Cdr. G. F. Grant, D.S.O., D.F.C.	2.11.43
Sqn.-Ldr. Cresswell	
Sqn.-Ldr. H. G. Travers, D.S.C.	7. 9.43
Sqn.-Ldr. A. P. Cranswick, D.S.O., D.F.C.	20.10.43
Sqn.-Ldr. C. A. J. Smith, D.F.C.	20.10.43
Wg.-Cdr. G. M. Dunnicliffe, D.F.C.	10. 2.44
Wg.-Cdr. F. W. Deacon, D.S.O., D.F.C.	8. 3.44
Sqn.-Ldr. C. P. C. de Wesselow, D.F.C.	7. 4.44
Wg.-Cdr. J. R. G. Ralston, D.S.O., D.F.C., A.F.C.	10. 8.44
Wg.-Cdr. K. H. Burns, D.S.O., D.F.C.	26.10.44
Wg.-Cdr. B. W. McMillan, A.F.C.	10.11.44
Sqn.-Ldr. J. R. Wood, D.F.C.	13. 9.44
Sqn.-Ldr. W. H. Robinson, D.F.C., D.F.M.	18. 1.45
Wg.-Cdr. J. D. Bolton, D.F.C.	1. 6.45
Wg.-Cdr. D. A. Cracknell, D.S.O., D.F.C.	24. 5.45
Sqn.-Ldr. H. Almond	21. 4.45
Sqn.-Ldr. R. C. Walker	14.11.44
Sqn.-Ldr. L. S. Thorpe, D.F.C., D.F.M.	20.10.44
Sqn.-Ldr. J. P. Crump	7. 1.45
Sqn.-Ldr. E. J. Greenleaf, D.S.O., D.F.C.	23. 7.45

Group Navigation Officers	*Appointed.*
Sqn.-Ldr. R. C. Alabaster, D.F.C.	25. 1.43
Wg.-Cdr. K. J. Lawson, D.F.C.	7. 6.43
Wg.-Cdr. A. G. S. Cousens, D.S.O., D.F.C.	23. 8.43
Wg.-Cdr. E. H. Bagnold, D.F.C.	20. 3.44
Sqn.-Ldr. L. R. Hastings, D.F.C.	26. 8.43
	(date originally appointed to Nav. Staff)

Group Met. Officer
  M. J. Thomas, B.Sc.

Group Intelligence Officer	
Sqn.-Ldr. W. J. R. Shepherd (later Wg.-Cdr., O.B.E.) (Int.)	25. 1.43

Group Engineer Officer	
Wg.-Cdr. C. F. Sarsby	1. 2.43

Group Armament Officer	
Sqn.-Ldr. W. Rathbone	10. 2.43

Group Signals Officers	
Wg.-Cdr. G. W. Adams	7. 5.43
Wg.-Cdr. E. L. T. Barton	20.12.43
Sqn.-Ldr. N. I. B. Harrison	16. 6.43
	(date originally appointed to Sigs. Staff)

Group Photography Officer	
Sqn.-Ldr. H. W. Lees	1. 7.43

S.A.O.	
Wg.-Cdr. A. W. G. Martin	28. 1.43
Wg.-Cdr. W. E. Carr	6.43
Gp.-Capt. F. R. D. Swain, O.B.E., A.F.C.	11.10.43
Gp.-Capt. H. McC. White	15. 5.44

Personnel	Appointed.
Sqn.-Ldr. F. B. Taylor	28. 1.43
Sqn.-Ldr. P. L. Burley	21.11.43
Sqn.-Ldr. R. M. Snow	18.11.44

Org.

Sqn.-Ldr. L. E. Barry	1. 2.43
Sqn.-Ldr. F. Vernon	18. 9.44

Group Equipment Officer

Sqn.-Ldr. J. C. Rose (later Wg.-Cdr., M.B.E.)	27. 7.43

Group Medical Officer

Sqn.-Ldr. J. C. MacGown, M.D., Ch.B.	10. 2.43

Stations—Commanding Officers,
1942-45

Wyton	Appointed.
Gp.-Capt. H. Kirkpatrick, D.F.C.	16. 6.42
Gp.-Capt. D. C. L. Wilson	5. 3.43
Gp.Capt. C. T. Jarman, D.S.O., D.F.C.	19. 4.43
Gp.-Capt. H. R. Graham, D.S.O., D.F.C.	22. 6.43
Gp.-Capt. L. E. Jarman, D.S.C.	28.10.43
Gp.-Capt. O. R. Donaldson, D.S.O., D.F.C.	27. 7.44
Gp.-Capt. D. F. E. C. Dean, D.S.O., D.F.C.	25. 2.45

Upwood	
Gp.-Capt. J. K. Kirby	1. 4.41–
	1. 5.43
Wg.-Cdr. R. P. Elliott, D.S.O., D.F.C.	17. 6.43
Gp.-Capt. J. H. Searby, D.S.O., D.F.C.	20.11.43
Gp.-Capt. J. L. Airey, D.F.C.	10. 2.44
Gp.-Capt. S. W. B. Menaul, D.F.C., A.F.C.	6.12.44

Graveley	
Gp.-Capt. B. V. Robinson, D.S.O., D.F.C., A.F.C.	1. 5.43
Gp.-Capt. S. W. B. Menaul, D.F.C., A.F.C.	23. 8.43
Gp.-Capt. G. F. Grant, D.S.O., D.F.C.	6.12.44

Gransden Lodge	*Appointed.*
Gp.-Capt. S. W. B. Menaul, D.F.C., A.F.C.	5. 6.43–
	4.10.43
Gp.-Capt. Dunlop, A.F.C.	10.43–
	2.45
Gp.-Capt. Womersley, D.S.O., D.F.C.	2.45–

Downham Market	
Gp.-Capt. W. H. Kyle, D.F.C.	7. 3.44
Gp.-Capt. R. W. Cox, D.S.O., D.F.C., A.F.C.	9.10.44

Little Staughton	
Gp.-Capt. R. W. P. Collings, D.F.C.	6. 3.44–

Oakington	
Gp.-Capt. N. H. Fresson	18. 3.43–
	1. 7.43
Gp.-Capt. A. H. Willetts, D.S.O.	1. 7.43
Gp.-Capt. T. L. Bingham-Hall	10.44

Bourne	
Gp.-Capt. N. H. Fresson, D.F.C.	1. 7.43–
	24.11.43
Gp.-Capt. J. L. Airey	24.11.43–
	10. 2.44
Gp.-Capt. R. W. P. Collings, D.F.C.	10. 2.44–
	6. 3.44
Gp.-Capt. H. E. Bufton, D.F.C., A.F.C.	6. 3.44–

Warboys	
Gp.-Capt. R. W. P. Collings, D.F.C.	7.43–
	3. 6.43
Gp.-Capt. J. H. Searby, D.S.O., D.F.C.	3. 6.43–
	24. 7.44
Gp.-Capt. T. G. Mahaddie	24. 7.44

Commanding Officers of the Path Finder and Light Night Striking Force Squadrons, 1942-45

(based on information provided by the Air Ministry)

No. 7 Squadron	Appointed.
Wg.-Cdr. B. D. Sellick, D.F.C.	10. 4.42
Wg.-Cdr. (later Gp.-Capt.) O. R. Donaldson, D.S.O., D.F.C.	2.10.42
Wg.-Cdr. H. H. Burnell	3. 5.43
Gp.-Capt. K. R. Rampling, D.S.O., D.F.C.	20. 9.43– 23. 3.44
Wg.-Cdr. W. G. Lockhart, D.S.O., D.F.C.	24. 3.44– 28. 4.44
Wg.-Cdr. J. F. Barron, D.S.O., D.F.C., D.F.M.	28. 4.44– 20. 5.44
Wg.-Cdr. R. W. Cox, D.F.C., A.F.C.	20. 5.44–

No. 35 Squadron	
Wg.-Cdr. J. H. Marks, D.S.O., D.F.C.	3.42–
Wg.-Cdr. B. V. Robinson, D.S.O., D.F.C.	3.42–
Wg.-Cdr. D. F. E. C. Dean, D.F.C.	5.43–
Wg.-Cdr. S. P. Daniels, D.S.O., D.F.C.	11.43–
Gp.-Capt. D. F. E. C. Dean, D.S.O., D.F.C.	7.44–
Wg.-Cdr. H. J. Legood, A.F.C.	3.45–

No. 83 Squadron	
Wg.-Cdr. M. D. Crichton-Biggie	14. 4.42–
Wg.-Cdr. J. R. Gillman	10. 2.43–
Gp.-Capt. J. H. Searby, D.S.O., D.F.C.	9. 5.43–
Wg.-Cdr. R. Hilton, D.S.O., D.F.C.	2.11.43–
Wg.-Cdr. W. Abercromby, D.F.C.	4.12.43–
Gp.-Capt. L. C. Deane, D.S.O., D.F.C.	3. 1.44–
Gp.-Capt. J. A. Ingham, D.S.O., D.F.C.	28. 8.44–
Wg.-Cdr. F. Osborne, D.F.C., A.F.C.	10. 6.45–

No. 156 Squadron	
Wg.-Cdr. R. N. Cook	30. 7.42– 28.10.42

No. 156 *Squadron* (Cont.)   *Appointed.*

    Wg.-Cdr. T. S. Rivett-Carnac, D.F.C.   28.19.42–
                                                      8. 6.43
    Gp.-Capt. R. W. P. Collings, A.F.C.   8. 6.43–
    Wg.-Cdr. E. C. Eaton, D.F.C.   15. 1.44–
                                                   27. 4.44
    Wg.-Cdr. T. L. Bingham-Hall, D.F.C. (later Gp.-
        Capt., D.S.O., D.F.C.)   5.44–
    Wg.-Cdr. D. B. Falconer, D.F.C., A.F.C.   21.11.44–
                                                  30.12.44
    Wg.-Cdr. T. E. Ison, D.S.O., D.F.C.   12.44–
                                                10. 4.45
    Wg.-Cdr. A. J. L. Craig, D.S.O., D.F.C.   10. 4.45–

No. 97 *Squadron*

    Gp.-Capt. N. H. Fresson, D.F.C.   1. 7.43–
    Wg.-Cdr. E. J. Carter, D.F.C.   1. 1.44–
    Wg.-Cdr. A. W. Heward, D.F.C., A.F.C.   25. 6.44–
    Gp.-Capt. P. W. Johnson, D.F.C., A.F.C.   3.10.44–
    Wg.-Cdr. E. K. Sinclair, D.F.C.   5. 6.45–

No. 105 *Squadron*

    Wg.-Cdr. J. de L. Wooldridge, D.F.C., D.F.M.   17. 3.43–
                                                    25. 6.43
    Wg.-Cdr. J. H. Cundall, A.F.C. (later Gp.-Capt.,
        D.F.C., A.F.C.)   7.43–
    Wg.-Cdr. K. J. Somerville, D.F.C., A.F.C. (later Gp.-
        Capt., D.S.O., D.F.C., A.F.C.)   25. 9.44

No. 128 *Squadron*

    Wg.-Cdr. K. J. Burrough, D.F.C.   15. 9.44–

No. 109 *Squadron*

    Wg.-Cdr. H. E. Bufton, D.F.C., A.F.C. (later Gp.-
        Capt.)   10. 7.42–
    Wg.-Cdr. R. M. Cox, A.F.C   27. 3.44–
    Wg.-Cdr. T. F. Grant, D.S.O., D.F.C.   28. 5.44–
    Wg.-Cdr. R. C. F. Law, D.F.C.   6.12.44–
    Wg.-Cdr. C. W. Scott, D.F.C.   28. 9.45–

No. 139 Squadron   *Appointed.*

Wg.-Cdr. R. W. Reynolds, D.S.O., D.F.C.   4. 5.43—
Wg.-Cdr. G. H. Womersley, D.S.O., D.F.C.   44—
Wg.-Cdr. J. B. Voyce, D.F.C.   7.10.44—
Wg.-Cdr. J. R. G. Ralston, D.F.C., A.F.C., D.F.M.   45—

No. 142 Squadron

Wg.-Cdr. B. G. D. Nathan   25.10.44—

No. 162 Squadron

Wg.-Cdr. J. D. Bolton, D.F.C.   18.12.44
Wg.-Cdr. M. K. Sewell, D.F.C.   10. 4.45

No. 163 Squadron

Wg.-Cdr. I. G. Broom, D.F.C.   25. 1.45

No. 571 Squadron

Wg.-Cdr. J. M. Birkin, D.S.O., D.F.C., A.F.C.   1. 4.44
Wg.-Cdr. R. J. Gosnell, D.S.O., D.F.C.   3.11.44
Wg.-Cdr. R. W. Bray, D.F.C.   2. 3.45

No. 608 Squadron

Wg.-Cdr. W. W. G. Scott   1. 8.44
Wg.-Cdr. R. C. Alabaster   23.11.44
Wg.-Cdr. K. Gray   29. 4.45

No. 635 Squadron

Wg.-Cdr. A. G. S. Cousens, D.S.O., D.F.C.   20. 3.44
    22. 4.44
Wg.-Cdr. W. T. Brooks   27. 4.44
Wg.-Cdr. S. Baker, D.S.O., D.F.C.   11. 7.44
Wg.-Cdr. J. W. Fordham   3.45

No. 692 Squadron

Wg.-Cdr. W. G. Lockhart, D.S.O., D.F.C.   1. 1.44
Wg.-Cdr. S. D. Watts, D.F.C.   24. 3.44
    11. 7.44
Wg.-Cdr. J. Northrop, D.F.C., A.F.C.   17. 7.44

No. 627 Squadron	*Appointed.*
Wg.-Cdr. R. P. Elliott, D.S.O., D.F.C.	15.11.42-
Wg.-Cdr. G. W. Curry, D.F.C.	3. 6.44-
Wg.-Cdr. B. R. W. Hallows, D.F.C.	22. 1.45-
Wg.-Cdr. R. Kingsford-Smith, D.S.O., D.F.C.	10. 4.45-

No. 405 Squadron	
Wg.-Cdr. J. E. Fauquier, D.F.C. (later Gp.-Capt., D.S.O., D.F.C.)	20. 4.43-
Wg.-Cdr. R. J. Lane, D.S.O., D.F.C. (later Gp.-Capt.)	22. 1.44-
Wg.-Cdr. C. W. Palmer, D.F.C.	23. 8.44-
	26. 9.44
Wg.-Cdr. H. A. Morrison, D.S.O., D.F.C.	26. 9.44-
Gp.-Capt. W. F. M. Newson, D.F.C.	1.11.44-

No. 582 Squadron	
Wg.-Cdr. C. M. Dunnifliffe, D.F.C.	18. 4.44
Wg.-Cdr. P. H. Cribb (later Gp.-Capt., D.S.O., D.F.C.)	25. 7.44
Wg.-Cdr. S. P. Coulson (later Gp.-Capt., D.S.O., D.F.C.)	11.44

P.F.F. Navigation Training Unit—Gransden Lodge
> Upwood, June, 1943
> Warboys, March, 1944
> Formed 10.4.43

Wg.-Cdr. R. P. Elliott, D.S.O., D.F.C.	10. 4.43-
	17.11.43
Wg.-Cdr. D. F. E. C. Dean (later D.S.O., D.F.C.)	17.11.43-
	25. 7.44
Wg.-Cdr. E. W. Anderson, O.B.E., D.F.C.	25. 7.44-
Gp.-Capt. L. C. Deane, D.S.O., D.F.C.	8.44-

No. 1655 Mosquito Training Unit—Marham; Warboys

Sqn.-Ldr. P. J. Channer, D.F.C.	10.42-
Sqn.-Ldr. J. R. G. Ralston, D.S.O., D.F.M. (later Wg.-Cdr.), D.S.O., A.F.C., D.F.M.	4.43-
	10. 8.44
Wg.-Cdr. J. S. W. Bignal, D.F.C., A.F.C.	10. 8.44-

No. 1409 (*Met.*) *Flight* — *Appointed.*

Sqn.-Ldr. D. A. Braithwaite	1. 4.43
Flt.-Lt. The Hon. P. I. Cunliffe-Lister (later Sqn.-Ldr., D.S.O.)	6. 5.43
	18. 7.43
Flt.-Lt. G. H. Hatton, D.F.C.	18. 7.43-
Flt.-Lt. V. S. Moore	28.11.43
Sqn.-Ldr. J. M. Birkin, A.F.C.	13. 1.44
Sqn.-Ldr. R. D. McLaren	11.44
Sqn.-Ldr. N. Bicknell (later D.S.O.)	17. 4.44
Sqn.-Ldr. D. G. Johnson	3.45

PATH FINDER FORCE—ORDER OF BATTLE

September, 1942

Graveley	35 Squadron	Halifax
Oakington	7 Squadron	Stirling
Wyton	83 Squadron	Lancaster
Warboys	156 Squadron	Wellington

December, 1943
Headquarters, No. 8 Group—Huntingdon

Graveley	35 Squadron	Halifax
Oakington	7 Squadron	Lancaster
	627 Squadron	Mosquito
Wyton	83 Squadron	Lancaster
	139 Squadron	Mosquito
Bourn	97 Squadron	Lancaster
Warboys	156 Squadron	Lancaster
Gransden Lodge	405 (R.C.A.F.) Sqn.	Lancaster
Marham	105 Squadron	Mosquito
	109 Squadron	Mosquito

December, 1944
Headquarters, No. 8 Group—Huntingdon

Graveley	35 Squadron	Lancaster
	83 Squadron	Lancaster
	97 Squadron	Lancaster
	692 Squadron	Mosquito
Oakington	7 Squadron	Lancaster
	571 Squadron	Mosquito

December, 1944
Headquarters, No. 8 Group—Headquarters (*Cont.*)

Wyton	128 Squadron	Mosquito
	1409 (Met.) Flight	Mosquito
Bourn	105 Squadron	Mosquito
	162 Squadron	Mosquito
Gransden Lodge	142 Squadron	Mosquito
	405 (R.C.A.F.) Sqn.	Lancaster
Upwood	156 Squadron	Lancaster
	139 Squadron	Mosquito
Downham Market	635 Squadron	Lancaster
	608 Squadron	Mosquito
Little Staughton	582 Squadron	Lancaster
	109 Squadron	Mosquito
Warboys	P.F.F. Training Unit	Lancaster

March, 1945
Headquarters, No. 8 Group—Huntingdon

Graveley	35 Squadron	Lancaster	
	83 Squadron	Lancaster	Detached to
	97 Squadron	Lancaster	No. 5 Group
	692 Squadron	Mosquito	
Oakington	7 Squadron	Lancaster	
	571 Squadron	Mosquito	
Wyton	128 Squadron	Mosquito	
	163 Squadron	Mosquito	
	1409 (Met.) Flight	Mosquito	
Bourn	105 Squadron	Mosquito	
	162 Squadron	Mosquito	
Gransden Lodge	405 Squadron	Lancaster	
	142 Squadron	Mosquito	
Upwood	156 Squadron	Lancaster	
	139 Squadron	Mosquito	
Downham Market	635 Squadron	Lancaster	
	608 Squadron	Mosquito	
	627 Squadron	Mosquito	Detached to No. 5 Group
Little Staughton	582 Squadron	Lancaster	
	109 Squadron	Mosquito	
Warboys	P.F.F. Training Unit	Lancaster	

Appendix B

CODE NAMES

NEWHAVEN	Ground Marking of Aiming Point by visual identification
PARRAMATTA	Ground Marking of Aiming Point by radar
WANGANUI	Sky Marking of Release Point by radar (Oboe or H2S)
R.D.F.	English for radar
GEE	A pulse phasing position fixer
H2S	A pulse reflector, air-ground-air
OBOE	A pulse responder, ground-air-ground
PINK PANSY	Early Ground Marker
T.I.	Target Indicator pyrotechnic Aiming Point Marker
WINDOW	Tin foil strips for radar confusion
FISHPOND	Radar warning of Fighter Approach
PPI	Plan Position Indicator (cathode ray tube)

Distributors and Co-Publishers

Goodall Publications Limited
Box 201
12, Liverpool Street,
LONDON EC2M 7BS
Telephone: 01-283 5924

Please ~~make cheque~~ or postal order (no currency), and allow
35p per book to cover the cost of postage and packing, to
the U.K.
D. C. Thomson
Fairh...
Denham, Uxbridge, Middlesex, UB9 9EQ